Cynthia Shepard Perry
Sept 2000

All Things Being Equal

One Woman's Journey

Cynthia Shepard Perry
United States Ambassador, Retired

Stonecrest International Publishers
Houston, Texas

Permissions Department,
Stonecrest International Publishers,
3602 South MacGregor Way, Suite 301,
P.O. Box 14503
Houston, Texas, 77221-4503

Library of Congress Cataloging-in-Publication Data
Perry, Cynthia Shepard
All Things Being Equal: One Woman's Journey

Includes Index and appendices
1. Women in leadership; Autobiography 2. Setting long-term goals, 3. Black writers. 4. African American Women. 5. Women – cross cultural studies.
Library of Congress Catalogue Card Number 99-096864

Cynthia Shepard Perry
All Things Being Equal: One Woman's Journey
ISBN 0-967-5571-0-0
ISBN 0-967-5571-1-9
Publication Date: March, 2000

The design of the Cover chosen by the author is taken from the navy blue standard reserved for the American Ambassador, which displays the Great Seal of the United States, on a field of white surrounded by 13 stars. The use of the Seal does not in any manner signify sponsorship or approval by the U.S. Government of the book or its contents.

Second Printing: July, 2000
Cover Design by DiGI Images, Houston, Texas
Printed by Prime Source Graphics, Houston

DEDICATED TO

My Prince Consort, James O. Perry,
For his unfailing love and support
To my six children
Donna, Jim, Milo, Paula, Mark and James
My many grandchildren and great grandchildren
Who willingly shared the time that was theirs
With the pursuit of my goal; and
To my friend and alter ego,
Valerie Dickson-Horton who shared with me
Her immense wisdom and good judgment.

And to all of those who will read and
Be convinced to set long term goals
In the act of becoming.

Thanks to all of you for believing in me

Acknowledgments

I owe a great debt of gratitude to many people, including members of my family, all of whom offered me assistance and provided encouragement along the way.

- To Alice and Paul Fowler from my hometown, Terre Haute, Indiana, who read and reread the manuscripts as they evolved, and who did final editing. Having known me for years, they provided reality checks and questioned my sources and logic to make me dig deeper. They believed the story should be told..

- To Dr. James Ward, professional editor and Communications professor at Texas Southern University, Houston, who performed the final editing of the manuscript and who found significant humor and pleasure in the reading, I owe him a great debt for making me believe readers would find the book entertaining and informative.

- To Marsha Stewart who undertook the initial editing of the manuscript at its earliest beginnings and many iterations, who researched my historical facts and also obtained the copyright from the Library of Congress.

- To Bette Van Ausdal, retired Foreign Service Secretary and my long-time friend, who edited the manuscript for sensitive inferences and information associated with the Foreign Service. She also helped to establish times, places and events of diplomatic ventures.

- To Stephen Horton, one of my first readers, for his sense of presentation of what the reader should be told, what things should be told to no one and what to leave to the imagination.

- To my sons, Milo, Mark and James, who soothed the savage computer throughout the production of the manuscript, and to their wives, Toya, Mirchaye and Nina, who allowed them the time. Without their helpful patience, this book would never have been written.

To all these above and the hundreds of others who assisted me in the production of this manuscript, I acknowledge the value of their contributions and can never thank them enough.

All Things Being Equal

The Prologue: The President Calls

BORN FOR A PURPOSE
The President's Call   1
Clearing the Hurdles   9
My Bloodline   15
Inside the Oval Office   29
The Swearing-In   33
All Things Being Equal   37
The Dream Recurring   49
Choosing a Party   55
On Our Way   65

WORKING TO MAKE A DIFFERENCE
Arrival at Post   75
My New Home—Freetown   81
Presentation of Credentials   87
My Prince Consort   95
The Dream Revealed   117
Passing for Black   133
Confrontations With Power   147
Representational Activities   157
Post Security Challenges   165
Tough Choices   179
My Constituency   199

IN THE AFFAIRS OF MEN
Rice Politics   223
When Diamonds Were King   229
Groping: An Indiscriminant Sport   235
Fish Poaching and the Russians   241
The Gullah Connection   247
Libations to the Ancestors   250
A Fond Farewell   261

The Epilogue   271

Afterword: The President Calls   275
Author's Notes   279
Appendices

Appendices:

A: Feature story in *Houston Chronicle*, on Black Career Women, February 8, 1978.

B.   Letter from George Bush, Vice President of the United States regarding possible appointment or placement in Reagan administration, March 1981.

C: Article appearing in hometown *Terre Haute Star/Tribune* announcing presidential appointment as Ambassador to Sierra Leone, May 1986.

D.   Appendix D: Letter of Congratulations from home state U.S. Senator Richard Lugar, Indiana, Chairman of Foreign Relations Committee, May 1986.

E.   Appendix E: Letter   of   Presidential Appointment as Ambassador to Sierra Leone, from Ronald Reagan, President of the United States, June 1986.

F: Letter from Ambassador Abbot Washburn to Vice President Bush, commenting on excellence of services rendered by Ambassador Perry, July 1986.

        Personal card from Vice President George Bush commending Ambassador Perry, to which was attached copy of letter from Ambassador Washburn, August 1986.

G: Article appearing in *Houston Post*, announcing Ambassador Perry's visit to campus of Texas Southern University, Houston, June, 1987.

H: Letter of Commendation from George P. Shultz, Secretary of State on her performance as Ambassador to Sierra Leone, December 1988.

I: Map of Sierra Leone and of the Continent of Africa.

The Prologue

Johannesburg, April 1986

I was awakened by Andy, urgently knocking at my door. "There's a call for you," he said. "I asked who was calling, that you were sleeping, and . . ." Andy was breathless. "He said he was the President of the United States. Big joke! But, I thought I should wake you—just in case."

Groggy from jetlag and interrupted sleep, I couldn't immediately remember where I was. I sat up on the edge of the bed, head in my hands, waiting for my brain to catch up, feet searching for my shoes, trying to give myself the needed push. Then, I leapt to my feet, stumbling over my shoes in my rush to the phone.

"Hello," I croaked.

"Hello, Cynthia," the voice said. "This is Ronald Reagan. How are you?"

My hair rose straight up from my head as I recognized the voice. My knees wouldn't hold me up. "I'm fine, Mr. President, and how are you?" I replied almost in a whisper.

"Where are you, anyway? South Africa?" He was laughing. "I thought I was talking to you right here in Washington. But, it's South Africa—sounds like you're next door. Well, what are you doing down there anyway?"

"I'm here on a special mission with the Agency for International Development, Mr. President, to develop human resources for the country. We are negotiating grants and contracts with non-governmental groups for training black South Africans who have been disadvantaged by apartheid . . ." I was babbling. I stopped.

"Well, that's good. Good!" he said. "I have had very good report on the development work you are doing, and folks here on my staff and people down in Texas seem to think highly of you. They think you would do a good job representing our country out there. I think so, too."

He paused. I wondered if I should say something, but he continued. "I'm calling to ask you if you would be willing to serve as my Ambassador to Sierra Leone. I understand you have considerable experience living and working in that country, too. I would be very pleased if you would accept."

"Mr. President," I breathed. "I would be honored to serve as your ambassador. I have worked toward this day for many years. It will be my great pleasure."

"Good, Good! Well, when you return to Washington, and formalities have been completed, I look forward to receiving you and your family at the White House." His voice was gracious and smiling.

I was nearly fainting but managed a weak, "Thank you again, Sir. I shall look forward to that."

"Thank you, too, Cynthia. May God bless."

"Goodbye, Sir."

I hastened to add, "God bless you too, Mr. President." But, he was gone.

All Things Being Equal

One Woman's Journey

Cynthia Shepard Perry
United States Ambassador, Retired

Stonecrest International Publishers
Houston, Texas

BORN FOR A PURPOSE

The President's Call

It was April 11, 1986, and I was on my way to Johannesburg, my third trip in one year. I had left Washington the day before, traveling by way of Nairobi on one of Pan American's last flights to the African Region. It had been a long, exhausting trip and it was going to be good to put my feet on the ground again. I was traveling in my official capacity with the United States Agency for International Development (AID) to head a team of professionals to design educational programs for the black disadvantaged in consort with black-directed, black-controlled agencies in South Africa. This project represented an unusual departure from normal protocols governing U.S. foreign assistance. In fact, there was no formal relationship between the two countries, because of American embargoes against the South African Government (SAG) due to its apartheid policies. Nonetheless, a program such as mine had been initiated with the consent of the American government. Under the watchful eye of the U.S. Congress, there could be no input from the official SAG, nor could any part of the U.S. funds expended for the projects pass through SAG coffers.

It was clear that apartheid was breathing its last breath, but those who supported the concept of separatism were fighting desperately to keep it alive, to keep control over the nation's black population for as long as possible. They knew their time was short.   On my previous visit in 1984, I had met socially with Bishop Desmond Tutu and Mrs. Tutu, at the home of my friends, Andy and Marion Torchia. As Chief of the Associated Press Bureau in Johannesburg, Andy had developed strong and broad relationships with both the white and non-white segments of the population. Bishop Tutu told me at that time he was absolutely certain that freedom would come; it would not be bloodless, but would ensue rather quickly considering that inclusion of the majority in the political system was right and just. I had also met with Alan Broasack, an impassioned spokesman of a black segment of the society, as well as Winnie Mandela, wife of the revered and imprisoned Nelson Mandela, and some of her closest advisors.

On my current venture, I would travel throughout the country beginning with Johannesburg, to Durban, Cape Town, Port Elizabeth and Natal, meeting for the first time Chief Butalezi, champion and impassioned leader of the Zulu Nation. The recognized leaders of the revolution, Joseph Sisulu and Nelson Mandela were in prison. Not all of the black leaders I had met thus far were happy with the prospect of accepting "tainted" money from the American government, money which they said would open the door to American "interference" in their internal affairs. To them, I was black but also an agent of the American government. They considered my presence and my allegiance questionable, and I was challenged to prove myself both friend to blacks in South Africa and an effective agent of the U.S. government.

The plane began its descent to the Nairobi airport. I had drifted off to sleep, my head buried in my newspaper, and was just waking when the captain announced our arrival. A middle-aged white woman dressed in bright yellow, sitting across the aisle, touched my arm.

"If you're getting off in Nairobi, dear, you'd better hurry. The next stop is Johannesburg, South Africa." She raised her eyebrows quizzically.

I peered at her from behind my newspaper. "I'm not getting off here. Are you?"

"No, I'm going to Johannesburg, but, I thought you— you know you can't—you can't . . ." She couldn't get it out. Her face turned red, and finally she just turned away. I returned to my newspaper. In time, the plane took off for Johannesburg.

I knew what she meant, of course. She thought that because of the color of my skin, the apartheid government would not permit me to enter South Africa. Some residents feared that freely admitting foreign blacks and allowing them to mingle with whites in public areas might represent a kind of shocking and dangerous example for South African blacks. Most of the black populations, especially urban and educated, were silently watchful and were certainly aware of the rapid changes occurring in their country. I shrugged off her comments, musing to myself that she might not be aware, herself, just how drastically things had changed on the surface since my first trip to Johannesburg two years previously. I was filled nonetheless with a strange anxiety as the plane rolled to a halt on the tarmac at Jan Smuts International Airport. It had nothing to do with apartheid, however.

During the past three months, I had been contacted by White House Personnel regarding a possible appointment as Director of Peace Corps Africa Bureau, in Washington, a rather visible post but not necessarily a "plum." I waited several weeks for confirmation of the appointment. Then, I received a call late one evening in January, 1986, from Bob Tuttle's office, White House Presidential Appointments, advising me with regrets that another prominent Republican from Texas, Bill Perrin, had been chosen for that position. When asked how I felt about it, I said I was of course disappointed, but I still had my job as Chief of Human Resources Development at A.I.D. with lots of projects on the table. Then, the caller said: "We want to put your name forward as the White House choice for Ambassador to Sierra Leone."

I dropped the phone, walked around the desk, came back and picked it up, dazed, while the voice continued with further advice. Although I was the choice of the White House, a highly qualified career Foreign Service officer would also compete for the position and a decision would be made on the best possible choice. I would be informed of that selection within a few days, and in the meantime, I could divulge nothing to anyone.

I tried to go on with my work and daily life as though this truly earth-shattering call had not affected me in the least, as though I had never received it. But, it was nearly impossible not to betray my anxiety. I needed desperately to share the good news and would have told Valerie, my friend, with whom my secrets could be entrusted, but she had been assigned to the Sudan the week before. How could I not tell anyone? I was now within days, hours, minutes, a heartbeat—a mere breath from achieving the goal that had directed me for nearly 30 years.

When the news finally came a few days later, I was as exhausted as I was elated. I had been selected and was now the Ambassador-Designate for Sierra Leone. But, I could not yet shout it from the rooftops. I told my husband, of course, who seemed to be in a state of shock, and I also sent brief, excited, and unpunctuated notes to my friend, Valerie. Interestingly, news of my selection traveled by some routes even faster than I had been able to broadcast it. My selection had even been announced in *JET Magazine*, though apparently it was noted by only a few.

The next step in the process was to complete the necessary security, financial and health clearance checks. I was filled to the emotional brim for several weeks. Could they possibly find anything in my life that would prevent my serving as ambassador? Some potential appointees had failed before they had cleared the White House, some before reaching the Senate. I was a nervous wreck all over again.

Before leaving Washington for Johannesburg, I completed exhaustive interrogations and investigations. I submitted financial disclosures to reveal my sources of income, real estate holdings, investments and possible conflicts of interest, and submitted to health examinations to determine my physical fitness and my husband's for overseas assignment. There were ethics probes into my previous assignments, jobs, and relationships; a federal income tax search was made to ensure that my returns were not delinquent or payments improperly filed. Even investigations were made into the lives of my six brothers and sisters, as well as my six children, with respect to possible conflicts or embarrassments in my appointment.

The waiting seemed endless. But, actually, within three months, Jane Mosselem, of the Presidential Personnel Office in the State Department, finally advised me that all investigations, including security, had been completed. No adverse comments had been heard from the Senate Committee, and my file had been passed to the White House for President Reagan's approval and formal nomination to the Senate.

"But," she warned, "it may take several weeks before the President calls, and he must telephone you personally. In the meantime, you cannot say to anyone that you have been nominated. That is the President's prerogative."

Even though Jane thought the call might be imminent, after what seemed an interminably long period, it still had not come. I checked with Pat Lynch Gates, Ambassador-Designate for Madagascar, who was also awaiting her call. She said, "Oh, I received the call last week, Cynthia. You should have had yours by now. Something must be wrong."

My heart sank. What could have gone wrong? I began preparations for my mission to South Africa. I would be gone for about ten days. Perhaps, he would call during my absence. I could not afford to miss this call. Just as a precaution, I left the telephone number of my friends in Johannesburg with just about everybody I knew in Washington, and then I boarded my flight for South Africa.

* * *

The reception at Jan Smuts International Airport had become more and more cordial each time I entered the country. Agents were now politely curious rather than condescending in their questioning as I passed through the customs booths. Perhaps my diplomatic American passport had something to do with it. It was like having a protective U.S. flag around me.

As I left the plane and entered the customs hall, I put the thought of Washington and its intrigues behind me and prepared for the adventure now at hand. When I queued in the line for non-South Africans, to my surprise, the woman in yellow followed me, her eyebrows knit together in a deep frown. I thought derisively, she was just another American like me; in fact, so were most of the passengers. Just for the heck of it, I flashed my diplomatic passport so that she could not miss seeing it, and for her edification, I conducted a spirited conversation with the official in the customs booth. He was tremendously cordial and helpful in directing me to the baggage area. The woman in yellow was obviously quite bewildered.

American diplomats in those days carried two official passports: one to be used only when entering and departing South Africa. When traveling further to some independent African nations, entry could be refused to persons because of the customs stamp indicating recent visitation to the embargoed apartheid nation. I was stopped and questioned once when entering Zimbabwe and another time when I entered Kenya on a business trip. Since most African nations participated in this embargo, the use of the second passport avoided further embarrassments of this type.

My friends, Marion and Andy Torchia, were waiting for me in the reception hall. Andy was now Bureau Chief for the Associated Press in South Africa, and Marion was a serious collector of African art and curator of her private museum. We had been close friends since we first met in 1974 in Nairobi where my husband was assigned to UNESCO and Andy was serving as AP's Bureau Chief for East Africa.

During our drive through the beautiful city to their home, we compared notes about our children, their successes and hopes, and the dynamics of racial confrontations since my last visit to Johannesburg. The Torchias, both equally competent political analysts, quickly and succinctly summarized the most recent developments and their predictions for the future. The atmosphere in South Africa had become increasingly tense and combative, and therefore the large cities were terribly dangerous, especially after dark. I explained to them my mission to South Africa, which was perhaps naively optimistic considering the enormity of the crisis in the country. I solicited their help in identifying the right people and organizations to make my program work. The Torchias were in an excellent position to do this and had even arranged a meeting for me with Archbishop Desmond Tutu in their home on one of my previous visits.

We agreed to have dinner that night at a particular German restaurant where people of different races were able to meet without intimidation, and where I might meet people who would be helpful during this visit. But, I had severe jet lag and we agreed I should first take a short nap before dinner. So, soon after we arrived at their home, I went to bed and fell into a deep sleep. It was in the middle of this deep, dreamless slumber that the miraculous telephone call came from President Reagan.

There are no words to fully describe my elation, my delight, my fulfillment—his words seemed still to hang in the air. I stood there, the receiver in my hand, stupefied. Marion and Andy, waiting discreetly in the kitchen, entered the room and virtually pried my fingers from the phone, replacing it in its cradle.

"It really was President Reagan," I whispered. Tears began to run down my face, dropping off my nose. I began to dance the holy dance, hugging the walls, screaming and laughing, hugging my two dear friends. Then, we all fell silent, in deep thought. For the next half-hour, the three of us spoke together in muted tones, full of wonder, bordering on disbelief.

I repeated my dialogue with the President, and with their help recorded it while the memory was fresh. It actually was President Reagan, and not one of his aides, who had spoken to me on the phone.

I felt very special. I would be the first black Texan to become an Ambassador and only the fifth black woman in the nation—only the fifth, in all of American history, to be named ambassador to a foreign country. It was a sad commentary on the patronage process of both parties as well as the career Foreign Service system. It was nonetheless a signal honor for me. I was the first and only black, female political appointee in the Reagan administration to serve as envoy to a foreign country and I would remain the only one throughout his administration.

"It's history in the making, Cynthia," Andy spoke in amazement, "and we're a part of it—to think it happened here in our house. The President of the United States called our house because you are here. We're proud to know you, Cynthia."

Finally, we exploded with energy and excitement, got on the phone and told everybody we knew—and finally my husband, J.O., who regretted he had missed my big moment. My two friends, Marion and Andy, had known about my goal for years; they had been there to share my happiness and one of the most exciting moments of my life. I had reached the goal toward which I had struggled for more than 25 years. I would now become an American ambassador.

We continued our discussions over dinner that evening at the restaurant, interrupted periodically by friends of the Torchias who wanted to meet me. We were glowing visibly from the excitement of our secret. Over the servings of lots and lots of delicious sausages, we plotted my social schedule for the next several days in Johannesburg to allow me to meet the most influential change-makers in the city and country.

Clearing the Hurdles

The next ten days seemed interminable as I tried to focus on the task at hand in South Africa, while anticipating events to come about in Washington over the next few weeks. I was told that following the president's call, the confirmation process would go very rapidly. Bidding farewell to my friends, the Torchias, I joined my team on the return flight to Washington to prepare for my new role.

Life in Washington for me had always been a carnival, but these few weeks were maddening. There were back-to-back briefings within the State Department, United States Information Agency, Peace Corps, the Pentagon, the Congress and all other agencies involved with our mission in Sierra Leone. I met with my predecessors to Sierra Leone, my old friend, Arthur Lewis, who was just completing his tour, and Theresa Heely, the first woman ambassador to Sierra Leone. I met with African diplomats and seemingly hundreds of private groups and businesses trading with Sierra Leone, or hoping to. During this time I also successfully completed the required, and often humiliating, physical examinations. The doctors left no bone unturned—no orifice unexplored.

Jane Mosellem, of the Presidential Personnel Office, informed me that I had passed the medical examination. Agrément, the formal acceptance of my appointment, had been received from the Government of Sierra Leone (GOSL), and everything else was going well with the process.

I was then scheduled for the Ambassadors' Seminar which covered two weeks (April 20-May 2, 1986), during which several other ambassador-designates and I were briefed by senior ambassadors on the expectations of our assignments around the world. The major convener was Shirley Temple Black, former child movie star and model for the famous golden-curled and dimpled doll. She had served as Ambassador to Ghana and the United Nations under President Nixon and shared with us a number of practical pointers from her experience. Two other senior professional ambassadors, Tony Mott and Brandon Grove, chaired various segments of the seminar. Most of the ambassadors in training were political appointees for whom even the City of Washington was a foreign country. My previous four years in Washington with A.I.D. proved to be an advantage in that I understood the diplomatic shorthand jargon and was familiar with most persons and agencies involved in the briefing.

On the other hand, my husband had spent only brief periods in Washington during my four years. He was completely bewildered during the training, as were several others in our seminar group. Now he was suddenly labeled the ambassador's spouse, a new and somewhat demeaning designation for him, he thought. For most of the seminar, spouses received their briefings separately from the ambassadors. Their briefings included how to inventory and order replacement china and silver, how to account for representational funds, how to head the Embassy wives at post and how to cooperate in charitable community activities with other diplomatic or U.N. women's groups. It was a completely new role and an immensely difficult mind set for my husband who had always assumed responsibility for major decisions in our family. He wanted to sit in on the closed sessions, the political, intelligence, and diplomatic briefings reserved for the ambassadors.

He did enjoy some of the special activities in the briefing phase, especially the luncheon and tour of the White House conducted by Nancy Reagan. He gained a sense of being in a special category. Nonetheless, the designation as dependent and "spouse" grated heavily on his sensibilities. While wives might be called erroneously "Ambassadrice" or "Mrs. Ambassador," a husband has no official designation or title, only "spouse" or "husband of the ambassador." He felt invisible, a feeling I'm sure was experienced by many Foreign Service wives over the decades.

There were, however, two other male spouses in my husband's spousal group, who after two days of this humorous training, quit the seminar to find other things to do. J.O. was left alone to cope with his indignation. Clearly the spousal briefings were never designed with male dependents in mind. Female ambassadors with accompanying husbands were a new breed, and J.O. and a few others were later asked to write a handbook for the brave men who would follow.

According to my State Department colleagues, my own greatest challenge was yet to come: the Senate confirmation hearings, a sometimes difficult hurdle in the presidential appointment gauntlet. In one of my briefings, I was again warned that the confirmation process could be quite grueling. With the help of the State Department's geographic office for the West Africa region, I had prepared a number of papers, all of which had been submitted to the Senate. Aides to the Senators had conducted their own investigations as well to ensure that all appointees—career and political—met the highest ethical standards possible in representing the American people. These investigations would provide the basis of their questioning. It was a powerful process.

In one of my earlier briefings, I had been asked by a friendly interlocutor, "Is there anything in your life, past or present, which if discovered by the Senate investigation, would prove to be embarrassing to you and to the President?"

I said, "Yes. They're going to find out I'm poor!"

Her quick laughter expressed some relief as well as amusement. She explained that on the contrary, it was in fact the millionaire appointees or those with politically sensitive histories or controversial investments who caused greatest concern.

* * *

It was June 11, 1986. I was truly uptight when I entered the Senate chambers for deliberations chaired by the angelic but very firm and persistent Senator from Kansas, Nancy Kassenbaum. She posed sensitive questions to me and three other ambassador-designates appearing before the Senate that day.

"What makes you believe that as ambassador, you can make a difference in that country? What uniquely qualifies you to carry out our foreign policy in a country that historically has little respect for women? How would you promote our policies of human rights and respect for the individual in a nation which for decades has had a horrible human rights record?"

These questions applied less to my situation than to others. Some ambassadors were being assigned to countries with strong Islamic cultures who restricted activities of women and whose idea of respect differed dramatically from ours. Each of us individually responded to questions regarding conditions in our posted countries. The committee hearing went quite smoothly for me, and ended with Senator Kassenbaum commending my years of public service both at home and abroad. She told me the Committee would send to the Senate their recommendation for approval of my appointment as Ambassador to Sierra Leone, and that I could be assured of their full support. And, indeed, I was confirmed by the Senate just three days later on June 14, 1986.

After the hearings, I was filled with an overwhelming sense of relief which demanded expression. I wanted to dance; I could barely contain my tears and other expressions of exhilaration possibly considered undignified of a new diplomat. As I drove home through the I-365 tunnel, I hung my head out the window, and screamed to the top of my lungs until I exited the other side. It felt good.

Over the next weeks, numerous ceremonies, receptions and celebrations were held in my honor. Among them was a prestigious reception given by NAFEO, the National Association for Equal Opportunity in Higher Education, which represents all the black colleges in the United States, arranged by my close friend, NAFEO vice president, Wilma Roscoe. One of our former Peace Corps Volunteers in the Washington area, Patrice Battle, gave a lavish barbecue at her house to which other Volunteers were invited. It was a great sendoff by the Volunteers, the majority of whom had served in Sierra Leone.

My Bloodline

The formalities were not yet over. There were still two major ceremonies scheduled before I would depart for Sierra Leone. Everything was now happening so quickly that I had little time to adequately prepare myself and my family for departure. Immediately following my swearing in, the last of the ceremonies in the process, I would be expected to depart for post as soon as possible to take immediate charge of the mission. We just had time to schedule one week in June 1986, to go back to our home in Houston to complete the packing and storage of our personal effects. A second week was scheduled to visit our old hometowns of Terre Haute and Indianapolis, Indiana, to say farewell to our extended families before returning to Washington. In spite of the many things to be done, I was anxious to get on my way to Sierra Leone.

Leasing the house in Houston was perhaps the biggest challenge. It was finally leased to a physician and his wife with five small daughters, and we were happy to have someone in the house who could fill it with love and laughter. Our son, Milo, handled the purchase of a minivan in Washington, and shipped it directly to Freetown so it would arrive before we reached

Sierra Leone. I was going to need the large family car to accommodate the needs of all the family members who would accompany me to post. I hired Johnnie Dickson, my former secretary at Texas Southern University, to manage our finances and our properties during our absence. I knew all would go well in her competent and discreet hands.

A beautiful reception was given for us by Jerry Gaither, a close family friend and former Peace Corps volunteer in Sierra Leone, in conjunction with Texas Southern University and other former Peace Corps Volunteers. Attending the reception were the former president of Texas Southern, Dr. Granville Sawyer, and his successor, Dr. Robert J. Terry, under whom both my husband and I had served as professors. Several parties, receptions and dinners were given in our honor during that one week in Houston.

Our daughter, Paula, a public school teacher in Houston, resettled into an apartment of her own. She had always lived at home and we simply transferred to the apartment her personal belongings and many household items we had no time or space to store. It was unbelievable how much "stuff" we had amassed in the past ten years, since returning from our last overseas tour in Kenya, in 1976. With little time to wrestle with a garage sale, we left what remained to charity.

Completely fatigued, we departed for Terre Haute and Indianapolis, to bid farewell to our large immediate families. Again, we were deluged with invitations to dinners and receptions, many of which had to be declined for sake of time and energy. We said farewell to J.O.'s. sister, Christina Stuart and husband Joe, his mother Anna Perry and his brother, Henry Perry, and their families, inviting them all to visit us in Freetown. We spent hours on the telephone with other members of the Perry family: sister Mary and her husband, Norvel Smith, and younger brother, Benjamin, in California; and his brother, Reverend David Perry and wife Gwen, in Florida.

In Terre Haute, George and Dolores Nichols, my old friends—George was also my first employer—gave a beautiful garden reception in our honor where we said hail and farewell to many old friends. We made farewell visits to my brother George Norton and his wife Alberta, to my brother Orville Norton and wife Ethel Mae, and to my sister Iona Wilcox and husband, Theodore, in Terre Haute. We telephoned my other sisters Madonna Austin and husband Harold, and Hazel Montfort and husband Dan, all in Cleveland, Ohio. We called on members of the Shepard family—Otto, my former husband and father of my four children, and his sister, Nola Wilford and husband Homer, who were very dear to me. We spent a brief time with some of our many friends still located in Terre Haute: Alice and Paul Fowler, former professor and colleague at Indiana State University; Bernice Lamb, widow of my high school principal and mentor; friends James and Barbara Ross, Lillian Stuart and others whom I had known all my life.

My visit to my hometown, Terre Haute, was not only nostalgic for me but was well covered by the media. In one newspaper interview, a journalist asked how and why I had chosen to become an ambassador. Out of a family of nine children, she wondered why I alone had aspired to achieve this particular, and untraditional, high goal? Who had inspired me and where had I gotten such determination? She did not ask the one question which still hung in the air awaiting opportunity: "Why Africa?"

I briefly reviewed for the benefit of the journalist, my own history, my childhood, and also my ancestry, or what I knew of it, dating back to Virginia in the late 1700's, and the migration of freed black families to Indiana prior to the Civil War. I also gave her an abbreviated version of the nearly 30 years I had spent in professional preparation for the ambassadorship. I told her of my purpose to make a difference in my lifetime, my concern for fairness in the world, my desire to improve the quality of life of all people, my determination to be a fitting spokeswoman and representative for my country, my hope to be a symbol of what America offers: freedom to become.

Where did I get the inspiration for such a high post? I was inspired most, in my early adult years, by Eleanor Roosevelt and her brave and masterful work in helping to establish the United Nations. She helped to steer a clear path after World

War II to lay the groundwork needed to secure a world peace. She became a living role model for me, as opposed to one that I might have chosen from history. I wanted to be like her in every way: rich, famous, intelligent, and gentle.

Assuming the journalist's question was more related to my bloodline, I told her it probably came from genes that I knew nothing about, that the history of my family before slavery was unknown to me. In spite of exhaustive research by family historians, that link with Africa had never been determined, and I refused to manufacture a connection. It was widely believed by black people, when I was growing up, that records of slave origins had been systematically destroyed during the centuries of slavery to prevent slaves and their descendents from ever establishing links and identification with the African Continent. Slavery could only have been effected among a language-less, culture-less, history-less, and therefore "rootless" people. The sad and ironic result has been that, for so many African American people in this country, the only direct connections that can be established with their Old World roots is through their European bloodlines.

"Perhaps," I said finally to the journalist, "one of my ancestors was the King of England, another a Zulu chieftain, another Pocahontas or Massaquoia, all great leaders of the past."

We both laughed.

But even as I laughed, I found myself searching for an answer closer to reality, closer to my own history. What was in my bloodline that had resurfaced in me, inspired me, I asked myself? Though I said nothing to the journalist, an image did begin to formulate in my memory. I knew from oral history that there were great scholars and leaders in my past on both paternal and maternal sides of my family on this side of the ocean. I learned these things sitting at the feet of my mother and her Aunt Evie as they discussed their early lives and their heroes of the past, especially Grandpa Josh.

My mother's grandfather, Joshua Hill, was the son of freed slaves. He had been reared in a Quaker village, Carthage, Indiana, where education for both sexes in both the black and white races was part of the social ethic. Carthage even boasted of having founded the first public library for Negroes in the State of Indiana during the 1840's. Grandpa Josh and his family all spoke fluent German as well as English. In 1871, he graduated with honors from Lincoln University in Pennsylvania, a college opened by the Presbyterians in 1854 to prepare young black men for careers as missionaries to Africa. Grandpa Josh also later earned a Master's Degree from Lincoln and returned to Indiana to work and teach in his black community. He was one of a very few highly educated blacks in the country, an intelligent and talented man, limited in what he might have become by the restrictive black codes and the machinations of racial separatism. These black codes controlled social and political access for black people, everywhere. Grandpa Josh married well and had two daughters, Eva, and Hattie, my grandmother. He supported the establishment of churches and schools for the education of black children and assisted poor families with their legal claims, such as they were. But his education, his linguistic ability, his knowledge of science and philosophy did not, in the end, serve to further him at all in the time and environment in which he lived. He was years ahead of his time, so to speak. A tragic story told to me by my mother, and later substantiated by news articles found in the local archives, provides a good example of the social and political climate of my grandfather's day.

My mother's father, Lee Phillips, husband of Hattie, worked in the deep, dark and dangerous coalmines of Burnett. Like most miners, he spent much of his free time, gambling and drinking in the local saloons. One day, he had a particularly fierce argument with a white miner, who shot my grandfather in the back as he left the saloon. Lee spun around on his feet and returned the fire, killing the white miner who died on the spot. He was immediately arrested for killing a white man and was sentenced to life in prison.

The newspapers account for the valiant, legal fight waged by Hattie, who without legal knowledge of her own, was coached by her father, Joshua Hill, who could not safely represent his son-in-law before the court. For two years, Hattie fought valiantly for the release of her husband, and public opinion seemed to be in her favor. I find it curious how well her efforts were documented by the local press. Unfortunately, she failed, and he died from the bullet in his back which had never been removed. What a terrible blow this was to my grandmother, widowed at an early age with three small children, and also to Grandpa Josh, who might have won the release of his daughter's husband had all things been equal.

When I learned of this tragic and violent event in my mother's childhood, I was tremendously impressed with the strength, intelligence and fearlessness of my grandmother. In the negative context of events in my mother's early life, this story gave me a totally different and positive view of my grandmother. It helped me to understand the undaunted later courage of my mother, of her determination and grit when things were rough. Even without my understanding, I believe these traits or values were passed down to me and I see them manifested in the behaviors of my daughter and granddaughters as well.

My father, George Norton, too, was a talented man and a great inspiration to me. He fought in France with the U.S. Army during World War I, and returned home in 1918 when the Great Armistice was signed. I was born exactly ten years later on Armistice Day. Each year on the 11th day, the 11th month at 11:00am, a massive celebration was held around the world celebrating the Armistice. Until I was a teenager, I thought the planes flying overhead, the fireworks, the sirens and factory whistles were all in my honor. My father told me so. He had many natural talents which, with nine children to feed and support, he was never able to fully develop. But, it was he who taught me to sing, to play the piano, to paint and to think broadly of the world. I believed him when he told me that I would be an important leader some day, and I became, as my mother later rued, an extremely proud and willful child.

Dad named me for his Aunt Cynthia, whom we also called our aunt rather than great Aunt. She became my great inspiration when I was quite young. She told me I had a magical name that had been applied to women in each generation of our family line for generations. The matriarch of the family, Aunt Cynthia's grandmother, was a woman of African and native American blood (thought to be Choctaw), known as Chena, whose name had an unknown meaning, possibly the same as my own: "moon." Chena's daughter was named Cynthia, who in death passed this name to her youngest daughter, my great Aunt Cynthia. I came along as my father's sixth child, following four boys, and became the next Cynthia. Cynthia, daughter of my elder brother, George, carried the name in the next generation. Latest in the line of Cynthia's is the youngest daughter of my eldest son, James Shepard.

Aunt Cynthia died a few years before I began the push to actualize my dream of becoming an ambassador, but she had long inspired me to do great things. I know she would have been proud of me. Without doubt, she was one of the greatest influences in my young life, especially in my formative years. Following the Great Depression, everything was so difficult for my family, for the families of our farming community, and for the nation as a whole. During these troubled times, she taught me decency, honesty, and pride.

* * *

My first memories of Aunt Cynthia begin at about age 5 or 6, when she was nearly 60. She would come to visit us out in the "country" in the largely black enclave overlapping Otter Creek and Lost Creek Townships, just outside Terre Haute, Indiana. Our house was located just up the hill from the coal-mining village of Burnett, with its narrow, dusty, graveled roads, blankets of mosquitoes and crescendos of croaking frogs. At night, it was pitch black; there were no street lights, in fact there was no gas or electricity—only the moonlight.

She would hire a Model T Ford, called the "tin lizzy," and a driver to bring her. All the children for miles around would rush to the roadside just to see the car pass. I can still remember vividly the sound of the horn honking miles away and the heaviness of the car as it hit the wooden planks of the bridge over the creek.

Aunt Cynthia was a city woman from Terre Haute, twelve miles or 1,000 light years away from Lost Creek. She would always bring gifts when she came, and we thought she must be tremendously wealthy. Dad adored her and called her "Sis," although she was his aunt. He was always so pleased when she would faun over his nine offspring. She put my elder brother, Walter, through high school and technical training, but I was aware that I enjoyed a special bond and place with her, as her namesake.

One Christmas, she sent me a Shirley Temple doll, immensely popular at that time, with golden curls and deep dimples. I refused it, not just the doll but the idea of having one, and gave it to my younger sisters, who thought I had to be crazy to give it up. My brothers got BB guns and slingshots, and jeans, and I failed to understand why I should not receive the same. My father's explanation that I was a girl seemed less than adequate. But my message seemed to have gotten across to my aunt and my parents: I never received another doll, and every Christmas after that, to my delight, I received a year's supply of paints, brushes and paper.

Aunt Cynthia had been born into the poor, but landed gentry of our community. Her father, George Washington Riley, a veteran of the Union Army, had purchased a large farm in Otter Creek Township and had provided all of his children a good schooling and upbringing. Aunt Cynthia was beautiful as I remember her, little more than 5-feet tall, petite, with a lovely, narrow waistline which allowed her to sport the fashionable clothes of the day. And, as I recall, her makeup was never overstated and was skillfully applied. She was completely feminine with her gorgeous brooches and pendants and the beautiful black Spanish comb that swept the heavy mane of black hair from her face. She always wore her hair in a large coil around her head, held by long, thick hairpins of horn or something. At night, she would let it down, allowing it to cascade to her waist, and sometimes she allowed me to brush it. She would work it into two thick braids, sometimes topping it with a nightcap, a white frilly thing that was strange to me. I was terribly envious of her elegance, her grace, her beauty, and always wished I could look a little like her.

It was out of her love for us that she shared her largesse with my father, which he accepted behind my mother's back. Mom would never have allowed it for her own reasons and her sense of pride. We weren't starving, far from it, but there were nine of us with many urgent needs, and my aunt's financial contributions were helpful.

When I turned seven, Aunt Cynthia asked Dad if I could spend my summers with her. I was delighted with the prospect of getting away from my three younger sisters. To spend the summer in the cool ambiance of my aunt's house was like a dream. My mother wasn't especially happy about it. I heard her shout angrily to my father that I would not spend time with that "dirty, awful woman." My father's voice in response was deadly quiet, as he declared I would indeed go. And, I did—every summer for the next several years.

But, I remembered my mother's angry statement—the strange words she used to describe my loving Aunt Cynthia who was certainly not awful, and not dirty. She had the nicest house in the whole community where she lived, with a white picket fence and gate and a front yard full of brilliantly colored flowers. I loved the opulence of the small house she had built for herself. Her great featherbed was covered always with a white, crisp, eyelet coverlet; the feather pillows, including the two bolsters, were fluffy, clean and fresh, smelling just slightly of lilac.

She had two giant steamer trunks in which she kept the most fabulous things—embroidered fineries, laces, albums, jewelry. She would open them occasionally when I visited, allowing me to search for some treasure or another. To this day, I associate the smell of mothballs with cleanliness, freshness and loving care for valuables.

I slept in her great bed when I visited. She would tell me stories of her life, her two marriages, and would weep a little for Mr. Howard, the husband she had loved and the child she had lost to influenza. Then, after I had chanted my prayers, she would hug me tightly and kiss me good night. I adored her and felt safe and very special in her presence. She taught me good manners—ma'am and sir, thank you and please, and especially not to reach across the table and grab. That bit of courtesy had to be taught and re-taught many times; I suffered relapses when I went home. With nine of us at the table, the fried chicken would disappear before my father had uttered the last syllable of his usually long dinner grace. But, she taught me to be gracious, and it was our private game to be used when I was around her. I gained new friends during those summers, both boys and girls about my age, especially Flossie and Marcellus, who taught me lots of new things. They taught me new words, too, but after having my mouth washed out with soap by my mother just once, I learned not to use them in her presence. How barbaric of my mother!

The little borough where Aunt Cynthia lived was called Highland, a poor, blighted area outside Terre Haute with a certain kind of enchantment and history. My father's parents, Grandpa Norton and Miss Suzy, and my Uncle George Riley, the brother of Aunt Cynthia, lived there, too. My parents were Baptist, but Aunt Cynthia went to a CME, Colored Methodist Episcopal, church. There was also an African Methodist Episcopal Church, AME, just around the corner. I questioned Aunt Cynthia why there were so many churches with so few members when they all seemed to have the same traditions, worship services, and so forth. She said some black people didn't want to be identified with anything African (AME) so they set up a CME church. That was crazy to me, but each Sunday morning—after a breakfast of hot pancakes with strawberry syrup, I would sit primly and proudly, smiling in the pew next to my beautiful aunt. I was special.

Foremost in my memories of my summers with Aunt Cynthia were our visits to the home of Cousin Annie and her daughter, Katherine, on Spruce Street. Visiting my great aunt and her "high-fallutin" cousins (as my mother called them), always made me feel like more than just a country bumpkin. It was a different world. They were all so genteel and refined. Perhaps that's why my mother's taunts to my father lingered in the back of my mind. I could not forget overhearing their argument regarding my aunt. One day I gathered the nerve to ask my Mom about it, but she gingerly skirted the issue.

"Mom," I asked. "What's a whore?"

She was startled and terribly embarrassed, knowing I had overheard her quarrel with my father. "It is not a nice word for a child to use. So don't use it." She chose her words carefully, "It means prostitute, a woman who sells her body to men for their pleasure."

"For what? How does a woman do that?" I was mystified.

Realizing just how young and truly innocent I was, she refused to pursue it further. But, each time I returned home after an extended visit to Highland, Mom would question me about my aunt's visitors, what she talked about with them, and whether she smoked all the time. What about the neighbors—did they visit? Did they ever speak to me of her "affliction?"

What affliction? Aunt Cynthia did grunt incessantly and cough a lot from smoking. She always complained about one ache or another, but I knew of no particular affliction. Instead, she just helped others who were sick or in trouble. I remember telling my mother about Helen Owens and her daughter, Ivy Wilcox, who lived up the street from Aunt Cynthia, who said they could not have survived without "Miz Howard," my aunt. She tended their illnesses, and nursed their babies back to health with her home remedies. When Ivy had difficulty birthing her twins, Miz Howard delivered them; one was named Cynthia in her honor. They told me about having school activities in the little segregated schoolhouse in Highland, and Aunt Cynthia could always be counted on to contribute delicious, white frothy cakes and pumpkin pies to their fundraising efforts. But, when they referred to her as a "saint," Helen's husband George, an AME minister, snorted loudly; and Helen narrowed her eyes, daring him to say more in my presence.

It was Aunt Cynthia who taught me the facts of life, in very gentle but realistic terms of what I might expect in my life as a woman. My father was very strict and my mother was not one to cross him or to persuade him to be more lenient with me.

I was nearly 16, never had a date, and did not at all understand my father's protectiveness. In my junior year, however, my Dad did not forbid my going to the senior prom, probably because he knew I had no dress and no date (there were no colored boys in my class). He also knew I was scared to bring it up. I was miserable. All my school friends were going and with dates.

On the eve of the prom, I visited Aunt Cynthia who listened to my woes. Looking at my tear-stained face, she said, "Your father is vehemently opposed to your dating before you are sixteen. Does your school have any rules against your going to the prom alone, without a date?"

"I don't know!" I answered hopelessly. I hadn't thought of it.

She said simply, "How badly do you want to go?"

When I hesitated, she added, "Would you dare go alone?"

I opened my mouth to say, "Yes, but. . .!"

She repeated as she moved toward one of the great trunks. "Would you dare to go alone? If so, I have the dress, one I purchased years ago. I was saving it for my burial. Here, try it on; it should be a perfect fit."

She pulled from the bowels of the trunk a beautiful, pink, floor-length gown, trimmed in pink lace, ribbons and rosebuds, carefully wrapped in tissue paper. It was the perfect gown, in excellent condition, a little old-fashioned, but so was I. I put it on, and it did fit perfectly. She placed her pearls around my neck and some shiny studs in my ears, and brushed my hair into a coil like hers. I was Cinderella and Aunt Cynthia was my fairy godmother.

I kissed her, finished dressing and departed by taxi for the prom at the Terre Haute House. When I walked into the ballroom alone, everyone looked startled but seemed genuinely glad to see me. My classmates and friends gathered around touching and admiring my beautiful gown.

I had a wonderful evening and returned home to regale my aunt with stories about people's reactions to her gown and my great pride in wearing it. She listened with tears in her eyes.

I have no doubt now that she had indeed been a prostitute when she was younger. I was told later that she had been a Madame of one of the most active "houses" in the city during the Depression. It had been an economic means to keep herself and her loved ones alive. She was also addicted to drugs. I refuse to judge her. I just know that morphine eased her pain, and it became an addiction from which she died at the age of 70.

By that time, I was a grown, married woman with children and plans of my own. Still, her death left me feeling cheated of my inspiration. I loved my Aunt Cynthia dearly in life, and in memory I adore her more for teaching me to be bold, to go after what I wanted and to persevere no matter the hardship.

* * *

By sorting through all of these memories, I had sought to formulate for the journalist a better answer than I had given earlier regarding my ancestry and inspirations, but there was no time. I had to return to Washington for the final ceremonies.

Perhaps I would have another opportunity in the future to tell her the full story.

Inside The Oval Office

Back in Washington, I still had to prepare for the two official ceremonies which would finalize my appointment as ambassador. The first was a formal visit to the White House to be received by the highest power in the land, the President of the United States of America. The magic of that moment on July 1, 1986, can never be replicated.

The *invitées* to that occasion included the immediate members of my family. Of our six children, the two eldest, Donna Ross and Jim Shepard, both computer executives, came to Washington for the swearing-in, but had to leave before the White House visit was arranged. However, my other children were there: Paula Perry, a Houston school teacher, resplendent in her new dress, wearing her lovely, shy smile; Milo Shepard, a marketing representative in Washington; Mark Shepard, a recent graduate from Washington University in St. Louis and on his way to Nepal with the Peace Corps; and James Perry, the youngest, a student at Texas Southern University, in Houston. James would accompany us to Sierra Leone for a year of study abroad.

All my sons were six-feet tall, looking their handsomest in their dark suits. Included in the entourage were two of our grandchildren, Kent Ross and LeShan Shepard, who would also accompany us to Sierra Leone for a brief visit. I suspect that my robust family group arriving at the White House was one of the largest in history, taking up all the seats in the waiting room.

Our entry to the Oval Office was delayed a bit by the Marine guard who, at the last minute, could not locate the security clearances for James and Kent. The boys were delighted with this bit of intrigue; it was a story to tell their children some day. While waiting for them, we were seated in the President's Cabinet Room with its long, polished table and antique oak chairs, each one bearing the engraved name of each of the President's cabinet members. The room was full of history.

Finally, the boys arrived with their security tags and shortly thereafter we were ushered into the Oval Office, where President Reagan stood to receive us. I remember thinking how tall, handsome and dignified he was.

He shook hands with each of my family members as they were introduced to him and presented each with a small token of the presidential office. The boys were given tiepins with the official presidential seal, the eagle crest. When he approached Mark, the President accidentally dropped the tie pin on the floor and aides rushed to assist him; but President Reagan gracefully bent over and picked it up himself, presenting the pin to Mark without a hitch. It was memorable gesture signifying the president's humility, an act long remembered by us all, especially Mark.

My daughter was given a similar pin; my husband received a set of cuff links bearing the same presidential seal. I was presented with a large gold replica of the Great Seal in a magnificent jewelry case.

As Mr. Reagan presented the gifts, he looked at each of the boys standing shoulder to shoulder with him, and with a bewildered smile, suddenly exclaimed, "Gee, they're all so big!" We all laughed.

The visit was fairly brief. President Reagan again thanked me for my willingness to serve as his Ambassador to

Sierra Leone, stating that it was an important post where he felt I would represent him well. He bid me Godspeed. I looked around the office, noting the exquisite plates and vases, the paintings, fireplace and white furniture. I remember thinking I might not ever get there again, and tried to commit it all to memory. It was to be, however, only the first of several visits to the Oval Office.

We all shook hands again with President Reagan in leaving. Official photographs were taken of each of us with the President to be sent to us later, bearing his personal commendations and signature. It was difficult to believe this was not all a dream.

The Swearing-In Ceremony

The big day arrived for the final ceremony of the long process: July 3, 1986, my swearing-in ceremony, a day never to be forgotten. It was held in the Diplomatic Reception Rooms on the eighth floor of the State Department, in the grand Benjamin Franklin Room. These rooms are reserved for ceremonies of highest protocol, and are frequently visited by the President and First Lady and high-ranking officials of the government for receptions and state dinners.

Symbolically, these elaborately decorated rooms introduce new ambassadors to the beautiful, formal settings in which they will be involved abroad. Therefore, the rooms are also used for the swearing-in ceremonies of American diplomats. Events in these settings are not only of domestic importance but also of international significance as ambassadors and prominent nationals of foreign countries are often entertained here. Few people, otherwise, see this part of the building, and for most of my guests, this would be the first and perhaps only opportunity to visit these spectacular rooms.

It was a glorious day. I had elected to wear a beige macramé dress, the only one of its kind, made of South African silk and hand-woven in Zimbabwe. I had bought it in Harare on one of my visits and reserved it for more than two years for such a grand occasion. I felt delightfully regal.

The swearing-in is the zenith of all the ceremonies that a new ambassador has the pleasure to experience. It is, however, the ambassador's own party, including the costs, and is what the ambassador chooses to make of it. Some ambassadors choose to keep the ceremony very private and low-keyed (therefore low cost), inviting only a few close friends and family members to the reception. Some close the event with dinner at a quiet but elegant private club.

But, I wanted to share this moment with my family and friends who had supported me along the way. I spent hours planning the reception and invested a small fortune in purchasing engraved invitations, cases of champagne, a variety of hors-d'oeuvres, white grapes and cheese, and large bouquets of flowers. I also hired several servers from a catering firm to make sure everyone was served properly. Nearly 300 people attended the ceremony and reception, some from my deep past. All had to be approved by Security before they could enter this level of the building. The event was beautifully orchestrated and went off without a hitch.

Present were Sierra Leone's Ambassador to the United States, Dauda Kamara, and half of the Heads of Missions of the African Diplomatic Corps in Washington. President Richard Landini from my alma mater, Indiana State University, praised President Reagan for having chosen "one of Indiana's best." George Nichols, who had hired me at his investment office in Terre Haute so many years ago, when no one else would hire a black secretary or clerk in that town, kissed my cheek, his eyes glistening with pride. Jim Bowie, who loyally shepherded support for my nomination through the tough Texas political maze, presented me a signed congratulatory statement from Texas Governor Bill Clements and a signed and sealed proclamation from Kathy Whitmire, Mayor of Houston. Lori Chance was there representing Texas Senator Phil Gramm. Delta Sigma Theta Sorority's national president, Hortense

Canady, presented me a lovely, engraved silver chafing dish, a recognition reserved for highly honored sorors.

Many people there were my colleagues from A.I.D., especially Keith Sherper and Valerie Dickson Horton, my alter ego, whose constant prompting kept me reaching toward my goal. But, the majority were members of my family: children and grandchildren, sisters and brothers, my only surviving aunt, nieces and nephews, cousins and a host of friends and associates from near and far who had made it all possible. Also present were children of my deceased sister and brothers: James Norton, Jr., Phyllis Norton Savage and Dolores Norton Jackson.

Present in spirit, were George and Flossie Norton, my mother and father and most faithful and loving mentors throughout the years, who passed away just three months apart in 1973. I felt their proud presence as I took the Oath of Office, my husband holding The Bible:

> I, Cynthia Shepard Perry, do solemnly swear that I will faithfully execute the office of Ambassador to Sierra Leone, that I will to the best of my ability preserve, protect and defend the Constitution of the United States against all enemies, foreign and domestic, so help me God.

Words of an old spiritual kept ringing in my head: "Somehow I made it, Through it all, God Brought Me Through."

Deputy Secretary of State, John Whitehead, speaking on behalf of President Ronald Reagan and the Department of State, enumerated my past accomplishments and wished me Godspeed as our country's newest ambassador. I was not the first black female ambassador. I was preceded by four others: Patricia Harris (Luxembourg) possibly a distant relative; Barbara Watson (Malaysia); Mabel Smythe Hait (Cameroon); and Ann Holloway Forrester (Niger). Unlike most female ambassadors, I was married and my husband would accompany me to post, a rare phenomenon indeed.

The United States Information Agency (USIA) videotaped the swearing-in ceremony to be shared with Sierra

Leone's public television and to preserve these memories for my own posterity. That was quite a launching, and the exhilaration I felt was indescribable. The great buildup would precede me to my post where I would be made to appear the most respected, competent and beautiful ambassador that Sierra Leone had ever received from the United States. I began to worry about how people would react when the real Cynthia stepped off the plane in Sierra Leone.

In my speech, I gave high praise to my family and my beginnings, and my thanks to the many persons who had made the day possible for me.

That night in the hotel, as I finished my packing for the next day's departure for London, I relived the events of my swearing-in and the visit to the Oval Office. Missing among my closest friends at the celebrations was Herbert Lamb, my high school principal and earliest mentor, who years ago had encouraged my interest in civics and government. Years after graduation, Mr. Lamb had helped me to set my specific career goal to become ambassador and had urged me to strive to reach it. He was a bald, blue-eyed, skinny man who was so tall, he had to stoop to speak to students. I was the only black student in my class, fully integrated at a time when segregation was still an accepted legal and social reality. But, I suffered with other black students all over the nation the racial taunts and discriminating incidents of our time.

I remembered how Mr. Lamb stood by me and for me, and I always felt the aura of protection that his presence gave. He died just two years prior to this glorious day, but I knew how proud of me he would have been. I wished aloud that I could tell him "thank you" once again. Perhaps he heard and shared my joy.

All Things Being Equal

We departed Washington on July 7, 1986, for Sierra Leone. Our itinerary included stopping for a few days in London, Stuttgart, and Paris before boarding the flight to Freetown. I had spent the last morning in Washington on the phone, checking and rechecking several matters, talking to my eldest granddaughter, Pam Hill, and her husband Raymond, and bidding goodbye to our many friends in Washington.

It would be a long flight from Washington Dulles to London Heathrow and as was my practice on long overseas flights, I would meditate and draft some notes in my journal. After such prolonged excitement, J.O. and the three children had all become tired and grumpy, and while they peacefully slept in the comfort of first class, I relived and exulted over the events of the past few days.

As we flew over the darkened clouds toward London, I thought again of Mr. Lamb and his career advice. He always prefaced his predictions about the future with the phrase, "all things being equal," meaning one must perceive that all things can be right, fair, and balanced with no distinct deficits or disadvantages in any given area, in order to pursue and achieve one's goals. What if I had been fearful and had not followed his advice? I certainly could not have foreseen the difficult choices I would have to make all along the way, nor could I have anticipated the constant forks in the road, and the difficulty I would have in choosing between two equally good things. But, my goal was ever before me, and I pursued it like a horse with blinders on to prevent distractions from the chosen path.

I remembered well the day when Mr. Lamb and I sat together in my kitchen and worked out each step of my goal-setting exercise. That was in 1956, the days when people like me were classified as "colored," and our hopes, career opportunities, and expectations were limited. Mr. Lamb paid a visit to my home at my request. It may have been somewhat unusual, but I had remained very close to my former high school principal, and at this time, had a number of matters on which I needed his advice. I was married by then and mother of three small children, certainly no longer the shy high school student he had known.

Mr. Lamb (no one dared call him Herbert except for perhaps, his wife, Bernice) sat across the table from me, long thin legs crossed at the knee, needing lots of room for his nearly seven-foot frame in my small kitchen. I seemed to have known him all my life, perhaps literally so. My first memory of him was when he visited No. 8 School, the black primary school outside Terre Haute in Otter Creek Township. I must have been in the second or third grade, and was frightened out of my wits by his steely, blue-eyed stare. He looked the same to me on this day as he did then, although we had bonded somewhere along the way, and I was no longer frightened of him. His blue eyes were warm as we recalled some of the activities and students at Otter Creek High School in North Terre Haute. This had not been our first encounter since graduation. He had come to see me in 1947 soon after the birth of my first baby, Donna. When he had asked to hold her, she did her normal thing, filling her diaper to overflowing. I had taken her from him just in time to prevent ruining his elegant suit. Having no children of his own, he had thought it was very amusing.

"You look the same, Cynthia," he said. "A little more mature, but, even more beautiful. Marriage seems to agree with you. How is your husband? How many children have you?"

I felt myself blush a little. "My husband is in good health, he is steadily employed and we are doing well. Donna and Jim Boy are attending Deming Elementary School down the street. It was just integrated a few years ago. Milo's going to be two years old in a month." I pulled my handsome child from behind my chair where he stood staring at Mr. Lamb.

He coaxed Milo to him. "What a beautiful boy, looks a lot like you," he said, tossing Milo's glossy, black curls.

I hadn't the heart to cut Milo's hair yet, despite the fact that my brother, George, constantly teased that he looked like a girl. At nearly two years old, Milo was very sociable, and I was surprised that he was reluctant initially to face Mr. Lamb. On the other hand, he had never seen such a long, tall, white man in his mother's kitchen before.

While we sipped our coffee, I told Mr. Lamb that I had left Indiana State University after two years to marry and start my family.

"My husband had insisted that I should not return to college until the two children had entered school. I didn't plan to have more children. My husband was stubbornly obsessed with a prediction a fortune-teller made many years ago, that he would have only two children and no more. He said she was right about many other things, so therefore she must be right about that. I believed him and as a consequence, there are now three."

Mr. Lamb laughed heartily. I blushed at my openness with him about my private life.

"Now, after having taken night classes at the University for a few years," I continued, "I want to enroll full-time this fall to finish my degree. I asked you to come by because I need counseling and I couldn't think of anyone who could help me better than you." He leaned forward, expecting the worst. I wondered if he thought I were having marital or financial problems.

"I am greatly bothered by the minutia and ritual of marriage, of cooking, housekeeping, laundry—things that perhaps make me a good wife and homemaker, but not necessarily a good person. I don't mean less of a person. I love my children dearly, but I don't like myself anymore. I know that I am capable of doing more. A little added income could improve our standard of living. But, it's not money or lack of it that is upsetting me to the point where I don't sleep well. It's my own self-image, my own lack of self-worth."

He nodded but said nothing.

"I first thought if I got a job, it might help my frame of mind. But, what kind of job can a colored woman get? Once, I saw an advertisement in the newspaper for an artist, one of those 'Can You Draw?' things. My declared major at Indiana State was art. I loved to draw and paint, and was always made to believe I was pretty good at it. So, I went down to apply, fairly confident of my skills. When I walked into the workroom downtown, I was met with a sea of white faces, everybody staring curiously at me. The foreman said coldly, frowning at my impertinence, 'Can I help you?' I panicked, and responded equally coldly, 'I came to see about the job you advertised. But, I assume it's already been filled!' I turned on my heel and quickly walked out. I could not bear to hear this man say those words to me."

Mr. Lamb sighed empathetically.

"Then, once, my girlfriend asked me to work in her place because she was sick. It was daywork. I was not accustomed to working in someone else's house, and was embarrassed people might think less of me for doing it. But, I agreed to fill in for my friend, because I considered myself a good cleaner and hard worker. But, each day I went, I wore a stiffly ironed nurse's uniform with matching white shoes and stockings, my apron in my handbag. And, later in the day I returned home on the bus, still spotless in my white uniform. No one suspected I had been scrubbing floors all day."

He shook his head sadly.

I continued, "I lost one of those cleaning jobs anyway by knowing too much. The woman asked me to proof a legal brief she had typed for her husband. I did and corrected a few grammatical and spelling errors. She thanked me for calling these to her attention, inscrutably peering at me over the top of her glasses. But, later as she paid my day's wages, she told me my services were no longer needed. No matter! As you can see, my husband provides well enough for the children and me. It is not a question of money, therefore I have no need to accept employment from people who offend my dignity."

I served him another cup of coffee.

"I want to go back to college, but maybe with a change of direction. My very wise mother says there is no future in art for a colored person, or else my father would have pursued it. Artists have been known to starve to death. There are few positions for art teachers. She thinks I should not continue to study art. But, painting is what I do best. I am a fairly good typist, but don't feel I have much else to offer."

"Oh, I wouldn't know about that," he reflected a bit. "I've watched you since you were in the third grade at No. 8 School. I perhaps know your potential better than you could ever guess. You were an excellent student and leader in junior high and high school, against considerable adversity. You are tremendously talented, and you always accepted challenges in many areas, in spite of the pain you sometimes suffered as a consequence. You didn't think I knew, did you? You never let anything stop you. You just plunged right in, over your head or not. I admired your stamina, and your determination to succeed. I think you are simply ready to move forward again with your life. Now, let me ask you an important question. What is it you really want to do?" He peered intently at me.

"I don't know. What's possible?" I asked. "I have good secretarial skills, I think, but no employer wants to hire a colored girl. The few colored businesses in the city can hire only so many, and then you have to wait until somebody dies, or has a baby or something—wait in line for your chance. If I finish my degree, I suppose I could teach, but the same problem exists. The colored schools have few openings and you have to wait until a teacher retires or dies, or whatever to find a place. Even integration has not resulted in more positions for colored teachers. It has just shifted them around. Two years ago there were 44 colored teachers in three segregated schools; today there are 46 colored teachers in 35 integrated schools. Some of my friends with college degrees left Terre Haute for better opportunities elsewhere. Some are running elevators downtown. Only one colored girl, who holds a university degree and deserves more, has been hired as a salesgirl in one of the department stores."

He patiently pursued his line of thought. "I had no idea things were that bad, Cynthia, but the whole racial, political spectrum is changing dramatically and rapidly. Perhaps I can see it better than you. There will be employment futures for people like you, jobs and careers you can't imagine right now. It will happen most quickly for those who are qualified and ready."

He took a breath, still looking steadily at me. "Normally, when I do career counseling, I encourage people to set long-term goals, not just five to ten years ahead, but 20 to 30 years. So, I must ask, what do you want to be doing when you are 50 or more, Cynthia?"

What a provocative question! I suddenly saw myself at my mother's age, 56. Just a little gray, she still had no middle-age spread, and was energetic and imaginative. She was interested in ideas and concepts alien to most of her friends, loved horse racing and financial speculation. Could she have become anything else than what she is, I wondered? Had she also hoped for more in her life, inspired by Grandpa Josh and Aunt Evie, who had raised her?

Shaking my head, I responded, "I don't know."

"Okay," he said. "Who in the world do you admire the most? If you had the chance, all things being equal, who would you want to be? Who is your model?"

I could see this was a very serious game. My first thought was of my elementary school teacher.

"I always thought highly of Mrs. Love, June Love, at School No. 8. I think you did, too, as her supervisor at the school. She was beautiful, hard working, and intelligent. She worked so hard with us kids to prepare us for junior high school at Otter Creek, and even cried when my class graduated. She wanted us to do our best to succeed at whatever we would do in the future. Then she went to Crawfordsville when school No. 8 had to close down. As much as anyone, she was responsible for my moral development, my value system and all my basic skills. I certainly wanted to look like her, to walk proudly the way she did even when things didn't go well, and certainly to handle the English language the way she could. She was my mentor and model in that sense. But, I don't want to be a teacher."

I considered Evangeline Harris, a local schoolteacher and nationally-known author of children's books. I thought of Nila Pettiford Manuel, a highly respected teacher and principal of one of the three colored schools in the city. They were all very successful women, but they didn't fit my mode. I considered Marian Anderson, a renowned diva, Mahalia Jackson, the gospel singer, Lena Horne, a beautiful actress—they didn't fit either. I saw no colored models in my environment whose careers I wanted to emulate.

"Does this person have to be colored?" I asked suddenly.

He laughed, "I did say, *all things being equal.* It is simply a matter of perception—your perception—that will determine the limits you impose upon yourself."

He saw that he had lost me.

"Try imagining yourself in a perfect world. It means that you can simply ignore obstacles, as though they don't exist: not race, not money, not gender or education. You can choose to be whatever you want to be. Why not be white, rich, and qualified? Or at least have all the same possibilities that someone like that might have?"

That was a funny idea! Then, I said timidly, believing he would laugh in my face, "My model is Eleanor Roosevelt."

To my surprise, he did not laugh.

"I have been following her life in the newspapers, on radio, and now on television. She is not beautiful, not outwardly at least, but she has such courage, and she believes passionately in this United Nations organization as a place to bring the world together to discuss peace and to end war. People listen to her, and people in high places seem willing to accept her lead. I want to be like her: brilliant, articulate, fearless, positive, selfless—and rich!"

"And, what would you do in Eleanor Roosevelt's world—all things being equal?" Mr. Lamb prompted.

"Perhaps the role she plays or a similar one is aiming too high, Mr. Lamb. After all, she's married to the President of the United States, and I can't hope to replicate that. And, I have not contemplated a role in the United Nations even in my wildest dreams. Maybe that comes much later in my life." I glanced at him to see if he were smirking. He was not.

"I want to be the United States Ambassador to Kenya," I stated flatly.

Startled, he sat upright, feet flat on the floor, mouth slightly open. I began to stutter: "I've read a lot in the newspapers recently about several African nations yearning to breathe free, and who are fighting hard for their independence. Many people are dying on all sides, but I believe the Africans will win, because their cause is just. They should and must be free. Our government does not seem concerned with Africa, because unlike European nations, the United States is not guilty of colonizing the African people. But, there is that guilt thing for having made slaves of Africans in this country, resulting in today's racial divisions and problems."

I thought seriously for a moment. "It seems clear to me that America is more sympathetic with the European colonizers than with the African people. I strongly believe the time will come that all nations in Africa will be free and our government is going to need some good ambassadors to help build strong relationships between them and this country. The millions of colored people in this country will also benefit from an improved relationship between this country and the land of our ancestors. We will assume a new kind of pride, of identity, not forgetting the past, but building upon it."

I stopped, believing I had said too much, but his eyes were dancing. He was clearly challenged with the idea and perhaps my naiveté.

Finally, he said, "I am delighted, Cynthia. I was afraid for a moment that you might set your sights too low. Remember

Robert Browning's words: 'A man's reach must exceed his grasp, or what's a heaven for?' Why did you choose Kenya?"

He pronounced it "Keenya" like the newscaster on WBOW, the local radio station. Just that morning, I had read an editorial in the Terre Haute Tribune about the Mau Maus, a fearless insurgent group of Africans, fighting with the crudest weapons and winning against the white settlers with their guns and explosives. It was like Nat Turner in the deep South before the Civil War, fighting with nothing but the ability to strike fear.

"I know little about Kenya," I ventured, "except it is a British colony on the East Coast of Africa whose economy is totally dominated by European settlers and traders. I know that many Kenyans are being educated in England, so they speak English as well as their own native languages and Swahili. English is taught in their schools. But, I think they're going to need a good American ambassador to help resolve their trade and development problems when the smoke clears." I knew so little, I realized. I hadn't yet tried to locate Kenya on the map.

He said, "You know quite a bit. But, do you know what an ambassador does or the process of becoming one?"

When I indicated I knew nothing, he said, "I will have to do some research on this myself, Cynthia, but to begin with, there are two ways generally an ambassador is chosen. One, is to join the Foreign Service and rise up through the ranks, eventually to become an ambassador if you play all your cards right. The Foreign Service has its own career path, and normally it takes 20 to 30 years to reach ambassadorial level. In fact, only a very few career officers succeed in becoming ambassador."

Thinking aloud, he continued, "You could go that way after you complete your degree. The other way is to be appointed by the President, that is, only he has the authority to name ambassadors. Some appointments he reserves as patronage for people who have worked hard or contributed financially to his campaign, people who have been loyal to his political party, those who have supported his political efforts throughout the years. It is a question of party loyalty and party favor. How do you vote—Democrat or Republican?"

Seeing the blank look on my face, he laughed as he said, "Well, I think your first step might be to register to vote. Presidential elections are coming up and now is a good time."

"Which party?" I asked.

He chuckled in amazement. "Well, that's a choice only you can make, and fairly soon, I should think. You are yet young enough to handle the enormous number of choices you will have to make. I can get an application for you for the Foreign Service exam, but without a college degree, you might not do significantly well. The process is highly competitive."

He paused. "Just how badly do you want to be an ambassador?"

I was excited. He had not laughed; he had never used the word "impossible," never even suggested that this was an impossible dream.

"I'll do anything," I said.

He looked me in the eye. "Then, in that case, you have much work to do to prepare yourself. You should set a long-term goal—not four years, not six years, but at least 25 years, in order to get all the schooling and experience you will need for the job. For example, you must return to university without further delay, and earn a degree in Political Science—as I recall you excelled at government, history, current affairs and debate. Earn a Master's Degree in English or in a foreign language. Aim for the doctorate in international law or international studies, an area concerned with world affairs. By my calculations, that should take you 10 years from where you are now."

He rose to pace the floor. "You're also going to need private sector experience, I mean real work experience with perhaps a global enterprise, like AT&T or IBM. You'll also need experience in that area of the world that interests you, Africa, to match your studies and research. That's how you become known as an expert. Travel to Kenya, learn to speak Swahili, study the broad range of cultures and politics of Africa. It's a huge continent. Learn as much as you can about the diversity of its nations, people, languages, cultures, politics, beliefs, and traditions. You'll need a university base for teaching, writing, and publishing about Africa in general, and the country of your choice, or an area related to the international arena."

"That's going to take you," he suddenly grinned broadly, "another 15-20 years, I would think, considering where you're starting from."

By that time, I would be about 52 years old. My mother's face flashed before me again. By the time I completed all the steps outlined by Mr. Lamb, I would be her age and older. But, I said without hesitation, "Okay. I'll do it."

Neither of us spoke for a few minutes. He stood, was pensive, no longer looking at me but, rather, off to some point in time and space. I cradled Milo, now sleeping in my arms, trying to comprehend the immediate sacrifices and barriers I would have to overcome. Mr. Lamb stopped pacing and began to move toward the door.

"Yes, I believe you will do it. But it will not be easy, Cynthia. Consider your marriage, your children. How is this going to affect them?" He looked a bit troubled. "I'm sorry I have to go now, but I will find some information on the appointee process and we'll talk again about the politics of all this. There's plenty of time."

I wanted to tell him about the dream, a recurring dream that had plagued me over the past seven years. But, he seemed preoccupied as he walked out the door. I watched him climb into his car, so deep in thought he forgot to wave goodbye.

It occurred to me in the months and years that followed, as I researched the appointment and placement of ambassadors, that the only black diplomats at that time were two special envoys to Haiti and Liberia, both black nations. Knowing that, Mr. Lamb might have encouraged me to choose another career. Only three women had ever been appointed ambassador in the nation's history at that time, none of them black, and all completing the appointments of their husbands who had died in office. Knowing that, Mr. Lamb could have warned me not to have such high hopes. But, he didn't.

What an extraordinarily rare and wise counselor, Herbert Lamb! Maybe, he had encouraged me to set a high goal in order to gain the most I could by trying to reach it. By establishing sub-goals, he had prepared me to stop, if I must, for any reason, without a sense of failure. I could stop at the Bachelor's, for example, and teach political science at a local high school. Perhaps with his philosophy of "all things being equal," he believed I could make it. Perhaps he envisioned that in the 25 years ahead, traumatic and dramatic social and political change would create new opportunities for me, if I were ready. He made me believe my long-term goal was achievable, with time and perseverance. It worked!

I wondered how he might have interpreted my recurring dream in terms of the goal the two of us had just set.

The Dream Recurring

It was a disturbing dream. Its details would remain in my consciousness with amazing clarity when I awakened from sleep. Its meaning seemed unfathomable. My first memory of the dream dates back to 1949, the year following the birth of my second child. I cannot recall any dramatic or traumatic event that might have triggered the dream, but from that beginning throughout the twenty years it recurred, I was nearly consumed with a search for its true meaning.

It was a simple dream. It began with a three-room house, presumably my residence, where I would spend hours busily matching color schemes, painting, varnishing, papering, making draperies—all the interior decorating I could possibly do. When finished, I would step back to take a final appraisal, and fold my arms together in satisfaction. Then, suddenly, another door would open all by itself, leading to a completely unfinished, undecorated room. I could see clearly the 2x4's and rafters exposed like the ribs of a starving animal. The fireplace was unfinished; only the floors and windows were in place. I would be swept by a wave of frustration as I would begin to replan the entire decorating scheme of the whole house to include the empty room.

Each time I had the dream, I would awaken, tense and unhappy, clearly remembering it all. Over the years, the dream changed little. The house increased in size to include more than three rooms; the rooms grew larger and the stone facade of the house turned somewhat darker. The new room itself got larger, but the story was the same. The task of rethinking, reorganizing, redecorating, redoing, grew more frustrating with the increasing sizes of the house and room. Finally, it wasn't the content of the dream that disturbed me so much as the fact that it kept recurring like an old memory. What did it mean?

I never told Mr. Lamb about this dream, but the goal-setting process we started that morning in 1956 brought the dream sharply into focus in my mind. Perhaps it was somehow connected with my desire to "become," but it was also a little mystical, perhaps eerie. I wasn't sure how to present it, as though it might somehow nullify the seriousness of my career goal.

I followed through immediately on some steps in the process we established; e.g., in 1956, I joined the Republican Party followed by full-time employment with Nichols Loan Corporation. For the next four years, the Company allowed me time to undertake part-time studies at Indiana State University, pursuing a degree in political science. I enjoyed these courses tremendously under the tutelage of Paul Fowler, head of the Political Science Department, and Arthur Dowell, my major professor who thought I hadn't a clue.

Most students in my classes were half my age, terribly quick and bright, and who knew all the answers. Evening classes were long and exhausting, and after having worked all day as well as caring for three children, I would sleep through a lot of important information. I could carry only six to nine credit hours per semester, and I knew it would take a long time to complete the program I had started. The important thing was that I had begun.

In 1961, I convinced my husband that we should serve as host family for a growing number of exchange students at ISU, especially those from Africa and the West Indian islands of Jamaica and Barbados. My understanding of other cultures was significantly enriched by my affiliations with these students. I was especially impressed with two graduate students from Jamaica who were my age: Hope T. Gooden and Jasper Wray. They were both scholars, and the classical education they had received in the former British schools in the islands had given them a breadth of knowledge and understanding unequaled by most of us. They identified with my ambitions and inspired me to excel in areas of art history and geography, about which I knew so little.

My psychology professor, Marguerita Malm, was a beautiful Swedish woman, around 35 years old. I found her soft approach to understanding the human psyche very intriguing, perhaps clairvoyant and mystic. Soon after my return to classes at ISU, I joined Psychology 101 and eventually requested her help in analyzing the dream.

She found it quite challenging.

"I understand that you have had this dream seven times in seven years. Describe it to me; try to recall every detail."

I described it in minute detail as she requested. "Why," I asked, "do I continue to have the same dream? Why can't I dismiss it? Am I losing my mind?"

She laughed a deep-throated laugh.

"I can see it bothers you greatly, and I believe also the dream has a meaning, very possibly a quite simple meaning. But, I need to know a great deal more about you personally, before I can try to make sense of it. I need to know more about your family, your parents, and your history. Have you sisters and brothers? What's your husband like, and your children?"

She glanced at her watch, laughing at herself.

"I have one hour before my next class, and there's so much I need to know about you. Let's see what we can get done today, and if not finished, we'll save another hour somewhere in the next few weeks."

As I began my story, she started taking notes. I hesitated. She hastened to explain, "I don't want to interrupt your train of thought when you get started with your story, and I will note only those things that need clarification. I am not a psychiatrist—I'm sure most people don't know the difference. There will not be a fee, Cynthia, and I promise you I will not include your life in my next book. Please do call me Peg."

Thus I began an analysis that lasted nearly six months, with intermittent meetings and discussions on every aspect of my existence. Peg loved to hear about my relationship with my husband. When I related to her Otto's comment that 'educating one's wife is like fattening frogs for snakes,' she snorted derisively.

"I've never heard that expression before, but its meaning is quite clear. With your high expectations of self, how can you be happy married to this man? He's a chauvinist. He doesn't deserve you. I guess I don't understand well this thing called love."

I was astonished; it was the first time she had offered her opinion. Apparently, my story had pushed one of her buttons, maybe several.

In the final weeks of our relationship, she scheduled a longer period of time to complete the analysis of the dream.

"This has been a most intriguing experience for me, Cynthia. I have learned a lot from you about how a woman fares in American society. More importantly, I'm beginning to see the difference in historical perspectives and aspirations of black women in comparison with the middle-class white women I normally counsel. Clearly, not all things are equal here."

She paused. "Your dream is simple, but quite sobering and full of hidden meaning. Perhaps you are now more aware of its complexities than when we first started the sessions. You certainly have a rich background. Your robust heritage, the knowledge you have of your own history is quite phenomenal. Your parents and siblings, your husband and children form a very rich legacy. I'm really quite envious. To be sure, you weren't born with a silver spoon in your mouth; things haven't always been easy for you, but none of this has hindered you thus far. You are a survivor, a winner."

She referred to her black notebook. "Your dream is telling you in a most compelling way that a special door of opportunity has opened for you, and will lead to a successful future if you pursue it vigorously and without hesitation. You can close that door without venturing through, thereby preserving your marriage and keeping the family intact. But, in your last dream, you peered inside that door and saw the vast emptiness that could represent a challenge in completing or continuing something already begun. I find that intriguing."

She shifted in her chair to look more directly at me. "There is something quite mystical about this dream, making it more a vision than a dream. I think the increasing sizes of the house and that special room are truly significant. The room could be a city within a state, a state within a country, a country within a continent or the world. Definitely, the room is a smaller but significant part of something much greater."

I was depressed, wanting so badly to end the pesky dream. She continued, "Your marriage has considerable merit, Cynthia, in spite of what I think. Your husband, Otto, loves you and his home, his children; he is faithful, reliable and resourceful. Many women would kill for that! He will resort to anything to keep from losing you, but can't find an acceptable way to hold you. Nonetheless, the dream is asking you to take the risk, to become what you must in life."

She finished. "This is my professional interpretation of your dream. It may not be accurate, but this is essentially what I see in it. Think through what I have said. Come back to see me again—in a month, a year, five years, I will be here for you."

What was there to say? I thanked her sincerely for her time, for her caring, for being there for me, and then took my leave. I wanted to tell her, but could not, that I was pregnant for the fourth time and was headed for an emotional confrontation with Otto and his fortuneteller.

Nonetheless, I was determined to have my baby and to continue working toward my degree. So, I attended classes until I could no longer fit into the narrow lecture hall chairs. Mark, my third son, was born in January 1963, and after two weeks, I rejoined my classes to complete the semester.

Before their return to Jamaica in 1962, my two friends invited me to visit Kingston as their guest. So, in 1964, with a one-year old infant in hand, the visit to Jamaica became my two-week "semester abroad" program. I also experienced my first terrific bout of "culture shock" over unfamiliar living conditions, strange new foods, tastes, and smells. But based on that experience, I became more conscious of my surroundings and political condition and was determined more than ever to push toward my goal.

Choosing a Party

I was startled from my reverie by the Captain of the TWA flight, who introduced himself and addressed me as "Ambassador." He told me how pleased he and his crew were to have me aboard for my "maiden voyage" to my assigned post, and if there were anything he or his staff could do to make me more comfortable, to please ask. Common sense told me that this attention was a ritual performed for all new ambassadors. Nonetheless, I was extremely flattered by this courtesy: it was a reminder of the new personality I had so recently become.

The flight was still several hours from London. I needed something to do. Rummaging through my portfolio, I found a briefing paper, informing me of the London airport protocol, persons meeting me, and a brief itinerary for the day. I smiled as I unearthed a lovely pen given to me by an old friend, inscribed, "It's lonely at the top." I glanced at my sleeping husband and hoped the inscription was not prophetic.

I carefully reviewed the post staffing pattern, an introduction to my staff and their roles. There were 28 U.S. government "direct hires," representing four different American agencies stationed in Freetown, Sierra Leone. None of these persons was known to me personally, although I had talked with key persons by phone. There were also Foreign Service Nationals, called "FSN's," Sierra Leonean professionals, who were classified quite separately from the larger number of contract and short-term staff hired locally. The FSN's were employed by the Embassy in supportive service roles under the supervision of the Administrative Officer and the General Services Officer, both Americans. Several FSN's had been employed for years at the Embassy and were intensely loyal to the United States. The total staff of our mission, then, approached 150 persons.

I looked forward to meeting all my staff and developing a good working relationship within the mission. At the same time, I began to wonder more and more how I, a presidential appointee, would be received by my "career" Foreign Service staff.

I had overheard pointed comments made by State Department colleagues and inferences during the ambassadorial briefings, that a political appointee was perceived as having somewhat lower status and as being of "lesser quality" than a career officer. The special White House briefing indicated that until 1924, only political appointees could serve as ambassador. Foreign Service personnel were prohibited from serving in this high post until the Rogers Act of 1924 was enacted.

Although I had not come up through the ranks, I felt equally prepared for the role and resented the distinctions being made. While I had chosen the political route to reach my goal, I believed, in fact, that my training and experience for the role were equal to or higher than the quality of training undergone by career officers. My formal education, in fact, exceeded that of most Foreign Service Officers; few had doctoral degrees. I had lived and worked six years in Kenya and Ethiopia with the United Nations, being exposed to both Swahili and Amharic. I had studied French and Spanish in my college years, although I would need further training to gain fluency. I had served for four years at policy and management levels in the Agency for International Development (A.I.D.) In Washington. I had managed staff, and had crafted and directed educational and human resources programs for more than 40 countries in Sub-Saharan Africa. I had traveled and worked in as many as 30 of them.

My domestic or civil service experience also was broader than the normal career service. Besides having served as professor and administrator of a university, I had conducted research and writing beyond my dissertation, worked with major land grant institutions as well as minority colleges in obtaining government grants to administer and staff programs for African universities. I had thereby gained experience and insights for designing, building, and managing programs within the entire spectrum of human resources development. Few career officers could boast of this level of governmental and non-governmental involvement. I felt totally equal to the task.

Perhaps I was indeed an anomaly, being atypical of the traditional concept of political patronage, and lacking the inculcation and discipline of the career service. I was neither political nor career, more academician than politician, but no less a competent and committed member of the Civil and Foreign Services of the United States Government. I decided therefore, that I would not feel intimidated by discrimination, if I should sense it. And after all, who at post, in his right mind, would discriminate against the ambassador? I put the portfolio back together and tucked it safely away again.

Intimidation, discrimination, these were things that I'd dealt with all my life: against my race, my sex, my lofty aspirations. I laughed at myself. It had never really happened to me before to be discriminated against on the basis of my politics and political connections!

* * *

I never really considered myself a "political" appointee, not in the traditional sense, certainly. For a long period in my life, to tell the truth, I wasn't "political" at all, in any sense of the word.

The one-room, segregated, elementary school I attended when growing up, School No. 8, served as the polling place for coloreds in our community in the outskirts of Terre Haute, Indiana. Whites voted separately at School No.10, the school for white children. The Democrat pollsters—most of whom were miners and union members—stood outside the polls, threatening with violence anyone attempting to vote the Republican ticket. These early memories of the democratic process created a bias, and greatly influenced my attempts as an adult to be philosophically neutral in my choice of party affiliation.

I was born in Burnett, Indiana, a small coal-mining town just outside Terre Haute, Indiana, an industrious Midwestern city with a population of 90,000 more or less. Terre Haute was the home of Eugene V. Debs, a dynamic individual very persuasive in trade unionism who, in 1920, came close to winning the presidency on the Socialist ticket. Theodore Dreiser, noted author of many novels including *Sister Carrie* and *An American Tragedy*, helped to influence popular thinking and action during his time. His elder brother, Paul Dresser, also born in Terre Haute, wrote the famous song, *On the Banks of the Wabash, Far Away.*

Terre Haute, located on the Wabash River and at the crossroads of Highways 40 and 41, was also the home of Clabber Girl Baking Powder. This large, industrial enterprise served the baking needs of the total nation and provided employment for hundreds of people.

My home and my legacy lay, however, in Lost Creek, a small black settlement a few miles east of Terre Haute, between the two great creeks known as Lost Creek and Otter Creek. These rich farmlands, yet inhabited by a few descendants of the original settlers, were purchased in the 1820's, long before the Civil War. The settlement became almost totally independent from white jurisdiction, had its own schools, churches and businesses supporting the farm industries, and was almost totally self-sufficient. This was all the more important as the community was socially segregated from the rest of the surrounding communities, almost uniformly white. The close and strong relationships between families and the discipline inherent in my Lost Creek community, had a significant impact upon my value system. We were not shielded, however, from the constant need to deal with the rights and wrongs of our social surroundings and to negotiate racial co-existence with the whites around us.

My husband, Otto, also came from a long line of farmers and landholders in the community, relatively prosperous and extremely conservative, who long believed their prosperity had come about through Abraham Lincoln and the Republican party. They had been far removed in thought and action from the transient mining settlement of Burnett, who were for the most part Democrats. But, my husband's family, my own father and many other colored voters from Lost Creek changed parties after Franklin D Roosevelt's first term. The Roosevelt administration's strong platform on poverty was very popular among black voters across the country, considering the bold actions the administration had taken to alleviate the plight of the black minority, especially in the military.

My husband expected that I would vote his family's ticket; I would otherwise, he reasoned, cancel out his own vote. If I would not vote Democratic, I might at least have the good sense not to vote at all. That would have been satisfying to more than just my husband, since, as I knew very well, "decent" women in those days were supposed to show disinterest in frequenting both the polls and the bars—where men passionately discussed the "relevant" issues of the day.

I was not totally ignorant of politics in Terre Haute. Remembering Mr. Lamb's advice that I become more politically active, I joined the local chapter of the NAACP shortly after our "kitchen conference." As the chapter's political officer, I was required to explain to the membership the role that political action played in supporting the eradication of racism and discrimination. I was knowledgeable of some of the candidates and their platforms, but unknown to many whom I counseled, I had never voted nor even registered to vote.

How I actually became a Republican rather than a Democrat was for more practical than philosophical reasons. Some months before, Herb Lamb had convinced me that choosing a political party and registering to vote was essential to my career. At the age of 28, I thought deeply about the matter, debating the merits of both—like choosing a religion radically different from that of my parents. The political process was somehow a little distasteful. Politics was considered among my friends as dirty, divisive, and boisterous. They had visions of smelly cigars and smoke-filled bars, drinking, swearing— certainly politics ought to be avoided, said the righteous few. But, I had to choose a party. Where to start?

President Eisenhower was the candidate for reelection that year, 1956, and it was widely speculated he would win by a greater margin in the second election over his opponent Adlai Stevenson, Democrat, from Illinois.

Life in Terre Haute had been dominated by the Democratic Party for more than two decades, led by the mayor of the city, Ralph Tucker, who had been in office for that period of time. Crime and corruption were rampant. His political machine was strong. He maintained control of the colored communities by ordering his police force to look the other way when it came to illicit businesses, such as prostitution and gambling. He gave controls to the black politicians who were involved in the numbers racket.

In 1956, incumbent Mayor Tucker was running for Governor of the State of Indiana and feeling confident that he would win. He feared, however, that if Dwight Eisenhower won the presidency, his Republican gubernatorial opponent would be swept into office. Mr. Tucker was, therefore, waging a very strong offensive campaign, especially among the minority strongholds throughout the state. He needed the colored vote to win.

I barely knew the local Republican candidate for Mayor, so overshadowed was he by Mayor Tucker. My review of party platforms and practices hadn't disclosed for me any outstanding differences in the two parties. Despite the evil I perceived in Mr. Tucker's politics, I was determined to have first-hand knowledge of how the political system worked.

I actually didn't know where to begin my political research and training, and after some consideration I simply decided to start at the top. I made a visit to the Mayor's Office at City Hall. The Mayor surprisingly granted me an appointment. I was, of course, a completely unknown quantity, but he greeted me pleasantly as I entered his office. After scrutinizing me closely for a few seconds, he asked charmingly, "And, what can I do for you, Mrs. Shepard?"

I sat up straight and prim in my chair and said with all seriousness:

"I know you are running a very serious gubernatorial campaign and only a few weeks remain before election. I know you hope to win."

He smiled beguilingly. "Yes, and I shall. There is much to do and it doesn't pay to become overly confident, but we believe we have more than a good chance of winning." He paused to light his cigar.

"Mr. Tucker," I cleared my throat, my eyes beginning to water from the smoke, and looked him in the eye, "If you will hire me on your campaign committee, I can guarantee your victory—not just in Terre Haute but elsewhere in the State." I marveled at my own audacity.

He leaned forward in his seat, blowing perfect rings of cigar smoke into space. I had piqued his curiosity and captured his interest. I saw it in his eyes. I was an unknown quantity in local politics, perhaps useful to the campaign. "Well, I suppose I could do that. I do need your help—not here in Terre Haute; we have the city covered—but in Gary and Indianapolis where most of the colored voters live, perhaps Fort Wayne. That's where I really need your help. Would you be willing to relocate to one of these cities to help build those campaigns?"

His words took the wind right out of my over-inflated expectations. I could not, of course, consider his proposal.

"No, I cannot, Mr. Mayor," I said regretfully. "My husband's job is here; my children are in school here. Terre Haute is our home. I pay taxes here and surely ought to be able to find work here."

He remonstrated, "It would be only a temporary relocation. When I take office, I will find employment for you here in Terre Haute and you can even determine what kind of job you want." He flashed his famous smile.

When I shook my head and rose to leave, he said: "I'll discuss this with my people and see what we might find for you to do here."

I knew that "his people" were the racketeers who had already sold out the community where I lived. They would turn thumbs down on any appointment he might consider for me. I was a church-going-housewife-turned-activist, not known as a political team-player, considered too clean, apolitical, unknown, and unpredictable. There were many others standing in line for jobs who could be trusted to support the mayor's campaign, despite the fact he was considered the crime boss in the minority communities of Terre Haute. Those others would be the ones rewarded by appointments to the less than meaningful jobs reserved for coloreds.

I left City Hall, disappointed that I had failed to accomplish getting my foot into the political process, especially at such an exciting and critical time. Yet, I was relieved that for all my yearning to accomplish that goal, I had not allowed myself to be bought cheaply, nor had I aligned myself with a campaign which I frankly did not respect.

I had not given up my quest, however, and knew precisely what to do next. I stepped out of City Hall and walked more determinedly than ever one block south from the Mayor's Office, where I turned the corner and arrived at the Republican campaign headquarters. The office was quite festive and bustling with activity. When I asked to see the person in charge, they pointed out George Nichols, the State Party Treasurer—a big man, smoking a big cigar. With little variation, I gave Mr. Nichols the same story I had given Mayor Tucker, and with the same outrageous assurances that I could lead the party to victory.

"Can you type?" Mr. Nichols asked without hesitation. When I indicated that I could, he hired me on the spot.

He turned me over to a secretary, who gave me a stack of cards to alphabetize, campaign literature to mail, and other innocuous, clerical kinds of things to perform like filing, answering phones, and running errands. But, I was there, and was even placed where I could be seen from the front window (instead of being hidden away in the back, as I might have expected). And, I was being paid a minimal salary for the work I would do until election day.

When Mr. Nichols checked on me later, he said, "If you do well, I have a business down on Main Street, a loan office, and I'll give you a job after elections are over." He didn't qualify his offer to say "if we win" or "if you pass an exam" or anything of the sort, although these conditions were probably inherent in the offer. He gave me hope for the future. I felt so good about myself. It was a kind of coup. That afternoon, I located the proper voter registration office and registered as a Republican.

General Eisenhower won that year by a landslide, so did the Republican Governor. Mayor Tucker lost his gubernatorial bid, but remained in the Mayor's seat until his retirement in 1967. I went to work for Nichols Loan Company for the next five years and thus began also my 30-year sojourn with the Republican Party. My active membership in the Party introduced me to many leaders, activities, cities, and places in the world and finally, through my many friends and mentors, to my goal.

I had formally decided to become a Republican after researching the history of the two parties. I believed the basic tenets of the Republican Party were most closely aligned with my personal philosophies, and so I remained loyal to the party. But the prejudices I now felt in 1986, as a political appointee, I considered to be without basis—at least not for those reasons traditionally given. I had made no large financial contributions to the party or to a candidate, which might have earned me political favor. Nor had I run for office or been defeated in a political race which would have brought into the party an appreciable number of new voters. I did not fit other reasons traditionally given for political favor, like mounting or directing a significant campaign in my area. The number of black Republicans across the nation was miniscule. Although I might have tried to win an appointment by increasing and encouraging black participation in the party, I had not done this either, to any appreciable degree.   I felt certain that my extensive experience and knowledge of Africa and diplomacy had been the decisive factors in my selection as ambassador.

I was grateful that the political route carried with it the added power and influence of the Presidency and the White House. It seemed certain that resentments would follow me, in fact had preceded me to post, and I decided that I should be prepared to deal with them, as I had with so many others all my life.

I peered out the small airplane window, fighting the sleep threatening to overtake me, exhilarated to be finally on my way.

On Our Way

We were awakened by the stewardess as the plane began its descent at London Heathrow airport. We scrambled to become presentable and to get our belongings together for customs. James, our youngest, had gone through these procedures many times in our past travels, but it was all new for my grandchildren, Kent and LeShan. They tried to appear as calm as James, who was feigning boredom with their excitement.

A courtesy cart was waiting for us at the customs gate and passed us quickly through the passport controls. My husband, LeShan, and I and were flanked by James and Kent, who were too large to get into the same cart. They looked very much like assigned secret service to those who didn't know better. They loved the stares and whispers of other airport travelers as they trotted to keep up with the courtesy cart as it whizzed along the corridors.

Our hosts from the United States Embassy in London guided us through a rapid, full day's tour of the city. It was the first opportunity for Kent and LeShan to visit London Bridge and to see the changing of the guard at Buckingham Palace, experiences they would never forget.

We departed the next morning by plane for Germany, spending the next few days in Stuttgart at the American military headquarters where I could familiarize myself with their IMET (International Military Education and Training) program in Sierra Leone. This was my first and very pleasant encounter with the formal, diplomatic protocol with which I would henceforth be met everywhere I went. Armed escorts met us at the airport and moved us quickly down the highways in fully-armored cars to the headquarters of the United States/European Command, EUCOM. The next day, I was given a detailed briefing on American military assistance programs for Sierra Leone. I was greatly impressed with the leadership training program being conducted by EUCOM to build the efficiency of Sierra Leone's military. One newly approved program for Sierra Leone had been reserved as a gift for me to present to the country's new president on my arrival.

While I was in the briefings, J.O. and the children visited the Black Forest, had lunch at an old German castle, and toured the area purchasing souvenirs with the help of a military guide.

Early the following morning, we were escorted overland by a military-chauffeured limousine with appropriate motorcycles and follow-on cars from Stuttgart to Paris. We spent the afternoon at the Eiffel Tower and walked along the Champs d'Elysées. We had planned to have lunch at the Eiffel Tower, where the children could experience the panoramic view of Paris. However, as we drove through the city, they spied MacDonald's, the first in Paris, and insisted that we have hamburgers for lunch. Knowing there would be no MacDonald's in Freetown, we gave in.

That evening, we boarded Air Afrique for an overnight flight to Sierra Leone. When we checked in at the first-class counter that evening, with ten large bags to be checked, the French pilot demanded that all bags be opened. They were all locked. I protested, waving my diplomatic passport under his nose.

"I am the American Ambassador to Sierra Leone and this is my family. As diplomats, we are immune to search—both our bags and our persons."

He saluted me and said very calmly, "Congratulations, Madame Ambassador. I wish you greatest success in your new post and hope you will travel with us often. You are quite correct. You have the right to refuse to open your bags. I am the pilot of this plane with the responsibility to get you and other passengers safely to your post. If you stand on your rights and do not open your bags, I reserve the right to refuse you seats on this plane. The choice is yours."

With great annoyance, I removed the locks and watched as the officers thoroughly searched each and every bag, and then took my seat on the plane much chagrined. I marked that one down in my little black book.

* * *

The flight to Sierra Leone was about 12 hours long. The plane stopped in Cape Verde, where we were all forced to disembark for refueling. That took about two hours. It was a miserably hot and humid morning, and a shocking introduction to the atmosphere and climate of West Africa. During the wait, I discovered that 50 Peace Corps Volunteers were on the same flight headed for posting in Sierra Leone. They were pleased to have the first opportunity to meet their new Ambassador, and claimed me as their very own. I was happy, too, that in addition to the new military assistance program, I was also delivering to the President of Sierra Leone, 50 new Volunteers.

They had many questions about the people of the country in which they would live and work for the next two to three years, although their training had well prepared them for their posts. I had the advantage of knowing the political side of Sierra Leone, having visited the country several times in previous years. From 1971 to 1973, J.O. and I had directed a Teacher Corps/Peace Corps project at Texas Southern

University in Houston, which prepared master's level teachers for inner city Houston schools. After teaching for one year in Houston, they were sent with Peace Corps to teach for two to three years in the nations of Sierra Leone, Ghana, Kenya and Liberia. Our three younger children had accompanied us several times during those years, when we returned to supervise the interns in Sierra Leone, and knew the country quite well. Many of the professionals we knew were still in place. Dr. Koso Thomas was now Vice Chancellor of Fourah Bay College and his wife, Olayinka, a medical doctor, was still practicing medicine. Dr. Dan Chaytor was still at the College and his wife, Trixie, was still active in nursing. Violet and John Smythe, the Queen's Counsel for British Commonwealth interests in Sierra Leone, were still there, along with Gladys and Salia Jusu-Sherif, who would soon be one of the Vice Presidents of Sierra Leone. We were looking forward to reestablishing these old relationships as well as making new ones.

To complement my first-hand experiences in the country, I had done a great deal of background reading to familiarize myself with developments occurring in the intervening years. The State Department had also briefed me thoroughly on recent political developments.

I found the history rather fascinating. According to historians, the Portuguese accidentally came upon Sierra Leone in 1450 during a severe thunderstorm, and because the two humps of the highest mountain peaks resembled crouching lions, they called it "La Sierra da Leona" or the "Mountain of Lions"—subsequently Sierra Leone.

The peninsula, with its deep natural seaport, on which the modern capital city of Freetown was established, and the nearby Bunce Island, served as prosperous way stations during the prolonged period of the African slave trade. When slavery was outlawed in England in 1772, the former slave ships were refurbished and their owners were contracted to repatriate 40,000 slaves from Britain, Canada, and the West Indies. The repatriated slaves—who stemmed originally from many tribes and countries in Africa—were resettled primarily along the fertile coastline of Sierra Leone, displacing many tribal groupings already established in that territory.

The seeds of war had thus been planted from the beginning, and these bore disastrous fruit in continuous conflicts even in the modern day, with many killed on all sides. The newcomers spoke English, and were called Krios, people of many racial mixtures and languages. They did not consider themselves a tribal group. In their minds, they were British and therefore "better" than the locals. In time, they became the powerful leaders and merchants in the new country and helped to colonize the country for the British. They eventually lost their overlord positions, so to speak, when England established an official colony in that country. The Krios, many having been well educated in England by this time, became instead the powerful, civil servants of the British colonists.

According to my briefings, the efforts of Krios to colonize Sierra Leone was not easy. The Mende, Temne, Sousou, Limba, Kono, and other native warring factions fought bloody battles to maintain their lands. And, this resistance was continuous. Notwithstanding, Sierra Leone eventually became a British colony, and the City of Freetown was founded in 1787. It took much longer to "tame" the interior with its many different tribal groups and languages. But, the colonists set up churches and schools and the missionaries went about civilizing the natives with a vengeance, rewarding those who best assimilated the new culture.

When Sierra Leone achieved its independence in 1961, strangely enough, the British did not hand over the reins of leadership to the minority Krios as might have been expected, but rather to the majority tribal groups—the Mende and the Temne, who had no previous administrative experience. This became and continued to be a bitter bone of contention within the country over the years. The Mende, Temne, and Krios seemed unable to form a coalition government, and there was always the threat of serious civil disturbance.

Eventually, power was taken by the Krio minority. The first president, Milton Margai, a Krio, was highly regarded as an advocate for education for the masses. The direction of the government was dramatically changed under the next president, Siaka Stevens, also a Krio, upon his return from exile in London in 1970. President Stevens had tremendous political strength and sense of direction, cementing his power through economic changes. He was not well liked, however, by the fiercely competitive tribal groups. During his administration, the Krio president felt it necessary to hire mercenary soldiers from Guinea, a neighboring country, as his bodyguard, his protection from insurrection. The newest president, Major General Momoh, who succeeded President Stevens in 1985, was from a smaller tribal group. He thought he could ameliorate the tension by appointing two vice presidents, thereby ensuring that the concerns of both major tribes, Mende and Temne, were heard and treated fairly.

Political and military control were but few of many issues impeding the successful stabilization of Sierra Leone. The major issue was control over the vast natural resources. Sierra Leone was at that time, and is still, an immensely blessed land in terms of its natural wealth. Diamonds were discovered in 1930, and Sierra Leone, still under colonialism, became the world's second largest exporter of diamonds. These were gemstones classified number one in quality in the world. The country's wealth of natural resources—particularly gold, diamonds, bauxite and rutile (a rare ore used in titanium production for jet engine construction, and paint manufacture among other things) brought sudden, new prosperity in mining and increased employment for local people after independence.

Due to mismanagement of these resources, however, and widespread corruption at the top, the government lost control over its resources and was, in fact, very nearly bankrupt by the time I arrived as its new American ambassador. Its immense wealth leaked steadily out of its ports into European and Middle Eastern markets and into "long pockets" inside the local government. Sierra Leone became known as a "kleptocracy." It seemed ludicrous that this small country in Africa, no larger than the State of Tennessee, could possess such tremendous wealth and yet suffer so much anguished and unnecessary poverty.

To be sure, things had drastically changed since 1973, when Sierra Leone was in its heyday, under President Siaka Stevens, who had been in power since the country became a Republic in 1971. Papa Siaka, a title he enjoyed, was an extremely powerful man on the West Coast of Africa, but had been forced to retire in 1985 under great pressure from his own people for lack of control over his government's extravagance. For example, in 1980, Sierra Leone hosted the 17th annual summit meeting of the Organization of African Unity (OAU), representing 50 independent countries of Africa. The summit was held in Freetown, and presided over by President Stevens. Just prior to the 1980 Summit, he built for himself, at the expense of the government, a great mansion overlooking the entire port city of Freetown, where with his binoculars and powerful telescope, he could see everything that moved. In addition to this well fortified castle, he also built the Bintimani Hotel with its modern conference center and a village of 52 completely modern bungalows to accommodate visiting heads of state. All of this had cost the government many millions of dollars.

The Bintimani was considered a "white elephant." Having been built to reflect the art and culture of Africa, it proved too costly to staff and maintain after the summit closed. So, it sat like the Taj Mahal, gleaming white in the morning sunlight; empty, rarely used, crowning the highest hill on the Bay. And, these exorbitant expenditures brought the government to a standstill, nearly totally bankrupt.

Even after Stevens was no longer president, as head of the ruling All Peoples Congress (APC), he wielded immense power. He selected his own replacement, Major-General Joseph Momoh, making it clear to his subjects and to diplomatic observers that Papa Siaka was still very much in control. Even in retirement, he continued to live with his extended family quite comfortably in the mansion on the hill, where like the Greek gods, he could oversee the machinations of mortal men. The continued use of his corruptive power became a critical question among the industrialized nations of the world. Would he continue to orchestrate the affairs of state from the top of the highest hill, no matter that a new president was in place? Was the party more significant and more powerful than the office of the presidency? How much authority did the new president actually have to make changes in the government and in the economic conditions of the country? Was President Momoh strong enough to take over the reins of government? Were U.S. funds safe in his hands? I thought deeply about these questions, to which I was to find answers during my tenure in Sierra Leone.

My musing over the future of this beautiful and potentially wealthy African country was cut short by the captain's announcement that we were landing in Sierra Leone.

WORKING TO MAKE A DIFFERENCE

Arrival at Post

On the bright, clear summer morning of July 13, 1986, we arrived at Lungi Airport, Freetown, Sierra Leone. From the plane's window, the countryside had looked the same as I had recalled it, very tropical, huge billowy white clouds, tall palm trees swaying in the sea breeze along the bright blue Atlantic Ocean. The airport gallery was alive with people clothed in dazzling colors, waving welcome to friends and family aboard the incoming flight.

James, the youngest of our six children, was only six years old the last time we visited Sierra Leone, but he remembered it all clearly and fondly. On the other hand, teenagers Kent and LeShan had never traveled outside the United States before this trip.

As the plane taxied toward the terminal, I heard James briefing the other two on what they would see and experience. Kent, staring out the window on his side declared in surprise, "It's not so big. It's just a small island. I can see all the way across it."

James, with an air of superiority, explained: "Lungi Airport is on a peninsula. The national airport was built here because the land is flat. Freetown is on a stony mountain straight up from the sea with no room for an international airport. After the plane lands, we've got another 45 minutes or so on the ferry before we get to Freetown." Kent and LeShan groaned in that expression of disgust typical of teenagers.

Kent mused. "A ferry—isn't that a flat-bottomed boat that carries cars, animals and people across the water? I saw one like that on a school field trip to southern Indiana."

James answered patiently, "Nope, well maybe a little. It's more like an excursion boat, with cars at the bottom, and people sitting and standing on the second and third decks. It has an inside bar with food and drinks, but no one sits in there. It's better outside on the deck where you can breathe and smell the air. It smells a bit like fresh fish."

LeShan sniffed petulantly. "I don't think I'm going to like it here."

The plane came to a stop, and as the newest diplomatic family, we were directed by the airline crew to disembark before anyone else. Standing stiffly at the bottom of the steps on the tarmac were protocol officers from the President's Office and the Ministry of Foreign Affairs to greet me and my family. This was a customary reception for an incoming Chief of Mission. Also there to welcome me were my Deputy Chief of Mission (DCM), Steve Eisenbraun, the Peace Corps Director, Habib Khan, and the USAID Director, James Habron, as well as other officers of the mission. We were greatly honored to see them.

The honor guard provided by the Sierra Leonean military smartly saluted and I was prepared to return their salute when I noted their attention was not focused in my direction. I turned to see my husband a few feet behind me, smartly returning their salute. Clearly, they hadn't been told which of us was the ambassador! Aren't all ambassadors men? He certainly looked the part, very dignified with his height and silver hair, almost regal. I raised my brows but pretended I didn't see it—for the moment.

With much pomp and circumstance (I could almost hear Sousa in the background) they ushered us into the President's Lounge, where we sat comfortably over soft drinks, waiting for our documents to clear. Steve used the time to brief me on formal events taking place the next few days after my arrival.

I had hoped to arrive at post before the Fourth of July to celebrate Independence Day with the expatriate American community in Freetown. But, I had opted to go to Stuttgart first which delayed my arrival at post. Our national day was the greatest representational activity that Americans living abroad had in any country, wherever we were, and I knew that Ambassador Lewis and ambassadors before him had always hosted huge receptions involving hundreds of people.

I asked Steve, who was Chargé d'Affaires during the celebration, "How did your Independence Day celebration go?"

"I gave a *vin d'honneur* at my residence," he said, "and invited about 50 to 75 top leaders and diplomats who came and seemed to enjoy themselves." He chuckled at my blank look. "The next day, the newspaper printed an editorial about the affair. They recommended that the American Embassy take a loan from the World Bank so it could celebrate its national day in proper fashion."

What was there to say?

My chauffeur, John, stood nervously by, waiting to drive us to the ferry and to the official Residence. Finally, all formalities completed, John seated me in the position of honor in the back seat on the right side of the limousine, and my husband on the left, and we departed for the ferry, the American flag flapping wildly on the front of the automobile. It had been explained to me in my pre-departure briefings in the State Department that, although I was Chief of Mission upon my landing in the country, until President Momoh had formally accepted my credentials, I was not yet the official United States representative to Sierra Leone. Until then, I could display the U.S. flag on the limousine only when accompanied by the Chargé d'Affaires.

That was certainly splitting some fine hairs, but so be it. With Steve firmly ensconced in the front seat, the Stars and Stripes waved vigorously in the breeze as we drove toward the ferry that would take us to the mainland.

The drive across Lungi Island was colorful; the narrow road was very much alive with people and animals, typical of the rural landscape of Sierra Leone. Along the bank, the heavy fishing nets were being slowly dragged in by as many as 20 men at each net. Women were cleaning fish at the edge of the water, while small children ran freely in the area, playing their games. The cement-plastered exteriors of the old houses were painted with graffiti of all sorts, some with Muslim prayers and symbols.

The poda-podas, small combi-buses designed to carry about 20 people, were loaded with possibly twice that many passengers hanging off the sides. The small buses, with roofs piled high with produce and flopping chickens, listed dangerously to one side. These vehicles were painted with exotic signs and symbols, some with familiar quotes such as, "In God We Trust" and more provocative quotations such as "Fools and Dey Money Soon Part."

The village children ran alongside the car, begging for sweets or "coppers." I waved to them with open hands, showing I had no treats. Steve advised that I should never give sweets to them. How would I ever manage that? The thick bullet-proof windows were sealed tightly and could not be rolled down. The limousine was a very heavy, semi-armored vehicle. The sign on the dashboard "No Smoking" warned that there was no outlet for the smoke should one dare. I was a bit dismayed that an armored vehicle was considered necessary. But, I was aware that terrorist acts occurring around the world demanded that certain precautions be taken. Ambassadors, especially American ambassadors, could become shooting ducks for terrorists, just to make a statement. Sierra Leone was considered a safe and friendly nation, but the many Middle Eastern inhabitants in the country could provide a haven for troublemakers. There were thousands of Lebanese, for example, and Shiite Moslems who claimed to be Lebanese. There was reason to believe, Steve explained, that a good number of Iranians and Libyans were illegally in the country, perhaps using it as a safe haven from which they could come and go in their various activities. The new Momoh government had a serious problem to resolve.

We rode along silently with this sobering thought. I checked to see that our kids were still riding safely behind us in their range rover, a heavy but unarmored vehicle. But, not to worry! We were being escorted by the Sierra Leonean honor guard, who seemed quite alert and mindful of their responsibilities. We arrived a little late to the ferry, but it was waiting for us, no doubt having received orders to do so. John drove the limo directly onto the lower deck. We left the car and climbed to the upper deck of the ferry to catch the ocean breeze and the first glimpse of Sierra Leone's shoreline. The water between Lungi and the mainland was deep and fiercely green, and choppy; but the ride was perfect.

The ferry was crowded with women traders on foot, bearing heavy baskets on their heads, full of food, fish and produce to be sold on the streets of Freetown. The baskets weighed up to forty or fifty pounds, and the women looked as if their slender necks would snap from the weight.

Steve read my mind. "It has been known to happen," he said, "if the load is not balanced properly and puts too much strain on the neck and spine. Very rarely do you see a man carrying such things on his head; they will help to load the basket on the woman's head, but carrying it is women's work—no matter how difficult."

I groaned.

After about forty minutes, the coastline began to emerge in the distance, the mountain range visible with its two humps jutting high over the city. The ferry slowed as it approached the landing, and in spite of the lingering sea breeze, a horde of mosquitoes descended upon us, causing the kids to slap vigorously at their arms and faces. Local residents seemed not to be terribly bothered, but the Westerners on the ferry donned light sweaters to fend off the insects.

I recalled from historical accounts that Sierra Leone was first termed "the white man's grave" by a British sea captain named Rankin in the late 18th Century because so many white settlers died from yellow fever and malaria carried by the vicious mosquitoes. An African historian told me, "We seriously considered building a monument to the mosquitoes. It was they who won our freedom from the British." I felt comforted that we had all begun our malaria prevention three weeks prior to our departure.

My New Home, Freetown

As our car left the ferry and began the short drive through Freetown, we marveled at how beautiful it was. The city was ablaze with color, primarily from the bougainvillea growing everywhere, climbing into the trees and overhanging the streets—yellows, golds, purples, pinks and whites. So little had changed in the environment over the years since I last visited. Most of the familiar landmarks were still in place, but the city showed little or no development or improvement. The buildings needed paint and repair; the streets had huge potholes.

Even on the approach to the Ambassador's Official Residence in the most affluent part of town, the holes were deep and wide enough to trap the limo. John skillfully maneuvered around them. The streets were teeming with people walking to and fro. The street vendors had pitched their kiosks along the main thoroughfares, despite city ordinances to the contrary. But, the magnetism, the high spirits of the people, always evident in the way the women carried themselves, seemed no longer evident, not the way it had been back in 1973 when I had first come to Sierra Leone with the Peace Corps.

Our stomachs became a bit squeamish as the cars began the approach to the Residence. The road was narrow and circled the mountainside. Although slow going up, traffic raced rapidly down the hill in the other direction. There were no guardrails; it looked as though cars could drop off the side of the road and land on top of houses below or even in the ocean. I checked to make sure the car behind us bearing the children was safely negotiating the curves.

Finally, we turned off the main road onto Signal Hill Road. The incline was steep; it seemed to go straight up with nothing but blue sky visible over the hood of the car. Signal Hill, Steve informed me, had gotten its name during World War II, when Freetown was an important base of the allied forces. The hill had been fortified by the British to warn of approaching German vessels and to fire on the enemy if provoked. The entire harbor could be seen from this position. A vast underground structure, containing a thick concrete bunker built to support the huge anti-aircraft cannon and to house the operators, was still in place. The structure was now totally abandoned except for one building with a sign declaring it to be the studio of the National Television Service.

So, there it was, my new home for the next three to four years, perched atop Signal Hill overlooking the city, overshadowed by the old gun position just next door. As the car approached the gate, I received my first glimpse of its entrance and its front door. I was not impressed. The entrance had no persona, no presence; it did not represent what I knew to be inside. I had reviewed the floor plans and photographs of its rich furnishings during my briefings with Foreign Buildings Operations (FBO) in Washington, but had not noticed the entrance itself. I made a note to design a new entrance as soon as possible.

I was delighted with the part of the gardens that I could see. The rest was almost all downhill, and its several different levels presented definite possibilities. Fantastically beautiful bougainvillea vines were everywhere, together with giant flame trees and all kinds of exotic flowering shrubs. A flagpole stood starkly alone in the middle of the concrete drive. I thought, I'll change that too. I'll surround its base with a free-standing stone rise or a rock garden filled with flowers.

The household staff—all men—formed a reception line just inside the drive. There were twelve of them including a cook and three stewards, three gardeners and five guards. They stiffly introduced themselves and welcomed us to the Residence. Several members of the Embassy staff were also there to greet us, and as a courtesy, had filled our refrigerator and pantry with goodies and essentials to last until our food order arrived from Houston. They informed me that the Embassy operated a commissary where I could purchase other essentials, if needed.

The Official Residence was tastefully furnished, but quite small, much smaller and less grand than my home in Texas. It comprised two levels. The first floor contained four small bedrooms, three bathrooms, the kitchen, a large dining room with a table that could seat twenty persons, and a spacious living room and entrance hall. The several windows facing the ocean and sky flooded the rooms with plenty of light (and rain as well, a problem which we later corrected). The lower floor had a laundry, a small storage area (later converted to a bedroom) and a large reception area with a serving kitchen. The balcony off the living room was the redeeming feature of the house for me. Most receptions, cocktails and dinners were held there, where visitors could get the best view of the Bay.

I had a sense of déjà vu as I inspected the house with Scott Harrison, the Post Security Officer. J.O. and I had visited the house twice before as guests of Ambassador Olson on previous visits to Freetown from 1971 to 1973. Some renovations had been made since that time. I could never have thought then that I would one day return to this house as ambassador!

I loved the view from my bedroom verandah, which stretched across the entire bedroom wing on the back side of the house. From this elevated point, I could look down at the crowds of people walking to work or to market. They resembled a colony of busy ants—that's how high up we were. I vowed to paint this view before I left the country. Unfortunately, my bedroom verandah also overlooked hundreds of unsightly tin roofs on the slopes below, browned from rain and rust, confirming the level of poverty and neglect in the country.

At the end of this narrow verandah, where I had just decided we would have our breakfast each morning, was a neatly coiled rope ladder. I asked Scott what it was for. He grinned broadly.

"That's your escape mechanism."

"Pardon me?" I rushed over to peer over the railing to a drop of more than 30 feet. "You've got to be kidding! I may as well be shot to death by an intruder, as to drop to my death from this little clothesline!"

"It's been there for years." He explained. "None of the ambassadors who preceded you has been happy with it, but none had occasion to use it either. The danger to you would be greater if we built an outside staircase to your bedroom. It could be accessed too easily by intruders. You need not worry, Ambassador. You are perfectly safe. This is merely a precaution that we have to take. As it is, unfortunately, you have no exit if someone enters the bedroom wing. Your only escape would be over the balcony, and the rope ladder is it! It's quite safe. Want to try it?"

There was a faint amusement in his eyes that I couldn't fathom. I think the horror in my face disturbed him a little, as I declined the offer. Then, he suddenly pulled off his jacket, neatly scaled the railing, and grasping the ladder, floated quickly and smoothly down to the ground below. His demonstration didn't at all allay my fears. J.O. would never attempt that rope.

This great concern for my personal security was more than a little unsettling. What was really going on in this country that no one had yet bothered to tell me?

J.O. and I sat down together at the end of the day on the verandah, after all our guests had departed, looking out over the beautiful bay. It had been a long, 30-year journey from Terre Haute to Freetown, and final arrival felt somewhat anticlimactic. The lofty experience of the past several days, the protocol with which I had been received in Germany and at the airport, were unimaginable when I first set the goal to represent my country in a foreign land. This was pretty heady stuff.

As we watched the glorious sunset over the bay, jetlag snapping at our energies, my thoughts returned to the interview I had with the journalist several weeks earlier in Terre Haute. I could have told her I would like to know my ancestry better, to know from what part of Africa my ancestors had come. I could have spoken to her of the importance of knowing one's roots, especially for black Americans whose known histories rarely ever point to any identifiable ethnic groups or nations of Africa. How envious I was of those who did know their origins.

Black historians in America have researched documents covering nearly four centuries of the black sojourn in America, looking for a history beyond the shackles of slavery and Jim Crowism. That history did not chronicle who we were before we were called niggers, negroes, colored, Afro-Americans, black, African American, and a variety of other names. The diverse black populations in America could not know—perhaps would never know—whether they were derived from Mende, Massai, Amhara, Ibo, Hutu, Tutsi, Zulu, or some other of the hundreds of ethnic groups in Africa, each with its own language, customs, traditions, style of dress, foods and culture. For most, the search has been elusive.

Certainly, I did not accept this post in Africa in search of my roots. But though I found myself surrounded by the foreign sounds and smells of Africa, none seemed totally strange to me. Could Sierra Leone be the home of my ancestors, I asked myself?

But, then the sun dipped below the horizon, turning the sea as red as blood, and the approaching night left my question unheard and unanswered.

Presentation of Credentials

It was Tuesday, July 16, 1986. I had been in Sierra Leone for three days. Each day was full of new wonders, new excitements, new situations to be managed as I got better acquainted with my country team and their individual staffs. The country team was comprised of the heads of the U.S. Government agencies functioning in Sierra Leone: the Embassy, with its division heads, the Peace Corps, the United States Information Services (USIS) and the United States Agency for International Development (USAID). The team was comprised of a total of twelve persons, whose role was to keep me apprised of their separate activities and to serve as my advisors on critical matters. Their assistance was extremely important to the success of my mission to Sierra Leone.

Although not a part of the country team, a Marine Security Guard was attached to the Embassy, comprised of five young but highly trained marines and a seasoned noncommissioned officer called a gunnary sergeant, or gunny. Their purpose was to secure the U.S. Embassy and I personally always felt safe with their presence.

This was a special day. Today, I would present my Letter of Credence to the President of Sierra Leone, my first official act as Ambassador. The following week, among other things I had to do, I would begin the two-week period of official visits to government ministers and to the Doyen and senior members of the resident diplomatic corps.

Steve sat with me on the front verandah of the Residence to provide last minute briefings before the day's big event, and to answer my questions. He was genuinely helpful and supportive, knowing I was nervous, no matter how confident I wished to appear. We were waiting for the government limousines to arrive to deliver me to the ceremony. I was prepared, with my speech and the official envelope containing the letter of credence and the letter of recall for my predecessor, clutched in hand.

I had taken care to dress appropriately in a two-piece white linen suit with red accessories. Had I been a man, I would have worn a formal morning suit. My appearance was extremely important, because being a woman in a traditionally male role was still curious although not unprecedented, and every eye, especially those of women, would be upon me. But, I had other concerns and priorities to think about in meeting President Joseph Momoh for the first time: his human rights agenda, the rice shortage and his request for food relief, the question of who was actually leading the country, the president or his retired predecessor, the matter of increasing tribal tensions and threatened instability. But, I knew all of those concerns would have to wait. Today I would bring only official greetings from President Ronald Reagan, the U.S. Congress and the American people.

I strolled to the railing of the verandah, looking across the bay to the peninsula. I could make out in the distance the bustling Aberdeen Village and the luxury hotels and casinos: the Sofitel Mammy Yoko, the Cape Sierra, and the Bintimani Hotel at the top of the highest hill on the peninsula.

J.O. joined me at the railing, probably more nervous than I. Pointing toward the bay, he talked about how much change had occurred since our last visit in the 1970's. The peninsula was then connected to the mainland by a narrow strip of golden beach dotted with dozens of palm trees bowing in the sea breeze. The beach and the road were sometimes inundated by the high tides.

"Remember, we stayed over there at the Cape Sierra Hotel, just built, which had a swimming pool for the children and was an exciting place to be. Remember that little road we had to take to get there? Now, there is a four-lane bridge, with a nine-pillar span swaddling the tough ocean to connect with the mainland. That's progress."

Steve came over to us, apologizing for interrupting our thoughts. "Madame Ambassador, the President has sent his personal car for you, a very rare honor, I believe."

Three limousines entered the compound bearing the protocol officers from the President's Office and from the Foreign Ministry. The National Television Service was there with myriad cameras to film the entire process, beginning with my departure from the Residence, highlighting my arrival at the President's reception, and even my triumphant return trip home! My husband and the children would ride behind me in the second limousine provided, and although they would take no part in the formal ceremony, they would be allowed to observe. The third vehicle was filled with security personnel. The motorcycles, which had arrived earlier, took up their positions outside the gate. The whole setup looked like a grand funeral procession.

The President's protocol officer introduced himself as Mansour Turey. He was quite young, I thought.

"Your Excellency," he said, "Have you any last minute questions regarding the ceremony? If not, His Excellency the President is waiting."

As I followed him to the limousine, I wished my mother and father could have been there; they would have been so proud of me. I felt their presence, like a force field around me, encouraging me, protecting me, and urging me to put my best foot forward.

The household staff and the gardeners all gathered at the gate to bid us Godspeed, and, we took off down the steep hill with sirens blaring, horns honking, people jumping off the narrow road into the ditch to get out of the way. Within a few minutes, we had crossed the city and pulled up to the State House, an old fortress formerly used as the residence and offices of the Colonial British Governor, now adapted to its modern use as the President's offices. I was amazed at its thick stone walls and its delightful, history-filled interior. I passed through several staging rooms before finally being invited to enter the presence of the President.

Smiling to myself, I recalled that nearly thirty years earlier I had dreamt of meeting a Mau Mau in Kenya; instead I was meeting a Momoh in Sierra Leone.

President Momoh sat upon what looked like a throne, looking dapper and relaxed in a business suit, amid a maze of wires connecting television cameras and microphones. Mansour presented me.

"Your Excellency, Major General Joseph Momoh, President of the Republic of Sierra Leone, may I present Her Excellency Madame Cynthia Shepard Perry, the Ambassador and Plenipotentiary of the United States of America."

As previously instructed, I advanced two steps forward, bowed from the waist—thank God, no curtsy required. When the President nodded his head bidding me to come forward, I took three steps toward his chair and began to speak:

> Your Excellency, I have the honor to present to you the letter from President Reagan accrediting me as Ambassador Extraordinary and Plenipotentiary to your government, together with the letter of recall of my predecessor. My nomination is recognition of the continued long and close ties between our two governments and peoples which began in the 19th Century through missionary activity. These ties include mutually shared values such as respect for human rights, national sovereignty and the peaceful resolution of problems. In this regard, my government wishes to congratulate you on the conduct of your most recent parliamentary elections and your government's recent acceptance of key economic reform measures.

Mr. President, I am confident that our two governments will continue to work together toward the peace and prosperity we both desire. I look forward to building on the existing foundation of good will established by the nearly 5,000 Peace Corps Volunteers who have served Sierra Leone since 1962. Your government is host to the third largest Peace Corps program in Africa. We are very proud to have assisted the Government of Sierra Leone through our focus on areas of economic development and will continue to assist in Sierra Leone's development.

I look forward to furthering the constructive and mutually beneficial relationship between the United States and Sierra Leone over the coming years

Having completed my speech, I proffered the large, brown envelope with my letter of credence and the letter of recall of my predecessor. Surprisingly I remembered to offer it properly with my right hand, my left hand supporting my right forearm, which is an important form of courtesy and respect throughout many African societies.

President Momoh accepted the envelope and responded:

> Your Excellency, it gives me great pleasure to receive the Letter of Credence by which His Excellency, Mr. Ronald Reagan, President of the United States of America, has accredited you as Ambassador Extraordinary and Plenipotentiary of the United States of America to the Republic of Sierra Leone. I also accept the Letter of Recall of your predecessor, Mr. Arthur Winston Lewis.

> Please convey to President Ronald Reagan my best wishes for his personal well-being and for the continued prosperity of the Government and people of the United States of America.

> Your Excellency, as you have quite rightly observed, contacts between the people of the

United States and the people of Sierra Leone which started since the 19th Century, developed rapidly over the years. Through several American Missionaries the people of Sierra Leone have been able to share with the American people similar Christian and moral values. Missionary activity in Sierra Leone contributed greatly to the spread of education throughout the country. It is in this spirit that we continue to look forward to greater support from the Government and people of the United States, to buttress the traditional ties of friendship and co-operation between our two countries and peoples.

The work of the Peace Corps Volunteer Programme in Sierra Leone has had tremendous impact throughout the country, particularly in the rural areas where health and agricultural projects, among others, spearheaded by the Peace Corps are yielding fruits.

I have no doubt that with your academic and professional background coupled with your experience of the African environment, you should find your assignment in Sierra Leone a rewarding experience.

Your Excellency, as you take up your duties as Ambassador of the United States to the Republic of Sierra Leone, I want to assure you of my support and that of the Government and people of Sierra Leone in facilitating your duties in this country.

Then, as directed by the Chief of Protocol, I took three steps backward, so as not to turn my back to the President, stepping gingerly through the maze of electrical wires behind me. The scene was like a page out of some ancient royal protocol. My heel caught momentarily in the wires; my heart began to pound wildly thinking I might fall and make a fool of myself. I managed to shake it free, however, and there was an audible sigh of relief from the perspiring protocol officer. Then I did a perfect about face and retreated to my appointed place.

This very formal presentation was followed by a private tête-à-tête with the President, where he and I sipped chilled orange juice and began our brief, confidential talk about my mission and what I hoped to accomplish during my tour. He enumerated the needs of his people and his expectations of continued and increased support from the United States government. I, in turn, assured him of the continued good will of the United States toward the government and peoples of Sierra Leone.

We would have many such talks, more pointed and serious in nature, during the next three years. I was pleased to find President Momoh warm and genuinely concerned about his presidency and the future of his people. I left his offices, feeling good about working with him and his government.

The Chief of Protocol then presented me to the smiling Foreign Minister, Alhaji Koroma, who in turn presented each of the members of the President's Cabinet, pronouncing their names and titles very carefully and precisely. They were all extremely pleasant, and welcomed me very warmly to Sierra Leone. It struck me as strange indeed that two Vice Presidents were considered necessary to keep peace in the country.

J.O. and the children joined us for refreshments, and I paused for an interview with the local television station and radio.

I took leave of the President, riding in my own limo with my husband at my side. The line of motorcycles and limousines took a wide tour of downtown Freetown before returning to my residence, sirens blaring, and the American and Sierra Leonean flags flapping, announcing the President's acceptance of the new American ambassador. People along the crowded streets waved greetings and smiled their welcome. That evening, Sierra Leone's national television played the video prepared by USIA of my swearing-in ceremony in Washington, D.C. I looked good, I must admit.

We held open house for the remainder of the day to permit the Embassy staff, both American and non-American, to meet me and to wish me well. I was very pleased that one of my neighbors on Signal Hill, former Foreign Minister Conteh, also stopped by. I was grateful for the competent household staff who prepared and served hors d'oeuvres to our guests. For the first time in a long while, I could sit in honor like a queen while my normal cares and concerns were expertly handled by others. I knew, however, that the new level of responsibility I was undertaking would make household tasks and all the responsibilities I had ever had appear to be child's play.

That evening, when all our friends and well-wishers had departed, J.O. and I sat on the verandah, watching the setting sun and the magnificent changes in color reflected in the ocean and skies. Taking my hand in his in a moment of tenderness, J.O. said, "Today, you have truly become the United States Ambassador to Sierra Leone."

We sat there in the twilight, caught in the romance of the moment, reminiscing about how we had made it, of how we had worked to make it happen, the two of us, from the time we first met, almost exactly forty years before, to the day. We sat considering and remembering with some emotion the people and the events in our lives that had brought us to this moment: the Ambassador and her "Prince Consort" to Sierra Leone.

My Prince Consort

It was the spring of 1945 when we first met. I was 17 years old, and would enter my senior year of high school in the fall; he was 21, finishing his baccalaureate degree at Wabash College, a private prep school for men in Crawfordsville, Indiana. I had traveled to Crawfordsville to visit June Love, my first and only elementary teacher at School No. 8 back in Burnett when I was a child. Mrs. Love was now teaching in that city. I had truly missed her and her daughter Marie, called "Babe," since they had moved from Burnett, and was happy to see them again. Eugene, Babe's brother, was also there, and it was good to be reunited.

On the Sunday morning of my visit, we went to the African Methodist Episcopal Church, which had a handsome young pastor who also had a handsome younger brother. They were David and James Perry. While Jim, as I called him then, was attending Wabash College, David was also studying and pastoring the church, following in the footsteps of his father, an AME minister.

We had little time together that morning at church, except to be introduced. I think I fell in love with Jim at first sight. He had the biggest ears I had ever seen, and his close haircut made them stand out, flop out, like an elephant's. He had the shyest and widest grin, virtually from ear-to-ear, with beautiful teeth and deep-set eyes. He was very skinny and the very picture of a budding scholar. Babe and I stopped by the parsonage for a short while after church, but returned to Mrs. Love's for dinner.

Later that evening, when I was expected to read or retire, I took Babe's bicycle without asking permission, and pedaled back to the parsonage. How I found my way in that strange town, I don't know. Perhaps it wasn't such a great distance, but I went directly there. The Perry brothers seemed surprised to see me, but made me welcome. We sat talking over cokes about a number of nonsensical things. I wanted to get closer to Jim, to have him touch me or try to hold my hand, but he just sat there and grinned.

David sensed the electricity between us and felt it necessary to warn me that James had no time for girls because of the heavy demands of his studies at Wabash College. He informed me that their father, Reverend Perry, would be terribly unhappy if James did not do well. All this time, Jim said little, as though he had no right to speak for himself. David sounded so authoritative and firm about it that I thought I must go. When I got up to leave, David said. "But, I have time to talk if you want to stay and talk with me!" We all laughed and I went off into the darkness on the bicycle.

I faced some sharp questioning and rebuke when I returned to Mrs. Love's house. She promised to report me to my mother. I was indeed remorseful and offered an apology for my undignified behavior, but getting to know Jim was something I had to do before leaving Crawfordsville. I was deeply, inexplicably attracted to him. It was, perhaps, my first sexual awakening, a consciousness, but more than that, it was the sense that I had truly found my knight in shining armor which overrode my normal caution and good manners.

I saw Jim Perry again in the spring of 1946 at Indiana University in Bloomington, Indiana. As a clarinetist with my high school marching band, I was participating in a marching band contest being held on that campus. Jim was attending IU, working on his Master's Degree in Education. He was polite but seemed distracted. After making sure he understood why I was visiting the campus, he left me to be entertained by one of his opportunistic friends.

I did not see or hear from him again for 24 years.

* * *

In November, 1946, at the age of 18, I married James O. Shepard, during my freshman year at Indiana State University. I called him Otto by his middle name. He was from Lost Creek, my home community, and from an old and highly respected family. He had just returned from World War II having served in France and Germany. He was 13 years my senior, and very knowledgeable about a lot of things.

My parents felt he was a good "catch" for me, but even without their prompting, I loved and appreciated him. I loved him all the more because he promised me his support in completing my college degree. We had a good marriage right from the start, in spite of my youthful ignorance, and together we had four children. With his savings and his army severance pay, he paid cash for a modest little bungalow in Terre Haute, Indiana, in a mixed community of blacks and Eastern Europeans. This was our home for the duration of our marriage.

The early years of my marriage were dedicated to developing a stable and comfortable home for my husband and family, but I still had hopes of returning to school. Otto's promises to allow me to return did not come to fruition, and I realized with the birth of our third child, that he never intended that it should happen. Each time I made plans to return to school, I became pregnant. In 1956, I had my "kitchen counseling" with Herbert Lamb, my mentor, and began to look for ways to shape and fulfill a new destiny for myself.

I followed Mr. Lamb's advice closely, immediately choosing a political party, and taking a job with Nichols Loan Company in Terre Haute in 1956. I returned to night classes at Indiana State University (ISU) in 1960. In 1963, I gave birth to my fourth child, Mark, and joined IBM Corporation as an educational representative. In 1966, I took an unpaid leave of absence from IBM to complete my Bachelor's Degree in Political Science, and returned to IBM Corporation after graduation. I began a Master's Degree in English at ISU and struggled to maintain a household with four children.

The period between 1956 and 1966 was extremely busy and complicated time for me and my family. It was so compacted. During those ten years, Otto and I grew more estranged it seemed, with each of my degrees and accomplishments. The marriage failed after 22 years, partially because of my high ambitions and unwillingness to give up my goal, all of which demanded focused study and experience building. My activities, including my night work at the university library, appeared to him unnecessary and he was more than a little suspicious of my being out "studying" at such late hours. With my continued self-improvement through work and study, I began to earn more money and to become increasingly independent.

The financial support my husband did provide me was minimal, by design. During my senior year at ISU, when I was on unpaid leave from IBM, I knew my husband would never subsidize my education. But, I received a full scholarship from the university for tuition and books, provided through a matching grant made to the university. My meals and transportation costs were not covered, however, and I had to ask Otto for assistance. He gave me an allowance of twenty-five cents per day. The bus ride to school alone would cost me fifteen cents, but it was useless to ask for more. Otto actually thought that he was being quite generous.

This was not a critical choice—to stay at home or go to school on twenty-five cents per day. I was determined not to miss my chance to go to school. I had to find a way around this dilemma. I resolved to get up in the morning early, fix Otto's breakfast and his lunch to take to work, get the children dressed for school, get Mark to his Aunt Henrietta who graciously offered to be his sitter, and then have Otto drop me off at the university, which fortunately, was on the way to his workplace.

I would splurge, spending ten cents on a cup of coffee with my friends before classes began, and used the remaining fifteen cents to take the bus home in time to make dinner for my family.

I was neither angry, nor resentful about this situation, although I would have appreciated more money. But the truth is, even with this meager assistance, my husband was nonetheless helping me to achieve my goals. I simply had to find the most efficient way to use his assistance. My great-great grandmother, I have been told, cared for herself almost to the day that she died, living on a fixed government pension of just $12.00 per month. And she even managed to acquire savings!

Could the marriage have been saved? In retrospect, I realize it was not possible for Otto to have fully understood my ambitions and determination to become an ambassador. He could not find his place in the process, feeling only that in some way it was a denial of him and all he could offer me.

As the marriage began to deteriorate, that strangely relentless and disturbing dream about a three-room house began to recur with increasing frequency. It began to take on greater meaning as I came nearer to reaching my goal. It actually helped to push me on toward my goal.

When I entered the doctoral program in 1968, taking me far away from home for three years, Otto asked for a divorce. He stated it simply, "You owe it to your family to stay in one place, to put your children's future first. Why the doctorate? Who else has one? Take the degree you have and teach in one of the public schools here in Terre Haute. All my friends and family are laughing at me, and I'm embarrassed. They ask me who is wearing the pants in this family. You are always on the road with IBM. You earn more money than I do. You're making all the decisions around here. Now, I'm asking you to decline the doctoral program, and remain here in Terre Haute placing your kids first. If you can't do that, I want a divorce."

Dissolving my marriage to Otto was one of the most difficult choices I had to make in my life. Marriage had given me a secure base to fall back upon when I was discouraged or risked failure. Divorce was like breaking away from my roots— and even though I took the children with me, I was concerned about how divorce might affect their lives. They loved their father. I did not proceed immediately with the divorce; it was nearly three years after filing that I decided to go through with it. By that time, Donna was married; Jim was serving in the Marine Corps; Milo was in boarding school at Howe Military Academy, and I had enrolled Mark in the Common School in Amherst, Massachusetts. However, my departure for Massachusetts in 1968 was the beginning of our physical estrangement and the marriage was dissolved in 1970.

* * *

My doctoral program at the University of Massachusetts in Amherst (U/Mass) was the apex of my academic training. The Commonwealth of Massachusetts had mandated that the new Dean of the School of Education, Dr. Dwight Allen, a talented and committed visionary, design a new school. The purpose was to revive and invigorate education and the training of teachers in order to improve education for the Commonwealth's young children. One of Dwight's first innovative programs was the recruitment of young, bright minds from across nation to enroll in a special doctoral program, working hand in hand with faculty, to develop curriculum and to propose a new configuration for administering creative programs for the new school.

I was among the original thirty persons recruited. We were called doctoral fellows, and we collaborated to put into place "Centers of Excellence," as a pilot experiment with a new administrative structure. Some curricular innovations were quite controversial at that time. Some Centers did not survive or were absorbed by others. There were a number of such Centers including the Centers for Urban Education, Educational Research, Early Childhood, Music and Behavioral Education, and others. Some, like the Center for International Education, survived and have continued to flourish to the present time.

I chose, of course, to be a Fellow in the Center for International Education. When I went to the first formative meeting—there were ten of us—I discovered I was the only black, the only woman, and the senior citizen of the group, obvious differences that shocked me, but not as much as it shocked them. I searched their faces and listened attentively to their views of the future educational program, looking for a friend.

Following the first weeks of broad lectures and orientation to the new concept, the total group—doctoral students, old and new faculty and staff—was flown to the mountains of Colorado on a 10-day retreat. The purpose was to bond with each other within and among our groups for the immense tasks ahead and to contemplate, apart from the demands of our daily lives, the opportunities facing us in building a new school.

When our Center group first met on the mountainside, I truly stood out—all my differences in full force. They were curious about me; I was an enigma to their world of thought. David Schimmel, an attorney and the major professor of our Center, seemed genuinely concerned about me, I think. Perhaps I appeared uncertain, aloof and a bit lost. I remember well how gingerly he approached me as I stood on the cold, windswept Colorado mountainside, internalizing (for later painting) the tremendous panoramic beauty of nature spread before me. He introduced himself as the faculty sponsor of the group and the Director of the proposed Center. He had served as Director of Peace Corps Training at one of the staging centers in the Virgin Islands, I believe, before being recruited by Dwight Allen as new faculty.

Speaking hesitantly, stroking his chin, he inquired about my family, my schooling, my aims, and goals.

"Cynthia," he began, "You are, of course, welcome, to join this group in International Education. But, you don't have to make a decision now. Visit the other groups. Perhaps you might feel more comfortable in Urban Education where all the others are?"

"I know nothing about urban problems," I said, ignoring his implication. "I'm from the country."

"Well," he explained, "In our proposed Center for International Education, we're trying to form a nucleus of thought based on a common experience, like international development or in-depth exposure to other cultures. All of the Fellows you see here have lived and worked for two to three years in another country, all but one have worked in the Peace Corps, which is itself a shared experience. Have you been outside this country before, and for how long?"

"Oh yes," I said. I remember stretching my neck to look taller and slimmer. "I spent two weeks in Jamaica and a lifetime dealing with benign neglect, poverty, bigotry, and ignorance in this country. That makes my experience more than equal to theirs."

Sensing that he was intrigued by my notion of equality, I told him about my goal to become an ambassador, and my reason for joining that particular Center. He reacted, repeating himself several times in fact.

"How interesting! How interesting!" And, he walked away deep in thought.

The only other non-Peace Corps person there, Joe Blackman, became my first real friend. We bonded immediately, possibly because we were both outside the Peace Corps nucleus that David had spoken of, and he became my tower of strength during the hectic times. While on retreat in the Colorado mountains, out of pure frustration I went alone to the higher elements and wrote a brief treatise on the condition of learning among black kids in America, and what education must do to harness their talents for the rebuilding of our nation. Building on my five-year old son's dreams, the paper was entitled, *The World Through Mark's Eyes*. Joe helped me to expand this brief introspective note into a serious article which was published in the Saturday Review, in 1968. I couldn't believe I was published and would receive money for the article. Joe and I collaborated on several other initiatives during the three-year program that helped to fund the Center and served to highlight the outstanding programs offered by the Center and throughout the new School of Education.

My first year as a Fellow in the Center for International Education was not easy. But, the Center itself was quite successful. We were viewed on the campus as exclusive, and even with my presence, our group was often charged with racism and sexism. Some of the "others" in the Urban Center became hostile and challenged my choice to study international development education when the inner cities of America were burning. The Fellows in my Center then came to my defense challenging my critics and defending my right to choose. We began to bond. While many Fellows in the New School were deciding where they wanted to go, I knew where I was going and was determined to focus my doctoral program on the knowledge and skills I needed to meet my goal in the shortest period of time.

In the second year of my studies, I declared myself a believer in the Bahá'í Faith, and thus began a spiritual odyssey which would take charge of and guide the rest of my life. Teachings of the Faith brought me closer to my inner being, to my soul, caused me to examine my relationship to God and to others. That determination, which I had called a goal, became a mission to assume a broader role in bringing to oneness and equality the total of humanity. Other issues in my life began to fall into place during the second year of my studies, partially because of my faith and its teachings, brought into focus by a supportive circle of friends and believers.

Being a single parent was difficult and I missed the shelter and intimacy of marriage. Center relations were often difficult. It often seemed to me that the "guys" met separately, at night, maybe over a bottle of beer, to discuss Center matters and made decisions that were *faits accomplis* by the next morning. I felt effectively excluded from substantive dialogue during our planning sessions. They delighted in "intellectual" discussion, arguing for hours about issues I considered inconsequential. So, I was often combative and became less interested in the development of the Center than gaining new skills, developing linkages and seeking funding for the programs I was writing. Because I was free to do so, I audited classes in a special MBA program at U/Mass, and the knowledge gained from this discipline became tremendously useful.

In spite of my impatience and reluctance to participate in activities in which I saw no personal benefit, I learned much from the other Fellows, from their combined knowledge and experience. They became in a real sense my teachers; among them Gordon Schimmel, Steve Guild, Jim Hoxeng, John Bing, John Hatch, Ash Hartwell and others as the Center membership expanded. David Evans became the new director of the Center and the programs and courses offered became more traditionally academic and focused.

During the summer of 1969, I was recruited by Operations Crossroads Africa as a team member from Colby Junior College (a woman's prep school in New Hampshire) to teach typing and shorthand to Kenyan women at the University of Nairobi. I was ecstatic. Sending Mark to visit his father for the summer, I took advantage of this golden opportunity to travel to Africa and to have an enriching experience in the country where I had hoped one day to serve as ambassador.

It was my first experience on the African continent. My first stop on the way was Addis Ababa, Ethiopia, where I discussed a concept with the United Nations Economic Commission for Africa (UNECA) for developing a broad-based commercial training program in Africa. One hindrance to business potential in all of Africa was the lack of trained indigenous personnel in simple office and communication skills. This obliged businesses to hire non-African secretaries and office staff. African employees continued to serve tea and coffee to office staff and visitors.

Colby's commercial training program took place on the campus of the University of Nairobi, and that experience broadened my vision of the mission for which I was preparing myself: diplomacy. The young women of Kenya, and a few men, were anxious to learn about the world, and to develop skills that would improve their economic status and provide for their families.

Although the program was exhausting, I still found time to take weekend excursions or safaris to Serengeti, the world's largest game reserve, in Tanzania. I also visited Malawi to participate in a close of service conference for Peace Corps Volunteers who were preparing to return to the States. I also recruited Volunteers from this conference for a master's degree program Joe Blackman and I were designing for U/Mass called National Teacher Corps.

The doctoral program at U/Mass represented the greatest and most focused phase of my personal and professional development. It prepared me to stand alone, to make hard decisions and to defend them, to stand shoulder to shoulder with men in an area of study dominated by men. It was great preparation for the major career I would assume years later as ambassador. The field of diplomacy had always been considered a bastion of white males. In retrospect, I concede that the shared experience of Peace Corps enabled the men in my group to communicate on a higher level than would have been possible with a diverse group. Under David Evans' leadership, the Center began to diversify and to grow. Some truly imaginative (and lucrative) programs began to develop as new Fellows were added to the group from around the world.

The doctorate I eventually earned in international education launched my career and my crusade for Africa. I used the knowledge and skills I gained to develop graduate programs for Peace Corps Volunteers, both going and returning from their African assignments. Later, it enabled me to assist A.I.D. to develop policies and programs for Africa, and to secure public and private funding for American universities to participate in African human resource development. The training and experience I gained enabled me to live in Africa, to work with the United Nations, and to prepare African professionals to serve the world. As an academician in development, I partnered with African governments and universities toward measurable success in this remarkable experience. I met and interacted with many influential persons along my journey, and eventually it was they who recommended to the President of the United States that I be appointed U.S. Ambassador.

In 1970, I was awarded federal funding to establish the graduate level National Teacher Corps Program that I had long proposed. This highly innovative program was designed to prepare Peace Corps Volunteers returning from service in Africa to teach about Africa in public school education. All thirty Volunteers initially recruited for the program were experienced professionals, holding university degrees in a variety of academic disciplines. None was a certified teacher. The goal was to develop a modular curriculum on Africa, building on their personal experience in a variety of nations, and to teach it to children in the elementary and secondary schools of Worcester, Massachusetts.

It was a unique pilot project and a highly successful program, spearheaded by these innovative interns who designed and tested new teaching approaches, as well as the new African Studies curriculum. By this time, my dissertation proposal had been approved and I had begun to incorporate data generated by this Teacher Corps project into my study. Many members of this initial group of teachers, particularly Marcia Perkins, Beth Malrey, Mary Lea, Sharon Carter, Roosevelt Thomas, Claudette Merrill, Pat and John Jacobs, John Groat and others, remained in touch with me over the following years.

* * *

One of the perks for being Director of the U/Mass Teacher Corps was the periodic travel to conferences and seminars across the country. One particular day in September, 1969, I prepared to leave Amherst to attend a National Teacher Corps conference in Washington where I would present a paper on "Learning by Behavioral Objectives." Directors from programs across the nation were expected to attend this annual event.

The very night before my departure, that curious dream came again, this time with some variations. The house was now much larger than ever before; its limestone facade seemed darker and was pitted with fossil shells. The unfinished room was of tremendous proportions, and there was a sense of sadness, something foreboding about its appearance. I awoke with a keener vision of the house itself, but bathed in perspiration and filled with a sense of premonition. The dream had become a nightmare.

I questioned its recurrence at the time when I had nearly completed my doctoral studies and when I had experienced a great wave of personal growth and challenge. I had begun to fill all the "voids" in my life and was consciously striving to fulfill my potential. If the interpretations of my psychoanalyst back in Terre Haute were correct, the dream should not be recurring. What had I yet to do?

Shaking off the lingering depression caused by the dream, I left Mark in the care of Marianne Nesler, one of the Teacher Corps team leaders. I drove from Amherst to Hartford, the closest available airport, through a deep snow that had accumulated overnight. I always enjoyed winters in New England. The trees were living sculptures, their limbs heavy with the clinging snow. The countryside was beautiful with its bizarre frozen shapes, and I wished, as I drove along, that I could stop and paint a picture of it. I dismissed the dream as I boarded the plane to Washington.

After checking in at the Sheraton Hotel where the National Teacher Corps conference was being held, I went down to the reception area to greet friends and colleagues arriving from all over the country. I waved at Margaret Chambers, one of the specialists from Washington, and Margaret Ainesworth from Detroit, Director of the Wayne State program, who were in animated conversation. I decided to join their discussion of current and future directions of Teacher Corps.

As we talked, I glanced from time to time toward the entrance to watch others arriving. Suddenly, I felt my throat constrict as if I were choking. Coming through the hotel lobby was Jim Perry! I couldn't believe my eyes, it was he, Jim Perry, my first love, whom I had not seen in 24 years! I recognized his large ears. He was of course older, with distinguished gray in his moustache and at his temples, tall and straight, still with the same wide, shy grin. I rose to greet him.

"Aren't you Jim Perry from Crawfordsville?" I breathlessly greeted him.

He halted in surprise.

"Yes! What do you know about Crawfordsville? Nobody even knows where Crawfordsville is. Do I know you?" He was flirty, I could tell by the way he was checking me out. When I gave him my name and explained how we knew each other, he pretended to remember.

During the next two days of the conference, we reminisced about the intervening years since our last encounter, about our families, spouses, our individual careers and lifestyles. He had completed his Master's Degree at Indiana University in Bloomington, and had become a professor at Texas Southern University at Houston, Texas, a black college still in the grips of racial discrimination and separatism. He had later completed his doctorate at the University of Texas in Austin, and was currently director of Texas Southern's Teacher Corps program.

He informed me that he was also a serious businessman, that making money was his great passion and his goal was to become a millionaire some day. I made a mental note that he must be a pimp and his business must be prostitution. He was wearing a $500 suit and the pair of shoes on his feet cost at least $200. But, he said he dealt primarily in real estate and investment brokerage. He had married a woman nine years his senior whom he had met while both were students at Indiana University, where she had earned a doctorate in education. They had two lovely children and their lives and careers in Houston were quite satisfying. He seemed happy and satisfied with the way his life had turned out.

He encouraged me to complete my doctoral program, no matter how tough, and invited me to visit him in Houston to speak to his interns on the subject of multicultural education, the new buzz word in Teacher Corps. They needed inspiration, he said, to set and achieve high goals. Of course, I said yes.

He was very anxious to talk more about Indiana and our old friends, having spent most of his life in Indiana where both his father and his brother, David, had been AME ministers and pastors. We found that we knew many of the same people. I couldn't help noting that he was even more handsome than I remembered and very sexy, solid, and intelligent. Now, he was also exceptionally polished and sophisticated as well. The old attraction was still very strong; but, although he was flirty and suggestive, he started nothing and I wasn't about to.

I returned to Amherst, musing over this chance meeting with Jim Perry and the possibility for consulting with his program in Houston. I told my colleague, Joe Blackman, about my encounter and he warned me to be careful, that old flames could be dangerous.

I didn't immediately pursue the Texas consultancy because of the heavy responsibilities I had for the Teacher Corps, my children, and my dissertation. I was also proposing a consultancy with the United Nations in Ethiopia, and had renewed my correspondence with the Director of Manpower Development, Mr. Edokpayi, at the U.N. Economic Commission for Africa in Addis Ababa. His response to my proposal indicated that UNECA was interested and eager to have me return to Ethiopia to participate in studies being undertaken. I got busy writing a detailed proposal for resubmission to UNECA for human resources development training in Africa.

The next six months passed quickly and I received notice of the next Teacher Corps conference to be held in Las Cruces, New Mexico, March 1970. This time, the thought of Jim Perry did cross my mind. I wondered if he would be there. I caught a plane for Las Cruces, an amazing city among the desert's white-sanded dunes with a particular old frontier atmosphere.

Surprisingly, upon my arrival, Jim was the first person I met, sitting in the foyer with his colleague from Texas Southern University, Dr. John Davis. I remember thinking that Jim looked rather strained, tired perhaps, with dark circles under his eyes. I tried to remember if he had them when I saw him last. He spoke hesitantly, searching for words it seemed, and without the bright enthusiasm he had before. I was curious about these changes, and sitting next to him at the banquet that night, I inquired about his family and life in general. He said everything was going well. I did not probe further.

My memories of the conference that day and the next are still somewhat of a blur, competing as they were with a much greater distraction. The final day, we all packed up before the final morning session to return to our homes around the country. I was rushing through a cup of coffee in the breakfast room when Margaret Ainesworth beckoned to me from the other side of the room.

"How well do you know Jim Perry?" She asked.

I explained that we were old friends and started to tell her more about him, thinking she also had an interest in him.

"Perhaps you don't know that his wife was killed," she said. I was thunderstruck. Noting my wide-open mouth, she hastened to explain. "Lucille died in an accident last November, struck by a taxi. She died instantly. It happened just weeks following the Washington conference. It has been extremely difficult for him to get through. She was an outstanding educator, one of this country's most prominent black Ph.D's, and a leader in the Houston community. We were good friends, and I attended her funeral in Houston. I just wondered if you knew."

I was in shock. She touched my arm gently.

"He's a good man. He is attracted to you, and I think he wants you to know. But, he couldn't tell you, because his pride would not accept your pity, your feeling sorry for him."

I thanked her rather humbly for telling me and headed out the door, to find Jim standing just outside, nonchalantly leaning against the wall. It was clear that he had engaged his friend to tell me of his sad situation, not being able to speak of it himself. We stood staring at each other for a moment, trying to think of the proper words. Neither of us mentioned the loss of his wife, Lucille. But, now I understood the change in his demeanor and the sadness in his eyes. We spoke again about my visiting Houston as a consultant for which I could be paid an appropriate consultant fee. I could stay at his home, he offered. There was plenty of room, and my son, Mark, should accompany me to meet his children, James and Paula, both very near Mark's age. I promised to set a date for the visit upon my return to Amherst.

We talked about it a number of times during the following weeks, and I began to make plans to go if the right time could be found. But, my program in Amherst became tremendously busy, and I was engrossed in seeking solutions to emotional and financial problems of my older children. My only daughter, Donna, was suffering heartbreaking trauma following the breakup of her marriage, and had come to Amherst for a few weeks for love and healing. The Vietnamese War was getting uglier and I was worried about my marine son, Jim, with naval intelligence in Hawaii. Milo, now 16, had left Howe Military and was attending school in Amherst; both of us were struggling to survive his defiant years. Mark, having graduated to first grade, had an energy and intellectual curiosity that made me wish I could afford a nanny. The children and my doctoral program dominated my thoughts and it was clear I could not leave Amherst.

Another conference was coming up within a few weeks in Oklahoma City, and Jim and I agreed to see each other again at that time. Our talks from time to time over the next few weeks began to become more intimate—a bit more confident. He was being pursued by lots of women, he said, who were all giving him grief, wanting to marry him, to trap him for his house, his car, and his money. He claimed to take none of them seriously, that he never intended to marry again. He just wanted to make money. It surprised me that he didn't seem to consider me a threat, perhaps because I was hundreds of miles away and busily occupied with my own agenda.

The time passed quickly. It was September, 1970, and I was off to Oklahoma City for the next Teacher Corps conference. When I saw Jim this time, he was much more relaxed and confident, still with the dark circles under his eyes. Several young women, mainly his Teacher Corps interns from Houston, were hanging on his arms. One young woman seemed reluctant to let go of him, and he was definitely not pushing her away. But, he did come away with me, and we spent the first afternoon of the conference together.

We were drawn together so completely; his first kiss made me cry. I was not opposed to his advances, but thought it was time to explain my agenda before we went further. I disengaged myself from his arms.

"You should know I am going to be an ambassador."

"So?" He arched his eyebrows, rattled at my sense of timing. I was rushing to get it all out.

"In my experience, a black man will never allow his woman to achieve a high goal, any goal that would force him to take second place, a back seat. Perhaps a white man might find it interesting and challenging, and I am seriously considering going that direction. I have some options. I am convinced that a black man's ego would simply get in the way. It has happened already once in my life and once is enough. I think I should make it clear here and now, that if you want to marry me you must understand that my goal will come first. I will be an ambassador. If you're the type of man whose ego will not allow me to achieve my goal, then let's not begin this. I have no time to play."

He laughed heartily, distracted for a moment from his pursuit of me.

"I can't believe you're saying this to me. I don't recall ever asking you to marry me. I don't want to marry again. But, just to set the record straight, I am a successful man in my own right. I have my own profession, my businesses, my own life. Being a man does not require that I hold anyone else back, especially a woman."

"Understand, it isn't just marriage we're discussing here," I said. "I don't have time to play with you, either. Whether we marry or not, I don't want to get involved emotionally with a man who in any way might deter me from my goal. I think you could have that power over me, and I don't want to risk it."

He stopped laughing. "I would never hold you back. I would only encourage you to become whatever you can or must. I would support you fully, even if you don't become ambassador." He sniffed. "How did you ever decide to become something like that, anyway. That's definitely not colored."

He was trying to make a joke of it. I told him I was now in the twelfth year of my 25-year goal, that I was totally committed and there was no turning back for me. I told him of my plan to travel soon to Africa on a consultancy that could help to launch my career, and that I was committed to serve at least five years in Africa as a part of my preparation for the ambassadorship. He was pensive but that twinkle in his eye said he thought I was just a little loony. I knew he found me challenging and intriguing and was sure he could change my mind. But, most importantly, I had his promise and I would hold him to it.

During that conference, he chuckled from time to time about my lofty aspiration, a truly alien thought in his world. He talked about Houston and his family, all professional educators. He was especially close to his sister Mary, who joined him at Texas Southern after finishing Ball State University in Indiana. She stayed in Houston until she married Norvel Smith, and moved to California, where Norvel became the President of Merritt Junior College in Oakland, home of the Black Panthers. I learned that Jim was greatly inspired by Norvel and his ability to guide black thinkers, even those who felt violence was as American as apple pie.

Turning to look me in the eye, Jim said pointedly, "Some people think there are serious racial and economic problems to be resolved right here in this country before we tackle problems in Africa."

I was annoyed. This statement reminded me of my first year at U/Mass when I was verbally attacked by other black doctoral students for majoring in international education rather than urban education. For a moment, as though time stood still, I was struck with the notion that Jim neither understood nor respected my mission in life. Why was I allowing him to toy with me? I did not trust myself to respond.

But, he sensed his *faux pas,* and quickly changed the subject. For the first time, he talked about his wife, Lucille. "We met at Indiana University in Bloomington," he began, "but we married about six years after she came to Texas Southern as a professor in the education department. She was a highly respected professional and leader, involved in all sorts of activities in Houston, a life member of Delta Sigma Theta, a truly beautiful person."

"How did she die? What happened?"

"It was my birthday. I was at home, had just come in with the children. We own two private kindergartens, and she had stopped by one of them for something, and was leaving for home. I'm sure her mind was on celebrating my birthday, a surprise perhaps that she had planned. She walked out in front of a speeding taxicab. It knocked her about 30 feet. An ambulance was called, but by the time I arrived, I knew she was dying, was already brain dead. We rushed her to the hospital but nothing could be done for her. She died the next day." He began to shudder, deep in memory, shock returning.

I knew I could not possibly comfort that depth of grief. I changed the subject, telling him about my belief and my life in the Bahá'í Faith.

"Tell me about your church," I asked.

He recovered after a few moments and began to talk about Pilgrim Congregational Church to which he was devoted. As president of the church's credit union, he said, he went to church every Sunday just to count the money. But, I sensed his devotion to the church went much deeper than that. He talked about the southern traditions so different from Indiana, his lifestyle, his friends, his private schools, Wheeler Nursery and Stonecrest Kindergarten. He described his real estate holdings, his work at the university and his goal to become a millionaire.

I found his lifestyle interesting, but cluttered and confining—reminiscent of the mounds of dirty laundry and dirty dishes in my past life. He talked and I listened until he relaxed and renewed his pursuit of me in earnest.

Late that night, the telephone awakened me from a deep sleep. The call was from John Hatch, my colleague at U/Mass.

"You received a telephone call from U.N. Headquarters in New York this afternoon. They received an unusual request from UNECA in Addis to contact you regarding a consultancy. The UN will fund your trip to Ethiopia to participate in a manpower symposium at the end of the year, and the caller was anxious to know more about you. It seems it is unusual for a UN agency to request a specific consultant, especially an unknown American."

I was elated, and asked John to advise UN Headquarters that I would return the call and send my *résumé* as soon as I returned to Amherst. I sat thinking about it for a while, considering the new relationship upon which I had so blithely embarked with Jim and trying to anticipate its consequences. When I told him the next day that the consultancy had been confirmed, Jim simply asked me for greater detail.

"I really thought you were kidding about this ambassador thing," he said soberly. "But I thought it was the most creative proposal of marriage I have ever had. Now, I see you are quite serious. I can't really let you go over there by yourself."

I stiffened. Was he possibly trying to tell me I couldn't go, I asked myself? I felt my hackles rising, ready for a fight.

"I will go with you," he said softly.

I was astonished and relieved that I wouldn't have to break up this relationship when it was just getting started. We agreed to make it a family trip with his two children, and my two youngest, Milo and Mark, for a 45-day tour of countries in East and West Africa. I was 41 years old. He was 45. In the days that followed, we took on that special glow, a kind of halo or force field that everyone around us could feel. There was no talk of marriage—no need, it wasn't being seriously entertained by either of us. We were merely exploring. He again invited me to come to Houston and talked about the timing for the visit.

We left Oklahoma City for our separate destinations, engrossed in our planning for the African travel, a new adventure with two sets of children. I found myself very much enamoured with him—a bit stiff and formal, very hung up on money, but yet exciting, sexy and very tender toward me. Lucille lived on in his mind. Except for the trip we planned to Africa, he was unable to think beyond what she had already planned. He always used the royal "we" when discussing family matters or the future. Clearly, he was deeply grieving and I debated in my saner moments whether I should enter into a relationship, no matter how right he seemed for me. But, we continued to plan our travel to Africa together.

Shortly after my return to Amherst, I received a surprising letter from Dr. J.B. Jones, Director of the Teaching Teacher Trainers (TTT) project at Texas Southern, inviting me to Houston as keynote speaker for his upcoming conference. Here, finally, was my opportunity and excuse for going to Houston. Why should I have been surprised? So, Mark and I flew down to Texas one fall day in October 1970 for our first glimpse of the "Bayou City" and home of the NASA Space Center.

It occurred to me about that time, that I was surrounded by men named James in my life. Jim told me his brothers and sisters always called him "James." My first husband's name was James; my eldest son was James, my brother was James, and now a new James was being introduced, Jim's toddler son James Perry, Jr. And, all were called Jim. To cut the confusion, I began to refer to him as "J.O.", not knowing that that was exactly how he had been called by his deceased wife, Lucille. Others in Houston called him Aloysius, a name he had given himself, he told me, to avoid being called simply James.

The Dream Revealed

In October 1970, Mark and I arrived in Houston for the first time. And were met by J.O. and his children. The weather was tremendously sultry, and I could feel my hair rising with the moisture. J.O. was driving a huge black town car, heavy, spacious and very bourgeois. His children were beautiful. Paula was ten years old, with beautiful black hair down to her waist, a little chubby with an angelic, shy smile. She said nothing, just clung to her father's hand and watched me suspiciously out of the corners of her eyes. He explained to me later that Paula had been seriously traumatized by her mother's death and had stopped talking as a result. She was having serious problems, also, with her schooling and he had hired a tutor to work with her on all subjects. James was a handsome four-year-old and the apple of his father's eye. He was wound up tight like a little yo-yo, bouncing all over the place. His undisciplined excitement with life was exhausting, and he needed constant watching to keep him from harm's way. He knew no fear, no bounds. I loved this little boy from the beginning, and he loved me, and was eager to call me his "new mommy."

Mark, nearly seven years old, was intrigued with the two of them as we drove from the airport. They were quite opposite from his playmates in Amherst. In his eyes, Paula and James were spoiled little rich kids who merely had to mention they wanted something and it would be given by their father. He decided it would be fun to visit them for a few days. An amazing child, Mark's lack of jealousy or possessiveness and his ability to adapt to new situations always surprised me.

After a seemingly endless drive, we finally reached the city limits of Houston, a great city, with skyscrapers and superhighways. I was impressed not only with its skyscrapers but its vast neighborhoods of single family dwellings. It seemed that everybody owned a home in this city.

J.O. drove into a fashionable neighborhood on South MacGregor Way, a broad street lined with huge homes, large old pin oak trees and spacious, manicured lawns. When he slowed to make the turn into his driveway, I literally lost my breath. There was that grand house I had dreamt about for 20 years! Its facade was the same pitted limestone I had seen in my last dream. He mistook my gaping, speechless mouth as a sign that I was tremendously impressed with his assets.

I could hardly wait for the car to stop in the drive. I rushed inside the house. His housekeeper, Mrs. Richards, welcomed me at the door and helped to bring in my bags. The children were running here and there introducing Mark to their rooms, games, and play space. It was a beautifully appointed home, with lovely furniture and decorations, a mixture of old and new. I hardly saw anything clearly. My heart was racing and my eyes were searching for that room.

I found it, on the second floor of the west wing, that empty room—huge, unfinished, waiting for me—just as I had dreamt it over the years. I leaned weakly against the open door, staring into the room at the unfinished walls, the gaping aperture for the fireplace, the empty wall sockets, the naked studs and ceiling joists. Only the unfinished hardwood floor on which we stood, was in place. The tears began to trickle down my nose. I was completely humbled by this incredible and unanticipated unveiling of my dream. "Why haven't you finished this room," I muttered through my tears. "Everything else is so beautiful, so well decorated. Why not this room?"

He frowned trying to understand what appeared to be bad manners on my part.

"Well, we tried many times," he said, "to make it a playroom for the children or to make it a game room with a pool table for me and my friends. But, in the five years we've lived here, we couldn't make a decision on what to do with it."

Then, weeping uncontrollably, I told him about the dream that had disturbed my peace for 20 years, beginning a few years after our first meeting in Crawfordsville, although I certainly never had associated the dream with him. I told him of my visit to an analyst who said the dream was related to my high ambition and would recur until I had satisfied my goal. So, I had gone on to the doctorate; but, even that had not prevented the dream coming on schedule each year, even just one day prior to our surprise meeting in Washington.

"It was more than a dream," I suddenly realized through my gulping. "I actually saw this house, this room without knowing it belonged to you. In fact, I know now it wasn't yours—it was being built at the time the dream first came. It was a vision of the future. This is just too incredible." I could not control the tears.

He listened without speaking for a few minutes as if trying to grasp the enormity of this mystical moment. Then, he turned me to face him. We both recognized the unseen Hand in our lives since the day we first met nearly 25 years before, in Crawfordsville. With his Texas accent and in typical John Wayne fashion, he said with some emotion, "Well, I guess I'm going to have to marry you."

Perhaps that wasn't really meant to be a proposal. It may have been an attempt to joke away the seriousness of the moment. But, it was the only proposal I received from him. If this were a fairy tale, I would at this point add, "and we lived together happily ever after." That would indeed be a fairy tale. The real story began where the dream ended.

We traveled that December to four countries in Africa with four children: Milo, Mark, Paula and James. That trip revealed all the differences between us in terms of life style, styles of rearing children, our concepts of the value of money, our perspectives of Africa, and so on, and so forth. It was his first trip to Africa, and he was more than intolerant and critical of everything he saw.

We were both certain when we returned to the U.S. in January, 1971, that we need not see each other again. I returned directly to Amherst, and he to Houston, to resume our lives. Within two weeks, however, I received an offer of a position at Texas Southern University, not quite a surprise. And, Mark and I began to make plans to leave Amherst to look for a place to live in Houston before February 1, when my assignment would begin.

To describe fully all that happened within the next six weeks, would require a book in and of itself. J. O. and I reconnected. Considering our differences, marriage was questionable. I offered to just live with him until we got to know each other better, but he said he couldn't live in sin. What would his family and friends think of him?

But, on March 20, 1971, J.O. and I were married in a Bahá'í ceremony, in historic Northampton, Massachusetts, in the home of my friend and mentor, Dr. Dan Jordan.

Our families thought it highly curious and amusing that we had to secure written permission from both sets of our parents before the marriage could be performed, as is the custom in the Bahá'í faith. However, my new husband insisted that we also undergo the civil ceremony at the courthouse, just to make sure it was all legal.

Mark and I moved to Houston, leaving Milo in Amherst to complete his final year of high school. I settled down to my new responsibilities at TSU and the enormous job of forging two families into one. Spurred on by the reality of the dream, I continued to push forward. I knew now for a certainty there was a divine plan for me, a divine purpose for my existence. I knew I was going to make it.

I never had the dream again. I finished decorating the room and made it my bedroom, my personal retreat, where, upon going to bed and arising in the morning, I would be pleasantly confronted with the reality of this mystical part of my life. In the years that followed, we found it necessary from time to time to remind ourselves that we were meant for each other, so different were our value systems, dreams and goals in life.

* * *

My determination to become an ambassador was stronger than ever. I considered my years in Houston not an upward move, not a final move, but a lateral move in my career plan. But, I consciously gave myself three years before I would again pursue an upward reach. During that time, I perfected the proposal I had conceptualized to do an innovative program somewhat the opposite of the Teacher Corps program at U/Mass. I proposed to train Peace Corps Volunteers before they departed for Africa, to provide the requisite teaching skills and philosophies prior to their African experience. All would hold university degrees in math or science, and our program would develop their teaching and research skills. They would record and evaluate that experience to serve them as teachers in Houston's inner city schools. The program received full federal funding.

J.O. and I shared the management and teaching responsibilities for this new program, and immediately began to recruit students of all racial and ethnic groups from all over the United States. Claudette Merrill joined me from Amherst, and in the course of time married her true love, Bob Ligons, a NASA engineer. This was where I first met Valerie Dickson, one of the Volunteers in training, and our friendship endured over the years. Although she was much younger than I, it was often difficult to determine at times which of us was the student. All the Volunteers who went to Africa (primarily to Sierra Leone) on this program were strong, competent people, but it was Valerie who held them together and helped to make this experience a meaningful part of their future lives. As years went by, our lives converged again and again, and she greatly facilitated my life in Washington as "ambassador-in-waiting."

J.O. and I traveled several times to Sierra Leone during the next two years, to supervise the academic training and research of this group of Teacher Corps/Peace Corps interns, as a part of their Masters Degree program at TSU. I was nearly overwhelmed with the demands of marriage, family and profession, but I remained firm to return to the pursuit of my goal. J.O. was very supportive and helpful, but his promise to help me reach my diplomatic goal had yet to be tested. Would he really be there for me when the time would come?

In the third year of our marriage, 1973, I lost both my father and mother, who died just a few months apart after 55 years of marriage. It was a devastating blow for me, leaving a vast void in my life. I desperately missed my mother and her encouraging voice which helped me move through the mazes of becoming, and who never allowed me to despair. It is a loss I have never overcome.

That same year, I received a letter from the U.N. offering me a three-year assignment in Bahar Dar, Ethiopia, to head a human resources development project. It was a great opportunity that would effectively utilize my skills as well as get me back into Africa, where my goal demanded I spend three to five years as planned. When I approached J.O. with the letter, he was adamantly opposed.

"There is no way," he said indignantly, "that I can close my businesses down, change my life completely to follow you around Africa. What am I to do over there? What about my businesses here in Houston? I thought I had made you forget that stuff. I thought you were happy here in the house of your dreams. I promised I wouldn't try to stop you. You can go if you wish. But, forget it! I'm not going with you."

Another fork in the road had appeared, and I was faced with another critical choice. I thought this could not possibly be happening to me again. I almost despaired; I had to go on. But how could I for the second time break up a marriage and place my children in jeopardy? For me, it was an untenable choice. What to do? I spent anguished hours in prayer and meditation. The answer came.

I wrote a letter to the project administrator at United Nations Headquarters in New York, informing him that I had married since our last encounter. My husband had virtually the same credentials as I, with a Ph.D. in Curriculum Development and several years as a professor and educator. Would they, I asked, consider him for the appointment to Ethiopia? I would gladly accompany him and the United Nations would get two professionals for the price of one. They were interested.

When the application arrived for him, I immediately filled it out, even signed his name, and submitted it with copies of his credentials. Only a few weeks later, an offer came from the U.N. addressed to my husband, requesting that he serve on a UNESCO curriculum team at the University of Nairobi in Kenya. J.O. was astounded and very proud that somehow his abilities had been recognized and rewarded. He attributed it to a number of people we had met on our trips to Africa. He, of course, accepted the U.N. offer. Within less than two weeks, he amazingly completed his physicals, placed his businesses in the hands of a manager, arranged for leave from the University and flew off to Paris for two weeks of orientation.

I remained in Houston for the next month, marveling at the power of ego to move immovable objects, like my husband. I stored the furniture, leased my beautiful house, removed the children from school, and departed for Nairobi. The children were excited, recalling their previous visit to Kenya. As for me, Kenya was precisely where I had determined to be when I first formulated my career plan with Mr. Lamb so many years ago. I did not have to be in charge or chief of an assignment to learn the language and the cultures of East Africa, in the land of the Mau Maus.

We arrived in Nairobi on January 11, 1974. Life was good and our immersion in this new culture caused us to bond, and get to know each other as a family. Our self-imposed isolation from television and other luxuries of our American existence helped to promote that bonding. The children were enrolled in the Nairobi International School and they grew intellectually from the freer atmosphere of the private school and relationships with the world's children and teachers.

After having spent nearly half his life at Texas Southern University, J.O. also blossomed in this new environment. He built strong collegial relationships with Kenyan academics, who in many ways changed his perspectives and values, especially Matthew Maleche, a professor in education, and a man of strong principles and determination regarding Kenya's future. J.O. mentored the doctoral thesis of Daniel Sifuna, with whom he held long philosophical discussions. Mike Savage, a distinguished science educator of Nigerian-British descent, inspired my husband with his innovative intellect and free lifestyle. We both mentored Mabel Mwaniki, an American-trained Tanzanian faculty member married to a Kenyan citizen. In spite of the difficulties she faced in her marriage and in an academic division dominated by men, she was able to hold her own with our help.

It was a marvelous and even idyllic experience for us all, one that our children would never forget and which would feature largely in their future lives and careers. During our second year in Nairobi, Dr. James McCoy, a cardiologist, J.O.'s former student and our friend, joined us for a year's internship at Nairobi's Teaching Hospital. McCoy and I developed a strong relationship, sharing philosophies and finding solutions to the many problems we both faced in the Kenyan environment. Soon after, my eleven-year-old granddaughter, Pamela, Donna's eldest child, also came to be with us for the remainder of our stay in Kenya. I was delighted with her and appreciated her hugs and her songs when she sensed my depression or preoccupation. The children found many friends and because of the size of the house, often invited them to spend weekends. Mary Opembe, a close friend of Paula's and her classmate at NIS, spent a lot of time in our home. Her father, a prominent Kenyan businessman, granted her permission to return with us to Houston to pursue her further education—at his expense—when we would eventually finish our assignment in Nairobi. Now, there were five children: Paula, Mark, James, Pamela, and Mary, who all attended the Nairobi International School.

J.O.'s younger sister, Christina Stuart, brave soul that she was, came to visit us one Christmas with her goddaughter, Cecilia Nolcox. Christina was the only other member of our family to visit us in Kenya, and she brought with her a welcome sense of home at Christmas. She and Cecilia truly enjoyed the spacious old mansion we called home in the city of Nairobi. It was their first trip to Africa and both had many exciting stories to tell their friends and students when they returned to Indianapolis.

During our time in Kenya, I worked with Peace Corps training programs in that country; one, a secretarial training project headed by a great new friend, Rainette Holiman, on loan from Bell Laboratories as a commercial trainer. We were delighted to meet Martha Ann Whiting, member of a prominent black family in Houston, who was working in Kenya on the staff of Africare. I also studied Swahili, and consulted with U.S. Government agencies in Kenya, Tanzania, Zambia and Nigeria, which enabled me to travel extensively and often to other parts of Africa. All these opportunities earned me greater knowledge and experience as well as important contacts in the field of international public service.

The time passed so quickly. We had been in Kenya for nearly two and one-half years when we were advised that J.O.'s contract and the UNESCO project would expire in July 1976. I reluctantly began to plan our return to Houston, and to build in broader international travel and experience for our children on their way home.

J.O. would route his travel homeward through Paris for debriefing at UNESCO Headquarters, stopping for three days each at Athens and Rome. He would take the three girls with him, to show them all the sights they had read about.

I planned my return to Houston with the two boys through Istanbul (so Mark, a budding gemologist, could visit the Topkapi Museum) and through Moscow, before returning to Houston.

We had three months remaining before our departure and before the children would finish school. In the midst of our planning, I received a telephone call from the United Nations

Economic Commission for Africa requesting that I come to Addis Ababa to serve as career development officer for the Commission on a short-term contact. UNECA had several hundred employees, primarily African, whose previous education and training required upgrading and expansion to empower them to handle their diverse workloads. J.O. reluctantly agreed that I should go for perhaps three months, postponing the decision for any longer-term commitment. He was very firm, however, about returning home to his professorship at Texas Southern and to his businesses which he felt had suffered immensely from his absence.

So, I accepted the position in Ethiopia, at least for the short term, in May 1976, leaving the children well cared for by my husband in Nairobi until the end of his contract. The five children came to visit me periodically while finishing the school year. When J.O. departed Nairobi for Houston, he took with him the three girls as previously planned, through Athens, Rome and Paris. Pamela, my granddaughter, was returned almost immediately by her mother to live in Indiana. I took an unpaid leave of absence from UNECA and traveled with the boys as planned through Istanbul and Moscow to Houston.

Although life in the United States was new to Mary, our children were happy to return to their old lifestyle and friends in Houston, and especially pleased to be in their old home again with its fond memories. They adjusted well to their new schools and generally to their new regimen. Two months later, after resettling the family in our home in Houston, I returned to Addis Ababa to complete my assignment.

* * *

Ethiopia was the first African country I had visited on my maiden voyage to the Continent in 1969, and I had developed over the years a special affection for that nation and its people. I was happy with my assignment to the UNECA and was challenged by the possibilities this position offered to upgrade the skills and experiences of the African experts.

I considered seriously taking the position on a long-term contract, but since the assassination of Emperor Haile Selassie and key members of his government, conditions in the country had become increasingly unstable under the Mengistu regime. It was a sad and dangerous period in the history of Ethiopia. My heart ached for the people who were suffering so deeply, and I wanted to be of help. I very often had to remind myself of my goal and the need to complete my two-three year experience and to "get on" with my career plan. An extended contract was impossible.

While in Ethiopia, I intervened to save the lives of two young children of an Ethiopian friend, whose bloodline connections to the imperial family put their lives in danger at the hands of the repressive Marxist-Leninist regime. Makonnen and Nardos Assefa were 14 and 16 years old at the time. J.O., on one of his visits to see me in Addis Ababa, took the two children back with him to Houston to complete their education. He now had a family of six teenagers to care for in Houston, and a wife living somewhere halfway around the world. The children loved their new freedom from a hovering mother, and were not always easy for my husband to manage. In fact, I spent most of my hard-earned money flying between Addis and Houston at fairly frequent intervals to keep my family together in my absence.

I spent two years in Ethiopia at UNECA designing training programs to enhance the competencies of individual officers and to improve the efficiency of the Secretariat of the Commission. That two-year period completed my commitment in my goal to work five years in Africa, and although I loved my work at UNECA, I was ready to go home.

Living in Addis without my family was a lonely experience, and represented a two-year sacrifice for both my family and me. Conditions rapidly deteriorated in the country with machine gun fire during the night, people shouting and bodies being laid virtually at my door. With the arrival of the Russian and Cuban militaries in support of the government's repressive measures, life and liberty changed drastically for us all at UNECA. Although I was protected from harm under the

U.N. agreement, I was nonetheless an American, and was subject to harassment from Soviet sympathizers. I left Ethiopia in 1978 to return to Houston to restore my family to "normalcy," and settled in once again to life in Houston.

The next year, 1979, I graduated three of the six children from Lamar High School in Houston at the same time. Later, Makonnen and Nardos were reunited with their mother, who managed to escape from Ethiopia and to establish residence in Houston, where she remained for the completion of their university work. After two years at university, our Kenyan foster daughter, Mary, returned to Kenya to work with her father.

I resumed my former professorship at Texas Southern University, serving as Director of International Student Affairs. Combined with my previous service, I had more than completed the five-year commitment in my plan for university teaching, public speaking and publishing.

I became more involved in community service, giving more attention to developing my political base. I began working closely with the Republican Party in the city and state, and established contacts with a large number of influential Republican supporters of the Bush campaign for the 1980 presidential nomination. When Mr. Reagan gained the nomination, I continued to work with a number of Reagan/Bush campaigners at community, county and state levels such as George Strake, Jim Bowie, John Fonteno and others. Chase Untermeyer, whom I came to know later in the political arena, became my powerful advocate over the next several years as we both moved through political appointments in Washington and abroad. He remains a staunch supporter and friend to the present day.

In 1981, I had completed my 25 years of preparation. Republicans were in the White House, and because of the plan Mr. Lamb and I had set, I fully expected a call to serve. But, no calls came. It became clear, when I paused to evaluate the process, that I had omitted the necessary bureaucratic experience in working with the Washington decision-makers. My friend, Jim Bowie, for years a black Republican activist in Houston, pledged to use his political relationship to George

Bush, to help me. On Jim's advice, early in 1981, I wrote directly to George Bush, then Vice President, about my desire to serve as ambassador. It amazed me that Mr. Bush answered my letter almost immediately, advising that only presidents had the privilege of naming ambassadors, but he would float my résumé, so to speak, among other influential managers in Washington.

I was first contacted by Loret Ruppe, Director of Peace Corps/Washington, who interviewed me as country director for Malawi. Although I was intrigued with the idea of living in Africa again for possibly five years, I felt I needed to be in Washington to gain experiences and contacts that would lead me to my career goal. I had to decline the position. Soon after, I was summoned to Washington to join the Agency for International Development for Africa, as Chief of Human Resources Development, serving the educational and training needs of 43 countries of sub-Saharan Africa. I accepted this position in September, 1982, because I would be stationed in Washington, and the position would provide me the experience and contacts I needed with the Washington bureaucracy. Under the able leadership of Frank Ruddy, then A.I.D.'s Assistant Administrator for Africa, I had responsible oversight for policies affecting human resources development programs administered by career officers assigned to those countries. My friend, Valerie Dickson, a career officer and Frank's administrative assistant at that time, helped to advise and guide my years at A.I.D.

Working for A.I.D. was a remarkable hands-on preparation for my future diplomatic role in Africa. As I managed the educational programs and staff, I also learned a great deal about international relations and the necessity for teamwork with other departments and other agencies in carrying out the missions mandated by our Congress. Our efforts were constrained by the limited funding available for Africa.

With the rapid decline in the federal government's commitment to education and decreased funds earmarked for education around the world, my division took deep cuts in staffing and travel allocations. The result was a tragic loss of programs and innovative contracting to carry out initiatives in

Africa. The noble perspectives of A.I.D. seemed to deteriorate into turf fights and reorganization for survival with devastating effects on its delivery of programs. With the assistance of my very capable staff, we managed to conduct two educational conferences in Africa that I felt made a difference, one on basic education in Nairobi and the other on agricultural education in the Cameroon. These could not have been successful without the loyal professionalism and ingenuity of Peggy Shaw, Marcia Ellis, Victor Barnes, Edna McBreen and Jacci Conley, among others, in the struggle to keep our operation alive. We later lost Peggy, my senior staffer and staunchest supporter, to cancer.

I fought diligently with others in A.I.D., like Al Harding, for set-aside funding for black businesses and black colleges to carry out projects in Africa, with the aim to increase participation of black Americans in our foreign policies and activities in Africa. It worked, primarily due to President Reagan's Executive Order, which established a White House Initiative on Historically Black Colleges and Universities (HBCU's) for delivery of certain areas of services. This HBCU initiative had some powerful set-asides, federal funds allocated strictly for those colleges and universities.

In light of all these changes, however, I began to question my remaining further in Washington, the only great incentive being the hope of an ambassadorial appointment. As in Ethiopia, a great percentage of my salary went to the airlines for the bi-weekly commute between Houston and Washington, D.C. J.O. had grown accustomed to my being gone for long stretches. He did not deny that he enjoyed the freedom and the breathing space that these separations afforded from the pressures and constraints of marriage. But, this period was most difficult for us both, and we had tired from being separated.

During my four years with A.I.D. in Washington, James, our youngest, had completed his final year of high school and had entered his studies in computer science at Texas Southern University. Paula had completed her bachelor's degree at TSU and was teaching in the Houston Independent School District. Mark, after taking his Junior Year Abroad in France at the Université d'Orléans, graduated from Washington University and was preparing to join the Peace Corps in Nepal. I no longer had children at home awaiting my return. Yet, the career goal I had set for myself had not yet appeared on the horizon; I began to question whether it would ever happen, and returning home to Houston was rapidly becoming a serious consideration.

In fact, during 1985, I considered returning to Texas Southern University, from which I had maintained a leave of absence. I advised President Leonard Spearman at Texas Southern University that I would be returning to campus the following semester, and he began to research the appropriate appointment for my return. Within ten days of my call to him, I was informed by White House Personnel that I was being considered for the position of Associate Peace Corps Director for African Affairs. I had no idea how long this process might take, and wasn't even sure I wanted the position. But, it was a ray of hope. So, I cancelled my return to Texas Southern, and continued my work with A.I.D. for Africa.

I was on a special "tdy" (temporary duty) in South Africa in early 1986, when I received President Reagan's call in Johannesburg. Thus began a whole new chapter in my life, a chapter I had been preparing to write all my life, a fresher and rewarding phase, culminating a thirty-year long journey.

* * *

So, here we were, J.O. and I together, now sitting on the verandah of the Official Residence in Freetown, remembering but not dwelling on the sacrifices, the separations, his single-parent experiences and other events over the past years of our life together. It all now seemed worth the struggle. In retrospect, our journey together from our reunion and marriage until this eventful day in Sierra Leone was a short fifteen years. As we left the verandah to retire for the night, arm in arm, passing through the darkened house, J.O., my good prince consort, sighed.

"Today is the beginning of a new life for us. It is a great honor, a reward perhaps for our diligence, our perseverance and our faith through some hard times. Somehow we made it; thank God we made it."

He began to hum the old tune of what had become our special anthem and song of praise. "Somehow God brought us through."

"Amen," I breathed.

Passing for Black

The first few weeks of my tour were particularly rough as I tried hard to understand my environment and the policies attached to the official American presence in Sierra Leone. I would return to the Residence when things were most perplexing, to sit and ponder the day's actions on my front verandah with its panoramic view of the Atlantic Ocean, the beautiful bay waters, and Lumley Beach. It was very relaxing and calming.

On a clear day, I could watch the approach of the cargo ships many miles out, loaded with containers of all sorts of imported goods for delivery at Freetown's harbor. Depending on the time of day, the ocean would change colors, with no discernable demarcation between the blue-gray water and the blue-gray sky. Only fluffy white dumpling clouds were visible where the water line would normally be. But, the sunsets were beautiful, especially during the rainy season.

The heavy, billowing clouds reflected the golden rays of the sun as it seemed to sink beneath the shimmering surface of the ocean, turning the clouds throughout the heavens into puffs of vanilla and strawberry ice cream. I mentally recorded all these changes to be reflected in my paintings when I would someday find leisure time. Friends advised me to take full advantage of this scenic view because soon the dry season would take over, and for nearly three months, the beach and peninsula would hardly be visible. The entire area would be shrouded with filmy dust from the Harmattan, when the fine sand particles blown by the stiff winds from the great Sahara Desert would settle over every thing. Then, the short rains would return, and the dust would simply wash away and all would be green and lush again. What words can adequately describe such natural beauty?

Late one afternoon, I sat alone as usual on the verandah envisioning the painting I would eventually make of this view: a triptych, I thought, to include everything in sight. I heard someone enter the verandah from the living room. Turning, I found my granddaughter, LeShan, standing quietly behind me, her eyes downcast in tears, twisting her handkerchief.

"Oh, my dear LeShan," I drew her close. "What could be the matter?" She put her arms around my neck and began to cry in earnest. After a few moments, she quieted herself but seemed reluctant to speak.

"There's no one here but us. Tell me, what is it?"

"Grandmother," she began hesitantly. "I don't want you to think I'm ungrateful. This has been a wonderful experience, traveling all over everywhere, seeing so many things and places I've only read about in books. I love being with you. But, I miss my mom. I want to go home."

She had been with us in Freetown for less than two months. Milo, my second son, wanted his daughter to have experiences similar to his own, living and traveling with me throughout Africa and experiencing a more sophisticated lifestyle. There was a more subtle reason for sending her with us to Africa, as I was about to discover. He had planned for her to stay with me another couple of months until school began in Indiana. What a loss for her it would be to miss this opportunity because of homesickness. I tried to coax her to telephone her mother, to telephone her best friend, Brandy, or to talk to her father. But, she shook her head at each option.

I wondered if Kent or James had said or done something to hurt her feelings, but she said no. She had certainly had plenty of attention. She was only fourteen years old, but was already a raving beauty. Members of the Marine Guard, most about nineteen years old, would gather around her closely in admiration. Her face would flush beet red and I would have to rescue her. What could be the problem? Finally, she stammered, still with her eyes downcast.

"Grandmother, I hope you understand. All my life, I've lived with my mom. I only visited you or Dad for short spells. My mom, her mom, her sisters, all my friends are white. I've never ever lived around black people. But, here, I'm completely surrounded; everybody's black; the streets are full of black people; the household staff, everywhere I turn, nothing but black except at the Embassy." She looked at my worried face. "I know you can't really understand, Grandmother. You think I'm ashamed to be black, don't you? But, that's not it. I'm not black. I'm white and I don't belong here. I want to go back to Sandcut, where I belong."

My heart ached for this child in my arms, so young, so beautiful, so confused, a sad pawn in a broken, interracial marriage. She had inherited Risa's fair skin, but not her blond hair. She looked Indian, or Lebanese, certainly not white. I thought she must surely have already faced problems and attitudes in her short life that should have toughened her. But, she claimed that no one ever made her feel "different." Her mother was like all the other kids' mothers in that lily-white existence called Sandcut, Indiana, and she was treated like all the other kids.

I assured her that if she really wanted to go home, I would make all the arrangements and would notify her father that afternoon. She began to calm down and to smile apologetically, brushing her hair from her damp face. It was clear that her problem was much more complex than mere cultural shock; hers was a deeper problem of racial identity. She was confused about who she was and was certain she had a right to choose being white or black in spite of societal judgments. Why not be black, I asked?

I recalled with a start that I had heard those words before, long ago when I, myself, was fourteen. On the surface, race relations had much improved in America by the 1980's. Opportunities appeared to be more equal. Interracial marriages, although not totally condoned, were becoming a common occurrence. Children born to these marriages were not a new breed since miscegenation had always been practiced in the United States, yet many of these children were demanding their own unique classification in society, neither white nor black. Were we reverting to the days when we were all colored, like in South Africa? As a rule, mixed-blood children took on the racial classification of the darkest-skinned partner. These children often became angry with both parents because of the painful dilemma thrust upon them, feeling lost in a world of stupid prejudices.

I thought it was time I made LeShan aware of her black ancestry, to give her a sense of pride, not just in me and my side of her family, but in the black race of which she was a part. I ordered tea and we sat together on the verandah. I suddenly remembered being fourteen again and sitting on Cousin Annie's front porch, sipping tea and eating cucumber sandwiches, while being taught my history by Cousin Annie and her daughter, Katherine. Now I was about to re-teach this history, myself, and LeShan and I would share the added benefit of sitting on my broad verandah facing the darkening ocean in an African country. I desperately searched my memory—to find the right words, the right story from the past.

"I want to tell you about your family, LeShan, my father's side of the family, a story that might help. It helped me when I was fourteen, like you. I had a great-aunt named Cynthia, for whom I was named, and until she died, she was a powerful force in my life, and remains so even now in memory. I dearly loved Aunt Cynthia and spent most of my summer vacations with her in Highland, just up Route 41 not far from Sandcut. She had a very positive sense of who she was and would often tell me great stories out of her past. You are almost her spitting image. Can you believe that? I must show you her picture one day."

I told Leshan that my Aunt Cynthia had wanted me to know my city folk, her cousins, my cousins, who were better off and better educated than most of the people of my acquaintance at that time. She had wanted to broaden my horizons, to show me a side of myself and my family that lay beyond my quiet, rural existence. So, she would take me to visit them. We would catch the street car with its clanging bells and glide quickly and smoothly to Cousin Annie Sims' house, where her daughter Katherine also lived, a fine home on Spruce Street in Terre Haute. At that time, in the 1940's, that's where all the black bourgeois lived or wanted to live. It was the epitome of success. Their home had hardwood floors and oil paintings on the walls and old grandfather clocks and luxuries I certainly didn't have at home and which, to my knowledge, no one had in Lost Creek where I came from.

In addition to being college-educated, Aunt Cynthia's cousins looked markedly different from me. They were absolutely white-skinned, with poker-straight hair and blue eyes. Yet, they let everyone know they were colored.

One summer afternoon, we visited Cousin Annie for tea. We sat on the front porch (as everyone did in those days), and drank tea poured from a beautiful little porcelain teapot in dainty little china cups, with tasty little cucumber sandwiches on white lace-trimmed napkins. Katherine was a schoolteacher and was very prominent in the Terre Haute community. She was tall and thin, and a little stoop-shouldered, very bookish, not good-looking, but not unattractive. She had this stringy, brown hair that used to be blond, and ivory-colored skin which completely mesmerized me. She was a 'spinster,' Aunt Cynthia explained to me once, and Cousin Annie always worried about dying and leaving Katherine all alone.

They seemed to have planned this moment, all three of them, to tell me my history. I had come of age, they declared, and it was a tradition in the family to open the chronicles of the past for daughters when they reached my age, fourteen. My cousin Katherine spoke first in her prim, schoolteacher voice, peering at me over her horn-rimmed glasses, while she opened two or three giant photo albums to support her narrative:

Perhaps you aren't aware, Cynthia, that each generation in our family since about 1800 has had a Cynthia. This naming tradition began with my great-great-grandmother Chena, a woman of Native American and African parentage, whose non-Judeo-Christian name may have meant "moon", like yours. She had been born into slavery on a Virginia plantation owned by a wealthy family named Hill. Because of her great beauty, gentleness and industry, she was chosen by Dr. Richard Hill, her master and plantation owner, to be his slave wife. Richard had come from a pioneering family in Virginia. The Hills owned vast properties and wielded great influence in their communities.

Probably the best known of Richard's ancestors was his grandfather, Dr. James Greenway, a brilliant botanist in Virginia during the late 1700's. Dr. Greenway had been born in England, but made his fortune in Virginia as a doctor, scientist, amateur musician, linguist, plantation owner, surveyor, and county judge. He wrote volumes of medical articles for learned journals, and his grandson inherited his intellectual prowess.

Dr. Richard Hill remained faithful to his slave wife, Chena, never marrying anyone else, and she bore him five children. As proof of his commitment to this "marriage," he made arrangements in his will for Chena's freedom and for financial security for his children even before their liaison began.

Of their five children, one boy and four girls, one was my father Jacob, and one was your great-grandmother, named Jacintha for the fiery color of her hair, but she was commonly called Cintha or simply "Cynthia," a name she preferred. With her red hair and green eyes, she was often mistaken for white, although she had been raised as, and lived her life as, a colored woman. She married your great-grandfather, George Washington Riley, called "Wash", a veteran of the United States Colored Troops during the Civil War, and bore him six children. She died unfortunately at the birth of your Aunt Cynthia, who was named for her. Your father, George, her grandson, inherited her red hair and green eyes.

Cousin Annie, I recalled, was quite aged at that time, but was very alert; her memory was keen and precise. She sat rocking slightly in her wooden rocker, long, thin white hair piled on top of her head in a widow's knot shimmering in the sunlight. Thinking of her now reminds me of freshly churned butter and buttermilk and a kitchen smelling like freshly baked bread. In a very soft voice, Cousin Annie began to speak, pausing periodically to reach deeply into memory.

As a family, we have come a very long way, Cynthia. We want you to know your lineage—your parentage, to pass it on as a true and valuable legacy to your own children. When I was fourteen just like you, I went to live with my Grandma Chena and she told me the story of how we, as a family, came to be split in two—just like our nation at that time—one side colored, and the other side, white.

When Richard Hill died in 1844, Grandma Chena was freed from slavery with all her children. He left her a lot of money and land, and she could have stayed on in Virginia, living comfortably on that plantation, but she didn't hesitate for a moment. She moved North to Marshall, Illinois, just across the Wabash River from Terre Haute, and in time married my Grandpa Evans, a colored farmer, with whom she had two more children. When he died, she eventually moved over to Terre Haute and bought a home of her own and cared for herself. She was a woman of great spirit and inner strength.

Grandma Chena's children were all fair-skinned like their father, but always claimed to be colored, all except for Jacob, my papa, who chose from his early youth to be white. When Chena moved on to Terre Haute, Papa chose to remain in Illinois away from all his colored relatives, and married my mother, who was German. They started a separate life from the rest of his family. Mama and my German grandparents, the Meehlings, always spoke to us kids in German. I almost knew nothing else.

But, then my mama died in childbirth, just like your great-grandma and in the same year, 1879, when I was just nine years old. Papa needed help raising us five kids, I knew he did, but I just couldn't forgive him for marrying again. He and his second wife had two sweet little boys, my brother Benjamin being one of them. But, Mama Mary and I had a rough time. I resented that she had taken my mama's place—and even had my mama's same name—Mary Hill! Papa finally had enough of our bickering, I guess, and he reluctantly sent me to live with my Grandma Chena Evans, his mother. I knew that Papa's mother lived in Terre Haute, but I had never met her. Papa had always said, "one day, one day." Terre Haute seemed so far away in those days—a horse and buggy trip took all day, and Papa always had an excuse not to take me there, until there was no choice.

I was fourteen like you when Papa introduced me to my Grandma Evans, and then I understood why he had tolerated my fights with Mama Mary so long. Now I understood why he had been so reluctant to send me to Terre Haute. Grandma Evans, my lily-white Papa's own mother, was a colored woman. Papa had never told any of us kids that he had colored blood.

I learned later as I grew up that the Jim Crow laws and the black codes of that time determined that anyone having at least 1/8 black blood in his veins was colored, no matter how white the skin. I was quite happy with my new identity. I dearly loved Grandma Chena, and wanted to be just like her. But in choosing this lifestyle, I was alienated from my Papa who kept his secret throughout his lifetime. I happily chose to pass for colored like my grandmother, and that's what I am today.

I turned to Leshan and continued, "Cousin Annie finished her story by telling me she had stayed in touch with her brothers and sisters throughout the years, all of whom lived as white persons. Katherine especially was bitter about this division in the family because of the hurt it caused her mother. She was uncomfortable hearing her mother talk about this side of the family, who now lived hundreds of miles away, as far away as Oregon. I thought how sad I would be to be separated from my father, or my brothers and sisters, no matter how difficult they were to live with.

"When eventually, Aunt Cynthia and I left to take the streetcar back home to Highland, I thought all the way home about Cousin Annie's story. I could not fathom why anyone who didn't have to be black would choose to be. It didn't make sense considering the vicious prejudice and discrimination we all had to face. No one knew about this family's history of mixed blood. That's why Jacob could continue his life as a white man. But, why did Cousin Annie, who was 15/16 white, choose to pass for black? And, Katherine, her daughter, did the same. There was nothing in her persona that would suggest she was not white, even though her father, Mr. Sims, was a black barber. It was a mystery to me why anybody would choose to be colored in America when they didn't have to."

LeShan was listening intently, as I continued.

"It was not easy to be colored in Cousin Annie's time, or even during my own childhood. I also endured many cruel remarks and insinuations in later years because of my race, even at Otter Creek High School, where people might have resented being considered racist. Some of these same people also came from Sandcut, where you live.

Thankfully, things have changed over the years. I remember clearly a number of stories listed as required reading in my literature class such as 'The Three-Legged Goose,' plastered with 'nigger' throughout and with other demeaning references to people of color. Not only were these stories read aloud in class, but the teacher also called on me to read them, supposedly because they were written in 'Negro dialect' and needed translation. I decided to read them in 'dialect,' so the meanings of the words remained obscure. Those were painful days when even the teachers would use racial slurs such as 'there's a nigger in the woodpile somewhere' or 'sweating like a nigger.' Our laws these days forbid such stories and racist references, so you've probably not experienced the same embarrassment.

"I remember Thelma and her brother Harry, our neighbors in the country, dirt poor and uneducated people who had the nerve to tell me they were better than I, simply because they were white. And, it was I who took pity on the poor girl, who was near my age, and combed the lice out of her thick, tangled red hair. I gave her soap to wash her face—it took several washings to remove the crut. Better than I? That's what wars are made of. Color was the major denominator, not economics or education, even in the minds of the poorest whites, who lived in less fortunate conditions than we. My mother used to take food to other white neighbors—the Settys and the Walters, very decent families—because Mom said they were half-starving, eating beans without meat, heaven forbid! She took them cured hams and sausages from our smokehouse."

LeShan laughed about the beans and then challenged: "Well, why would anyone choose to be black if they could be anything else—if they could avoid the pain?"

I studied her face for a moment. Then taking her hand in mine, I continued:

"Remember, that's precisely the question I asked Aunt Cynthia. She said Cousin Annie told me that story for a purpose—to give me pride in being what and who I am, just as she was. She said, to choose to be anything else would be to deny our ancestry, to deny Chena and all the black people before her and since, who endured gross indignities to allow us to become what we are. Their struggle made it possible for me to be what I am today, Ambassador of the United States, the impossible dream. Aunt Cynthia told me slavery is not a measure of our shame or our weakness—it's the shame of those who by their strength and might made money from human suffering. Generations later, their descendents went further to use skin color as a basis for determining superiority and inferiority in this country.

"We are derived from Africa, although life in America has given us a mixture of bloods and nationalities. It is important that as a people, we identify precisely our African roots. Knowing our African ancestry is a missing part of the puzzle, but is an essential part of our being, our pride, and our true identity. Can we ignore, forget, or just throw away the suffering, the plight of all these generations of people, generations of struggle, generations of hope? Their strengths are our strengths. Their hopes for a better future are finally being realized through us. Why not be proud of that—the distance we have come despite all the obstacles in our way, despite things being so unequal? We have endured no matter. Why not choose to be black? Yes, why not?

"Cousin Annie made me to know that being 'colored,' as we were called, was not just about color. That would be easy! No, being black is hard, and being black in America takes character and strength. Being black means knowing your history, knowing where you come from, and loving your origins even when everybody else tries to make you believe you have no history, you have no traditions, you have no culture, no true home. Being black means having to believe that you can make it, that you are equal to any other human being on earth, even when they tell you otherwise. Being black means having to love and honor yourself, even when it seems like everyone else on earth despises you. Being black is tough! But you have come from a line of tough black people—from strong genes over many generations. We have survived death itself, the slave ships, the indignities of slavery, the beatings, the rapings and the castration of our sons. We have borne half-white children, who have fared no better than their black mothers in American society, and yet we and our daughters have all endured. Black women have an indomitable inner strength and we know the future is ours. Why not pass for black, LeShan?

"We must have faith in ourselves and our abilities to be whatever we wish to be. I would hope that my act of becoming has made it even more possible for you to become whatever you wish to be. That is the legacy I will leave for you.

"I remember that Aunt Cynthia wept as she told me, 'It's too late for me to be anything but what I am. Time and circumstance have cruelly disadvantaged me. But for you, Cynthia, you can choose—not whether to be black or white, not whether to be male or female, but to be yourself and to be successful in whatever role you choose to play in life. Most importantly, you must be proud of who you are—you came from a long line of strong and brave people. There is a reason to pass for black when one could choose otherwise!'

"It was her words that perhaps first challenged me to become something that no one I knew had ever dreamt of in my time—an ambassador of the United States. We all know that in America racial bias is still a reality, but the good news is the law, which allowed me to exercise my rights as a citizen. Who could better represent the opportunities that democracy has guaranteed—than we, as successful black women?

"I went with Dad to Cousin Annie's funeral, in 1954. When I joined the long line of mourners and viewed her frail body lying in peace, I remembered her concern that Katherine should marry before she died, so as not to be left alone. Prior to her mother's death, Katherine had fulfilled her mother's wish in her much-celebrated marriage to Dr. Winton Jones, a prominent black pharmacist, who owned the only black pharmacy in town. Both had seemed a bit old to me to be marrying for the first time. Doc Jones, as everyone called him, was a big man and perhaps the darkest-skinned man I had ever seen. I felt that in marrying him, Katherine had also made her own statement about who she was. They made a strange-looking couple as they drove about town and were often harassed by the local police, mistaking them for a forbidden interracial couple. They were both wonderful people, dearly loved by everyone. They had one child, a son, Dennis, who was quite brilliant. Over the years, together as a family, they built a prosperous pharmaceutical business in the city of Terre Haute.

"Cousin Annie passed many years ago, but her story— Chena's story—will remain alive through me, and now through you, and all those who will follow us. You must include this history in your own life's story some day and pass it to your children. Perhaps this has little meaning for you now, LeShan, but in a few years you will understand that America has even less respect for 'brown' people than for black. In a society so divided into black and white, there is often little voice for those who choose to be lost in the middle. The world of blacks, browns, coloreds and others in apartheid South Africa, another bad example of racial division and hatred, is likely to explode soon unless there is rapid change in that society. Laws, even good laws, cannot force people to love one another; they can only help us to peacefully co-exist in a civil society. You are obliged to strive to change your own attitudes, LeShan, and the attitudes and behaviors of others around you toward racial mixing, for the sake of your own children."

LeShan rose to lean over the railing on the verandah. "That's a great story, Grandmother, and I'll always remember what you've told me about my ancestors. But, I have the right to pass for white, just like Jacob in your story. My mother is as white as my father is black. I don't look black; it's just easier not to have to spend my life fighting prejudice and discrimination if I don't have to. I am very proud of you, Grandmother, and I love you very much. When I told all my friends about you and that you were black, they were surprised; but it didn't seem to matter, and it shouldn't matter. Their attitudes toward me didn't change. It's like coming from Germany, or from Vietnam or China, and you become an American—that's all that should matter. I am an American because I was born in America, and white is what I choose to be, because that's what I am."

I knew that down the road, LeShan would face many hurts and pains from whites and blacks alike, to force her to yield to the pressures of society. But, today the sun was setting in Sierra Leone, placing the peninsula in silhouette and casting a weird silver glow over the rippling Bay.

After a few silent moments, LeShan laid her head on my shoulder and said, "I love you, Grandmother."

"And, I love you, precious heart," I sighed. "Let's go plan your travel back to Sandcut!"

Confrontation With Power

Over the ensuing weeks and months, I missed the sweet innocence of LeShan's presence in our household. The heavy social calendar, together with the altitude, humidity and the heat, was exhausting. As Chief of Mission, I was ultimately responsible for the policy and programs of all U.S. government agencies as well as the security of their personnel in the country. Total personnel approximated nearly 200, including Foreign Service Nationals who worked hand in hand with American officers and staff.

One of the largest contingents of the Peace Corps worldwide was serving primarily in the rural areas of Sierra Leone, nearly 250 Volunteers, significantly diminished from the nearly 400 in 1973. There were another 650 or more American missionaries, and one of the largest private American mining investments, Sierra Rutile, in the south of the country. I was concerned that responsible Embassy officers should be always fully apprised of local conditions and therefore should travel often and meet with American constituents, especially in the rural areas. There were reports also of trouble brewing in the other cities of Sierra Leone—Bo, Kenema and Makeni.

I found myself working long hours to keep the paper from mounting on my desk and to avoid delays on actions that had to be taken. The most pressing issue for the first months, and, indeed, for my entire stay in Sierra Leone, was Embassy security, with warnings of terrorist plots throughout Western Europe and attempted assassinations of diplomats around the world.

Terrorist events would escalate over the years of my tour. In 1988, the world would be stunned by the tragic Pan Am 103 crash over Lockerbie, and controversy raged over the possible involvement of Middle Eastern saboteurs. A later crash in 1989 of a French UTA flight over Niger, would kill all on board, including the wife of the American Ambassador to Chad, would also be attributed to Middle Eastern sympathizers.

We, in Freetown, became increasingly aware of our own vulnerability. Sierra Leone had begun to experience serious domestic problems. There were rumors of growing political unrest in the country. Reportedly, there had been an attempted coup d'état and President Momoh had narrowly missed being assassinated by a missile launched at his car, just outside the city limits of Freetown. Although State House authorities never substantiated this particular rumor, a gaping hole in the road near his Residence gave moot testimony to its occurrence.

Tensions began to mount throughout the country between the two major tribal groups, the Mende and the Temne. The situation became almost palpable. Authorities were extremely nervous. The President placed his military forces on high alert, just short of declaring a state of emergency throughout Sierra Leone. Reportedly the French government, or perhaps the U.N., gave President Momoh a helicopter and he hired an American pilot with flight experience in Vietnam, who doubled as security while shuttling the President from place to place about the country.

The First Vice President, Francis M. Minah, a Mende and a brilliant, British-trained lawyer, was accused by prosecutors in 1987 of being the primary instigator of a plot to overthrow the government, although reportedly other men carried out the specific actions. All alleged plotters, a small group of government employees largely from Mr. Minah's Pujehun district, were placed on trial. Being declared guilty by jury, they were put to death. Mr. Minah was later tried and imprisoned after being found guilty of treason by the high court. He remained in prison throughout my tour and, in spite of protests from highest levels of Western observers throughout the world, some months after my departure in 1989, Vice President Minah was summarily hanged to death.

In 1988, the rapidly detoriating political situation became a greater concern among my diplomatic colleagues in Freetown. Many were already considering evacuating their non-essential personnel, with the possibility of closing their embassies. I did not concur with the severity of threat against our mission, and so advised the State Department in Washington. But, I cautiously summoned the Post Security Officer (PSO) for daily briefings on local disturbances and the specific precautions being undertaken by the Embassy. I was especially concerned about the hundreds of Peace Corps Volunteers and American missionaries who lived and worked in the deeply isolated areas of the country. Our early warning system was quite limited in range and we relied primarily upon personal visits and the missionary radio band. The missionaries in the country had their CB radio connections and the ability to send messages throughout the country. The PSO evaluated the warden system for me in terms of its efficacy in alerting American citizens to potential disturbances and advising them how to follow the emergency evacuation plan.

I was equally concerned about the security of the Chancery and the 35-40 homes and apartments of Embassy families spread out across the city. There was no identifiable American compound which might have been easier to secure, but which could also have become an easy target.

My staff prepared an emergency plan which I endorsed to send to Washington. Then, I focused on evacuation procedures for the Chancery, should the building come under siege, fire, bomb threats, etc.

"A problem does exist with Chancery security," the PSO warned. "There is no egress from the executive floor should an emergency arise; for example, a fire on the lower floors or along the stairway would invalidate both elevators and the stairway. How would you get out? The windows are all shielded by an ornamental brick facade; the only escape route in the case of fire or attack or disturbances from this floor is via a sky genie, from the fourth floor balcony."

To my raised eyebrows, he explained, "Oh, the sky genie is a simple escape mechanism authorized by the previous ambassador. He left before it was installed as a safety measure, and employees have not been trained to use it. I respectfully request your thoughts on the matter, and if you agree with the procedure--which you have the authority to change," he hastened to add, "I will need your agreement to set up the training."

"So, what does training entail?" It seemed too simple.

"Basically, all employees would have to be trained to evacuate the premises quickly and orderly utilizing the sky genie. A memo to that effect has to go out over your signature setting up preferably at least two Saturday mornings for the training, and requiring that all employees in the building participate. They should be dressed in appropriate casual attire." He waited.

"Why every employee?" I was still not clear on the procedure.

"Security regulations require that every employee, American and local hire, understand and follow safety rules. So, even though they don't work on this floor, they might be on this floor at a particular point in time that an emergency occurs; therefore, they all have to know how to manage their own and others' escapes. We can't wait until an emergency occurs, however, and this procedure has to be detailed in our emergency plan, due in Washington next week."

I thought of all the horror stories I had heard about embassies under siege. "Is it safe?"

"Yes, if carried out properly," he sounded very convincing. "Other embassies of our size have followed similar procedures and have experienced no problems. The marines will demonstrate the use of the equipment for the employees. It's quite simple, and they will work to reassure everybody that it is not only safe but necessary."

I stared at him for a few seconds, and thought I saw a faint flicker of amusement in his eyes. I had seen that look before, at the Residence, when he introduced the rope ladder. I was uncomfortable with it! There was a catch somewhere.

"Okay, I'll have Bette type up the order and get it out to everybody. Let's take the first Saturday morning next month, beginning at 8:00 a.m. for the first half of the employees; the rest, the second Saturday."

After he left my office, I sat tapping my pencil against the glass desktop for a few seconds, pondering.

Bette buzzed. "Barbara wishes to see you rather urgently, and Boima, your cook, is on the line about tomorrow's dinner. I'll tell him you'll call him back."

When Barbara Johnson, the Consular Officer, entered, I was surprised to see with her, Peggy Gorth, a senior Peace Corps Volunteer, who was subbing for the Peace Corps Director on short leave outside the country. They told me a bizarre story about our Peace Corps women being strip-searched at military roadblocks on their way down to Freetown from the northern provinces of the country. Apparently, several Volunteers had attempted to reach Freetown when rumors of an impending civil uprising became persistent. Some had witnessed actual hand-to-hand combat in remote areas. Most of the Volunteers utilized their mopeds to leave the northern regions; others rode the local buses which were being stopped at the roadblocks.

Reportedly, no one else was being searched or detained at the roadblocks, except the white female Volunteers. None of them apparently had been molested or harassed by the soldiers, but several described in tears how the local women employed to search them jeered and belittled them as they disrobed. "Is that all you've got?" they would hiss at the quaking young women. It also was not clear whether the male soldiers could see through the thatched walls of the huts. The question was why weren't the male Volunteers being searched or detained? Why not all the local men and women who were also riding the crowded buses?

I called in my deputy, and asked that he investigate and lodge a protest with the government's Foreign Office, being sure to follow all the protocol procedures demanded by this situation. Bette made a call to the presidential protocol officer who, considering the gravity of the situation, set up a meeting for me with the President the next morning at the President's Residence. By the time I arrived home that evening, several frightened young women had gathered in the American apartments next door, spending the evening with sympathetic Embassy families. I invited them to speak to me, and over Boima's hot apple pie and coffee, they tearfully related their experiences to me. I vowed to convey their concerns to the President the next day.

The next morning, I arrived on time at the Presidential Residence for my appointment. I was amazed and a little intimidated by the scores of armed soldiers at the gates, on the roofs, and covering the perimeter of the compound. President Momoh was holding meetings with several groups and with prominent individuals. His waiting room was packed. When First Lady Hannah Momoh learned of my arrival, she very graciously came down from her apartments to greet me and to offer me a cup of coffee. Although curious, she did not ask the purpose of my visit.

Shortly, the President's protocol officer ushered me into a small office on the second floor. I was surprised to find the President alone, assuming he would have a member of the foreign office or security present for the discussion. But, he seemed well briefed and deeply concerned about possible insurrection in the country. He was certain that the threat was absolutely real and imminent. We talked briefly about security measures he was instituting to quell the violence and to prevent further civil disturbance. I then repeated for him the stories told me by the Volunteers about being strip searched by his military and also informed him of the levels of concern being raised in Washington about these incidents.

"The situation in the countryside is very tense at this time," he explained. "We have proof of insurgents entering the country from Liberia, former soldiers from our own ranks, who have every intention of taking over this government. Verified attacks have occurred in the provincial offices in our major centers of Bo and Kenema. These renegades have many friends who are hiding and feeding them; therefore, a number of houses have been searched. Now, rumor has it that a group of insurgents is headed toward Freetown aboard local transport and in private automobiles from the regions. I understand that my soldiers at the roadblocks have been less than cordial with travelers from the regions, and I regret that Volunteers have been caught up along with others for search and questioning."

"Mr. President, why would only the Peace Corps women be searched," I asked. "And for what reason? For weapons?"

His eyes grew round. "I was not aware that Peace Corps girls were being body searched until you informed my office. I'm positive that many local citizens are also being searched and detained. But, it is possible the soldiers may be taking unauthorized measures to secure the area at the roadblocks. They might also be searching for diamonds. It was rumored that the Lebanese merchants are using women to transport illicit diamonds from Kono in their clothing, their hair, and wherever they could be hidden. One Peace Corps Volunteer, identified as the girlfriend of the most notorious Lebanese trader, was searched, and alleged to be found carrying a sizable cache of diamonds hidden on her person. As a result, possibly some of my men, many have little education, may have given the order to strip-search all the Peace Corps girls coming through the roadblocks."

He paused a moment. "I sincerely regret that it has gotten out of hand. I will send the officer-in-charge to investigate. We are pleased to have Peace Corps here—you know that I am a great supporter. I ask that you excuse this unfortunate incident, Madame Ambassador, and I will personally issue an order to correct the situation."

"Mr. President," I was nervous that he was nervous. "This accusation brought against Peace Corps is quite serious, one that I cannot ignore. Could you please give me the name of the Volunteer accused of collaborating with the Lebanese, and the Director will take appropriate action?"

"I'll have to consult my Chief of Security and the Foreign Affairs Office," he back-pedaled. "I did not bring this matter to your attention at the time it was reported to me because I could not verify the charge." He paused slightly. "Please understand, Madame Ambassador, my men are on full alert; we are convinced that my government is in danger of being overtaken. I cannot weaken our security posture by asking at this time that our men make exceptions at the roadblocks. Most are common foot soldiers who are incapable of making such distinctions. They just follow orders. But, we will investigate the matter. Please advise the Volunteers to stay in place, not to travel at this time. I cannot guarantee that the searches will be immediately discontinued."

"Thank you, Mr. President, for understanding the seriousness of our concerns." We both rose to our feet. "I am sympathetic with the security position you feel you must take. But, my government is requesting your immediate action to protect these women. All are white women, easily distinguishable by the most illiterate soldier. I will advise the State Department of our discussion this morning and the action you have proposed to take. I'm sure you are aware that Sierra Leone has one of the largest contingents of Volunteers anywhere in the world, the program has been here for many years without a break. They are not soldiers; they are not clandestine; they are not entrepreneurs, but are here to assist you in meeting your development goals."

He was nodding, looking very disturbed.

I continued, now more softly, "I am sure Washington will ask for my recommendation on this matter. Regrettably, Mr. President, if I receive just one more report of a Peace Corps "girl" being body-searched at a road block, I will recommend that the total Peace Corps program—all 250 Volunteers, be immediately removed from this country, and that our agreement be terminated."

He blinked hard, but thanked me for bringing this serious matter to his attention and wished me a good day. I wished him success in restoring peace to his country and his people and assured him of our concern and goodwill. Before I could get out the door, I saw him reaching for the telephone. He knew it was not a laughing matter and that he personally, as well as the country, had much to lose.

I returned to the Embassy to advise Washington of the action I had taken and presented all the required justifications for the recommendation. The strip search episode became a hot item during the next few days. The Peace Corps office and the Embassy were flooded with calls and cables from parents who had heard on American and international newscasts about the searches. Journalists were calling from the U.S. and Europe for information. American parents were sure their daughters were being molested and worse, raped, by "those Africans" and were contacting their congressmen who were also calling the Embassy. They were calling Loret Ruppe, Director of Peace Corps/Washington, demanding to know what she was doing about this shameful episode.

For procedural reasons, Peace Corps/Washington was not happy with the action I had promised President Momoh. They questioned my authority to make such a threat without the advice and consent of the Peace Corps Director. My country team, on the other hand, in the absence of the Director, had concurred with the action taken believing it was most propitious and that my unprecedented access to President Momoh had averted a major incident.

Then, I received a cable from Assistant Secretary of State for Africa, Chester Crocker, stating that he stood behind my decision, and if the situation were not remedied immediately, he was prepared to endorse the evacuation order. I felt vindicated although I had made no friends with the Peace Corps bureaucracy by my action. The Volunteer who had been reportedly caught with the large diamond cache was never identified. Most importantly, however, not another Volunteer was searched, and Peace Corps soon resumed its normal activities in the country.

On later examination of this crisis, I felt for the first time that being a woman diplomat in this case allowed me to speak directly and persuasively to the President of a sovereign country without causing serious offense. A male ambassador would have found this approach difficult because of the risk of offending this president or losing face or prestige should his ultimatum be ignored. He would probably have taken a different tactic. I will always appreciate a remark made by my deputy.

"Ambassador," he said seriously. "I want you to know how pleased I am to serve an ambassador who's got balls."

According to the Volunteers, word of the incident and my "facing up" to the President reached even the most distant corners of the country. The leading women of Sierra Leonean society used the incident to tout their own gender-related issues and the Peace Corps case became the cause célèbre for all women in the country.

Representational Activities

The relatively rapid resolution of the Peace Corps crisis allowed the Embassy to return quickly to business as usual. I had planned a number of representational activities, designed to introduce to our important contacts in the country some aspects of American lifestyles and culture, including art, foods and music. These activities were also strategically designed to bring together top decision-makers within Sierra Leone's government with members of the American mission. These activities often included selected members of the diplomatic community as well to build camaradry between and among international missions in the country. The activities provided a forum for resolving sticky matters in a fairly neutral and informal atmosphere, much as male ambassadors might do on the golf course or the tennis court.

I chose to meet these important groups for discussions over dinner, breakfast, lunch, or receptions whenever possible, knowing that the act of sharing a good meal was always a most effective icebreaker in Africa. I personally loved to cook and took great pleasure in setting a sumptuous and bountiful table. I made certain that everyone was always pleased to receive an invitation to a meal at the American Ambassador's Residence. I entertained small groups and large groups, one-on-one settings, or up to 1,000 or more for our Fourth of July celebrations each year. My dining table easily accommodated 20 persons for a formal sit-down dinner. For larger groups, I could set 10 round tables to seat 80 persons if desired. Larger receptions or buffets were often set up in the beautiful tiled garden terrace with a stupendous view of the Bay. My front verandah was most often used for smaller, formal functions.

The State Department provided limited funds for these affairs. It was necessary to do some creative budgeting to cover the costs of my representational program. In the three years of my tour, I normally overspent my allocated amount and therefore had to dip into my own personal funds. At the end of the fiscal year, however, I could apply for funds left over from other missions to refund my out-of-pocket costs. Fortunately, fish, shrimp and oysters were plentiful in Sierra Leone and fresh fruits and vegetables were available in the local markets at modest prices. My pantry was stocked with dry foodstuffs and spices which I replenished regularly through the Embassy commissary.

I can say with pride that my Residence was considered the most elegant and indeed best appointed official Residence in the city of Freetown. It was expected to be. The wife of the French Ambassador and I competed for first place position in selection of cuisine. She did better in the quality and quantity of wine and cheese. The cook and three stewards comprising the domestic staff of my Residence staff were well trained in traditional American cookery, but had to be re-oriented to cook and to season foods to my liking, and to adapt to my particular style of preparation and presentation. They loved it. When additional cooks or servers were required, I usually recruited temporary domestic help from other missions, such as the French, British and Belgian embassies.

Representational activities were sometimes difficult to manage, but I did them nevertheless, and tried hard to ensure that my guests all left impressed and satisfied with the meal or activity. Even if willing, my husband lacked the necessary skills or experience to supervise the staff, as a wife might have delighted in doing, and to orchestrate the total affair for me, including hiring additional staff when necessary. In fact, his efforts to organize events often served to confuse matters, especially those involving the kitchen staff.

A number of special occasions were presented at the Residence each year to bring together interested and engaging groups of people such as visiting American dignitaries and congressional delegations, visiting family members, church groups, etc. The most popular event was perhaps the annual visits of American ships to Freetown. The arrival of these ships, involved in West African coastal security, always created great excitement within the host government and the harbor city of Freetown. Sailors on shore leave always brought a lot of money and excitement to the economy. When the USS *Barnstable County*, visited Freetown in July 1987, the sailors aboard ship carried out joint military bivouacs with Sierra Leone's small navy, later joining them on brief shore leave excursions.

My role normally was to invite and accompany a small group of top Sierra Leonean officials to lunch aboard ship with the Admiral. Embassy officers would also set up meetings for the ship's junior officers with local military officials, and our Marine Guard would plan social evenings at the Marine House, in American homes, or at the American Club and local entertainment places.

Secondly, my role was to host a formal dinner at the Residence for fifty or more high-ranking dignitaries and VIP's in honor of the visiting Admiral. The most influential persons in the city, the government and diplomatic corps were always invited to meet our distinguished guests. We weren't always given a lot of time for preparation and things had to be done rather hurriedly.

On one occasion, I was informed by telex that within the week we were to be visited by the USS *Harlan County, LST 1196*, a part of the West African Training Cruise program, known as WATC. We were to host a dinner honoring Rear Admiral Dalrymple, and his top officers.

Kamara, the chief steward, and I had already discussed the table arrangements, protocol seating and table service. Extra servers had been hired; the champagne and wine were being chilled and the butter properly pressed, very importantly, into small daisies. We had purchased a huge tuna fish, one that could have been someone's proud trophy, to bake in two parts because the oven was too small. It would be served with a delicious crab and shrimp stuffing. The menu included several dishes of fresh and stewed vegetables and condiments. Over the weekend, I personally made up all the table menu cards as well as the seating cards, and ensured that all other details had been arranged. Freshly cut flowers from the garden were placed throughout the public rooms and arranged with candles as centerpieces at each round table. I loved doing all this with my staff, but it was time-consuming, taking me away from other priority tasks, and I often wished my husband could have been a better wife.

I knew Kamara would carry out his part, including overseeing the cook, himself. But, just to be sure, before retiring for the evening the night before, I walked through the plans with Boima, the cook. He had been the head cook for several years at the Residence, with previous experience in local hotels, and was considered the best cook in Freetown. He assured me all would go well.

The night arrived for the dinner. I was delayed at the Chancery with a call from Washington. I rushed home, regretting that unlike my male counterparts, I had no wife who would have managed everything so that things would go just like clockwork. But, thank goodness! When I walked in, the house looked elegant and festive, just as we had planned.

Boima, dressed in his white chef's cap and apron, met me at the door, smiling and exuding self-assurance.

"Everything is in place, Ambassador. The fish will be placed in the oven as soon as the first guests arrive for cocktails."

We had decided earlier to go buffet style because the presentation of the fish would otherwise be lost. Boima had baked some of his delicious lemon meringue pies. All was in order.

I dressed quickly in a floor length caftan of West African cloth, and J.O., looking very handsome in his black tie, helped me to greet visitors as they arrived. Admiral Dalrymple arrived first with five of his top officers, all very impressive in their dress whites. We had placed a table in the entrance just to hold their white hats. The officers mingled freely with our several guests as they arrived from the government and the Diplomatic Corps, all impressed with the view from our verandah. For the next thirty minutes, they took their cocktails watching the sunset, with its resplendent colors. Finally, we all sat down to dinner and were served our appetizer. When finished, the guests formed a queue to be served or to serve themselves the main dishes. I stood at the serving table to assist and supervise, as a good hostess would commonly do. I was proud of the giant fish, now put back together and expertly garnished with lemon slices arranged to resemble fish scales. It was beautiful to look at and would be enjoyable eating.

But, where were the vegetable dishes? Wishing I were invisible, I marched quickly to the kitchen, smiling warmly at my guests as I passed, trying not to look panicked.

"Boima, the fish is beautiful," I complemented the smiling chef, "but where are the vegetables?"

"Vegetables?" He looked at me blankly.

"The country greens, the buttered mushrooms, the rice."

"Oh," he smiled reassuringly. "They're all stuffed inside the fish just as you ordered, Madame."

Then I panicked. I was mortified. What to do? I could not allow my guests to witness my loss of composure. In these matters, the Ambassador is expected to be unflappable. Of course, "he" would have been, and his wife would be having fits in the kitchen like me. I summoned Patti, a volunteer helper for the event, who ordered the serving staff to flood our guests with champagne and wine, hot rolls with plenty of butter, and green salad. The vegetables were inedible. Out of respect for the hostess, some people tried to eat them; others raked them out of their fish, salvaged the crab stuffing, and ate the fish which was, fortunately, delicious. The lemon pies and coffee saved the day; guests took more than one serving, and when they departed that evening, thanked me graciously for the wonderful American meal.

The need for communication and close supervision, even of seasoned staff, was an unanticipated complication. The entertainment and representational part of my responsibility was the most difficult task of all for me, because there was no other woman in the house. I found the negotiating and reporting responsibilities of my job much more manageable, primarily because expert officers assigned to post did an appreciable percentage of the actual work. But, the management of the Residence took hours of my time and sapped my energies. Like most men, my husband was concerned about his image, not wanting to appear house-broken, and insisted he did not accompany me to become the maid.

With my secretary's help, we managed to spend more planning time with the staff to avoid any future embarrassment like the stuffed fish. Nonetheless, these mishaps occurred from time to time. I tried a number of management schemes and none worked well. I became convinced that a woman's touch was necessary to manage these affairs—some other woman's touch, that is—so I would be free to concentrate on my other diplomatic duties.

Since the State Department would fund no additional household employees, it would have been necessary to lose one of my male staff to hire a woman. Instead, I chose to use my own personal funds to hire a young British woman who immediately began to organize the men in the house. She coordinated the ordering of food and accounting of expenditures for my representational budget, and took general charge of my many breakfasts, luncheons and dinners throughout her tenure. When her husband returned to London at the end of his contract, he took my marvelous staff sergeant with him and I went looking for a replacement.

I later found Sandra Bullock, an American Bahá'í resident in Freetown, who also spoke the local language fluently. Under her diligent eye, my representational activities soon normalized, and I was grateful to her for her assistance. Before I departed post, however, one of the stewards resigned, allowing me to hire a young, Sierra Leonean woman, Alice, as a permanent housekeeper. Although she at first found the three men in the house quite domineering, she soon wound them around her little finger and returned to the Residence a woman's touch—and smell.

The point must be made that not all wives of career ambassadors have enjoyed the burdensome role imposed upon them as household managers, and a number have refused to go to post with their husbands for that reason. The social responsibilities are often quite demanding and it is a thankless job, considered more an act of love than duty. More recently, a stipend was approved for wives who chose to carry out such responsibilities. I argue that the training of an accompanying male spouse should also include household management, and would be a fitting topic for the Ambassadorial Seminar.

Such training, if and when it ever takes place, however, will come too late for J.O., my prince consort.

Post Security Challenges

Within my first year, the operation of the Residence and the Chancery had vastly improved. But, due to continuing threats of terrorism, particularly from the Middle East, all foreign missions were required by the Inman Commission to upgrade the security of their principal offices. In Freetown, the post security upgrade began in 1985, the year prior to my arrival, and was scheduled to be continued by a detachment of Seabees, a playful acronym for CB, which stands for the naval Construction Battalion. This group of young, energetic construction men, "worker bees at sea," between 18 and 22 years old, was led by a senior naval construction officer. They arrived shortly after I arrived at post.

Their 13-week task was to tear out and rebuild those parts of the Embassy believed to constitute a security risk. The Embassy had sat for years in the center of town, on the busy intersection around the historic Cotton Tree, under which tribes and governments for generations had negotiated peace settlements. It faced an avenue which circled upward toward the State House and the Parliament Building. This had been a most prestigious location for the American Embassy in times past. At this time however, it was a hazardous location. The four-story building sat squarely on the corner, directly on the sidewalk, with no setbacks on any side. Few possibilities existed for providing any secure distancing of the building from the public. The building, moreover, was not U.S. Government-owned but had been acquired years before on a long-term lease from a local merchant. We could not get authority to deface the building to provide greater security and were advised by the State Department that no funds were available for constructing a new building or for purchasing a more suitable one. Available monies were reserved for embassies at greatest risk, located primarily in Europe and Asia.

African missions, they reasoned, were not under threat from external sources, and were at considerably greater risk from internal, civil uprisings than from Middle Eastern terrorists. Sierra Leone was a prime example. We were advised, however, to keep an eye and ear open for possible changing conditions involving the Middle Eastern presence in the country.

So, most of the security upgrade would involve certain internal renovations and an enlarged Marine Guard detachment. Large cement planters were placed along the sidewalks to prevent trucks or automobiles with potential explosive devices from being driven up close to the entrance. We were painfully aware, as terrorist threats and actions escalated around the world, that our building only minimally met the new security codes, and because of our position in Africa and the limited funds available, upgrades if done at all would be minor. We felt extremely vulnerable.

The nation-wide alert, put into effect following the attack on the President's motorcade and rumors of an imminent *coup d'état*, persisted beyond reasonable expectations. Each day presented new challenges for the nation's military. At the same time, threats posed by Libya around the world built new levels of alarm. A number of locally-based Iranians and Libyans had been declared *persona non grata* by the Government of Sierra Leone for interfering with the country's internal affairs, and were given 24 hours to leave the country. Shortly thereafter, Libya temporarily closed its Embassy in Sierra Leone, but the Islamic "Green Book" cultural library and the Libyan commercial community continued to function. Their bitter political denouncement of the United States appeared daily in local newspapers as paid advertising and in printed leaflets widely distributed throughout the country.

For the first time, the Iranians opened a fully staffed Embassy in Freetown, and the increasing numbers of Iranians together with the continued presence of Libyans in the country became a matter of concern to the U.S. government. It was my task to bring those concerns to the attention of the Foreign Minister. Unfortunately the Foreign Minister was not available due to travel outside the country. I was encouraged by Washington to discuss the matter directly with the President of Sierra Leone.

President Momoh graciously and warmly received me and one of my senior officers for a discussion of Sierra Leone's relationship to Libya, in light of increasing threats emanating from that country's leadership. Without a great many preliminaries, I opened the subject of Libya and the propaganda war being conducted in Sierra Leone against American interests. Acknowledging the sovereignty of Sierra Leone, I asked President Momoh if he would clarify his country's relationship to Libya.

"I think our position is quite clear," he stated flatly. "We discovered that the Libyans were making mischief in the country, promising support and weapons to our opposition, and preaching discord. Those identified as instigators were asked to leave the country. Libya closed its mission here, but made it clear that they were not severing diplomatic relationships. They said that due to the high costs of operating a formal mission, they wished to consider their options. Their former Chancery has now been offered to public bid. They decided to maintain their Green Book operation and, together with the Iranians, to undertake a number of religious and educational projects with our Muslim communities."

I shifted in my seat, formulating my response, while he continued, "You may have noticed the magnificent mosque the Iranians are currently building in the heart of the city. But as for the Libyans, I can say without hesitation we have no relationship, nor do we have any communications with Colonel Qadhafi."

"My government will be pleased to hear that, Mr. President," I began. "And considering the recent actions you have taken with Libyans in this country, your position on Libya seems quite clear and is greatly appreciated. Therefore, I was a bit startled to note in one of today's Tripoli newspapers that the Foreign Minister of Sierra Leone, Alhaji Koroma, had paid a courtesy call on President Qadhafi this morning."

"When did you say?" The President asked, attempting to disguise his astonishment.

I repeated the information. My economics officer began to twitch, to cross and uncross his legs, feeling uncomfortable and needing to clarify the source of my information.

"It's public information, Mr. President," he offered. "And, it is apparently true. Minister Koroma is in Tripoli today."

President Momoh smiled sardonically, and was speechless for a moment, collecting his thoughts and composure.

"I assure you," he said, "that I did not know that my Minister was going to Libya. I take your word that he is indeed there. He is not there by my authority." He was thoughtful. "But, he is the Foreign Minister, and some authority comes with his job. I don't order his every move, although I would want his actions to reflect our policies and stances in the public forum."

He was agitated; his fingers drummed the top of his desk, and he was frowning. Then his face brightened and his infectious smile returned.

"On the other hand, he told me he was going to Addis Ababa for the Annual Minister's Conference of the Organization of African Unity. Libya is a member of OAU and we are pledged to support each other's sovereignty. President Qadhafi's minister may have issued an invitation to Minister Koroma for talks in Tripoli about the possibility of restoring relations currently in limbo. Since Libya is in the same neighborhood, so to speak, with Ethiopia, the Minister may have found it convenient to stop there before returning home. He is a devout Muslim, you may know, having journeyed to

Mecca last year, so he and President Qadhafi have the religion in common."

He paused. "He will report to me when he returns, but I assure you, Madame Ambassador, although we have not officially broken relations with Libya at this time, we are also not encouraging their return."

We left the President deep in thought. We had delivered a bombshell for which he was hardly prepared. But, he was also a general in Sierra Leone's military and I was confident he would handle the matter. The outcome would not favorably impact my relationship to the Minister, which was at best, strained. I silently applauded the president's ability to recover, and to some degree, regretted having told him in the way I did. I also realized the breach between the President and his Foreign Minister may have been seriously widened by my information.

Over the ensuing weeks, the country's internal atmosphere steadily worsened and the military began to move troops in long convoys to the interior and along the coast. Rumor had it that confrontations between the military and the insurgents in the interior were steadily occurring. Tension began to mount in the mission, especially among our Foreign Service Nationals who were primarily Krio. They had no great confidence in the ability of the tribal groups to run the country, and there was no trust in the military.

The very air in Freetown was filled with trepidation. I encouraged my staff to look for ways to reduce stress in their lives, and the regional American psychologist, a medical officer based in Nairobi, arrived to discuss with all of the American staff their concerns and fears. I handled my stress by painting when time allowed, huge canvases in oil depicting scenes of the countryside, portraits of the wonderfully human faces of Sierra Leone, and I began to keep a diary of those things that bothered or impressed me most during those days.

To relieve some physical tension, I started jogging early in the mornings, when I felt it was needed. One morning, I rose early to do a two-mile jog on the road below Signal Hill. In most places, the road was on a gradual incline, especially at the nearby military installation, so heading out was tough. Coming back down the hill was a breeze. I was easily identifiable by this time by my white hair. Local people frequently stopped to watch me slowly jogging, my hair flopping with every step. I remember being told by a female Krio friend that no self-respecting African woman would display her gray hair in public; she would color it, shave it off, wrap it up, but never show it. I consequently always bared my head like a badge of distinction.

So, there I was, before six o'clock in the morning, running with my white hair shapeless and damp with perspiration, a stricken look on my face due to exertion, struggling for breath. I went up the incline past the military installation to the crossroads, where normally I turned around for the return downhill stretch. Not many people normally were on that stretch of road at that early hour.

I passed only one man, in fact, walking in the opposite direction along the road, loaded with a huge stalk of green bananas across his back, headed for the market. He stopped to stare at my sweating, distorted face; his eyes searched the road behind me toward the military camp. Seeing nothing, he determined that, nonetheless, something or somebody must be chasing the American ambassador, and he'd better run too. He threw the stalk of bananas into the bushes, turned around and in record time, passed me at breakneck speed. Stopping at the crossroads for breath and gesturing wildly, he urged two men standing there waiting for the bus to run for their lives.

They bent over laughing hysterically, slapping each other on the back and hooting loudly. Finally, the poor man got the picture. He walked slowly back to retrieve his bananas from the bushes, shaking his head and muttering derisively as he passed me on his return, "crazy old American woman!"

That incident brought home clearly to me the level of nervousness in the country. Almost anything could start a panic. I curtailed my jogging for a while.

Amid reports of attacks and threats against American embassies and installations abroad, the Post Security Officer called on me again, to urge immediate testing of evacuation procedures from the Chancery. I agreed and signed the order.

Half of the Embassy staff gathered one Saturday morning to begin testing the weird escape mechanism. Everyone had been advised to wear jeans and tennis shoes.

I arrived promptly at 0800 hours, to find about 25 persons lined up on the fourth-floor balcony on the backside of the building. I cheerfully took my place at the end of the line as the PSO and the marines began the training session. To demonstrate the procedure, one of the marines buckled himself into the genie and nimbly jumped backward off the roof. We all gasped, and stared at each other. Were we expected to do that, too? This was asking too much! I had imagined that one would sit in a canvas seat to be lowered quickly but "gently" to the ground below. Apparently, I was not the only one under that impression. Everybody, men and women alike, looked very pale and drawn around the mouth.

The PSO came over to where I stood, mesmerized, at the end of the line. This time there was no mistaking that sarcastic amusement in his eyes.

"Madame Ambassador," he began respectfully. "We are pleased that you have endorsed this security measure by being here this morning. You realize, of course, that protocol dictates that the Chief of Mission is always the first to leave. No one leaves before you. Therefore, we await your presence on the ledge. Here, let me give you a hand."

I knew I was being challenged—as an ambassador and as a woman! Should I meet it? I could refuse, but that's what I felt "they" expected. I could see it in their faces. I was fairly athletic, although somewhat overweight. I had no fear of heights, but this was ridiculous! All eyes were on me, some urging me to back away, others hyping me up, "our fearless leader!" The marine gunny escorted me to the ledge. I stood looking down four floors below me to the ground, where another marine stood waiting to assist me if needed.

Another marine buckled the harnesses around me. I looked at the one slim cable hooked to the genie contraption over my head and the other looped around my arm and waist. There was nothing else. Where was the canvas seat?

"Bend your knees, Madame Ambassador, and shove yourself backward over the ledge. Brace your feet against the building to slow your decent as you go down," the marine yelled above the din of the traffic below.

My knees would not bend. I tried. My joints had locked. My muscles had frozen in absolute terror.

"This is how lives are lost, Madame Ambassador," he shouted through clenched teeth. "People freeze at the most critical moment, trapping all others behind them. Just bend your knees and shove off!"

I acknowledged the truth of his statement and for that reason, I turned around to climb down off the ledge.

I know I did not jump! He shoved me! I was mad, no—furious and outraged—and called him every bad name I knew as I whizzed by the windows on each floor. I vowed to ship him out when this was all over. Too angry to be afraid, I landed with a WHOP, the hard ground jarring everything inside me and injuring my pride, but doing no serious harm to my body.

Everybody at the top cheered wildly as I picked myself off the ground, and declared me brave—in spite of my age and size and gender. At that moment, I recalled that when Mark was born, I had vowed to get that mean old nurse who assisted the delivery. But, after the trauma was over, I couldn't remember her face. Luckily for the marine, I could not later identify the one who shoved me off the building.

Perhaps if terrorists were truly bursting through the door, I would feel grateful rather than insulted! But, my life was not in danger; we were not in an emergency situation, and his push seemed spiteful and senseless.

Hearing cheering and applause behind me, I looked across the main street to see literally scores of Sierra Leoneans lining the boulevard, attracted by this bizarre circus on the roof of the American Embassy. They knew about the increased security measures at the Embassy and had first thought there was a fire or that I was being kidnapped by terrorists. Being star of the show, I managed to put on a smile and cheerfully waved to them to assure them that all was well.

The word got around, I was later told, that the new American Ambassador was a tough old bird. Interestingly, many employees on the roof refused to jump. One said she would let the terrorists shoot her first, or I could shoot her myself, but she wasn't jumping, and walked away. I instructed the PSO to find an alternative to this evacuation plan. This matter was left on the drawing board for the next Ambassador to finalize, and fortunately, there was never a need to test or to use the sky genie again during my tenure.

* * *

However, the security upgrade continued with the Seabees, who were exceptionally good at tearing down things, even things that weren't in the plan. Rebuilding was much more difficult. For weeks, important work by my staff was almost at a standstill because of the pounding, knocking, and hammering that shook the building. Wet cement was unavoidably tracked everywhere. It smelled bad, too. The two elevators were clogged with cement and debris. When the elevators eventually stopped working, climbing up and down the four flights of stairs became my new daily regimen.

Among the smaller tasks to be performed by the Seabees was the installation of a small duress button on my desk. In the event of a threat to me in my office, I could press the button and alert the Marine Guard to come to my aid. The officer-in-charge requested that I vacate my office one weekend so the Seabees could work without disturbing me. When I returned the following Monday, the button had been installed—in the ceiling directly over my head. I inquired facetiously of the officer-in-charge if I might be issued a broomstick to poke the button, or should I perhaps leap upward from the top of my desk to reach it? He was flabbergasted, and apologized profusely. It turned out that the Seabees had read the blueprints upside down. The duress button was eventually installed properly within reach of my fingers.

I remembered the advice of Shirley Temple Black in the Ambassadors Seminar, that one must keep a good sense of humor and a positive outlook. It was sometimes a struggle. Every day was filled with the unexpected. I was never bored. On the contrary, I met a new challenge every day and some were not easily resolved.

As a prime case in point, the International Monetary Fund (IMF) had demanded that Sierra Leone's currency be devalued; i.e., decreased in value until it met the level of local demand, thereby defeating the vigorous black market in the country. When I first visited the country in 1972, one leone equaled nearly three U.S. dollars. During 1989, the leone's value had "floated" to fifty leones to the dollar, and was still declining rapidly. People began to hoard the large bills, and soon, there was not enough paper currency in circulation to meet public demand. Banks began to postpone cash disbursements until money could be gathered from depositors who were speculating on its rise in value. The Government ordered the issuance of new currency from their mints in London, to lessen the possibility of panic.

The Seabees and our local contract employees were paid in local currency. To protect our own employees, we borrowed leones from external sources to maintain our payroll and to meet emergencies. Eventually, no large denominations were to be found in the country, and payrolls were issued in bills of two-leone denominations.

One afternoon, I had an urgent call from Chief Anoka, the Nigerian High Commissioner, whose Embassy was located next door. "Ambassador," he said excitedly, "There is money coming from the top of your building. What are you doing?"

I told him, "I don't see anything from my window, Ambassador." I had no idea what he was talking about.

He cautioned, "You'd better check again."

And, sure enough, when I checked the windows on the opposite side of the building, leone notes were falling like autumn leaves. The normally rapid traffic around the circle at the Cotton Tree was now at full stop, with people jumping from their cars to retrieve the bills. There was absolute pandemonium.

The phones began to ring. One call was from Foreign Minister Koroma, demanding my presence in his office immediately. Before going, I took stock of my own house. Security officers brought in two young Seabees, no more than 18 or 19 years old, who confessed to tossing the money from the roof of the Embassy. Shaking in their boots, they explained.

"We got paid today. Each of us received nearly a bushel basket of two-leone bills—a basketful! We couldn't believe it. The people have no money—we had plenty that had very little value for us. We thought we'd give it to the people. What's wrong with that? It's our money; we earned it; we had the right to throw it away, give it away—even burn it, if we wished, didn't we?"

I left them in the hands of the Deputy and their superior officer to explain that this was not New York or Chicago, that these were not U.S. dollars, and to explain why I was being summoned to the Foreign Office. They were much chagrined.

Foreign Minister Alhaji Koroma very firmly demanded that the two Americans who had been seen throwing leones from the Embassy roof depart Sierra Leone within the next 24 hours. I thought this action too drastic, and said so in a few words, explaining they were just boys. Moreover, they were part of a larger renovation detail that was vital to our presence in the country. In fact, I said, their job was nearly finished and they would all be leaving within one week. I humbly asked for his reconsideration.

"Your Embassy is party to an egregious insult to the nation of Sierra Leone," he said without blinking. "By this act, your people have poked fun at our current financial condition. They have treated our currency as 'play' money, worthless paper to be thrown on the streets. This act created a traffic hazard in which many citizens could have been maimed or killed. Therefore, I cannot excuse them. They must be out within 24 hours, Madame Ambassador, or I will hold you personally responsible and will take whatever action necessary with the Department of State regarding your refusal to act."

Did he intend to demand my recall over a simple matter like this? He did not buy my story that some Americans had been known to throw money from the rooftops from time to time, even from planes, or to burn it for no reason other than it belonged to them.

He sneered: "You'll never make me believe that anyone would willfully throw away or destroy an American dollar!"

He refused to change the expulsion order. I returned to the Embassy and issued an order to pack out the two Seabees. I then learned that six Seabees had actually been involved. If that were discovered, the security project would be jeopardized by the loss of half the team. I felt that I, myself, and the Embassy staff could not endure possibly ten more weeks of dirt, grime, noise and delay, which would result from posting a replacement demolition and construction team.

The next morning, I received a very strongly worded diplomatic note from the Foreign Minister, formally demanding the departure of the two Seabees within 24 hours. I telephoned the President's Protocol Office, and in the humblest tones I could muster, requested a meeting with the President. President Momoh granted me a brief audience and I explained to him the conditions under which the thoughtless action leading to my dilemma had occurred.

He responded gravely, "Ambassador, I suppose to some of my people this was a grave insult. We are under terrible, financial straits with no currency to pay our workers. People are sitting on their money, keeping it out of circulation hoping it will soon regain value. Perhaps we can blame the IMF and their stringent demands for all our woes." He looked at me squarely and sternly.

"I don't like to cross my Foreign Minister in these matters. But, I can understand from your explanation how it really happened and that no offense was intended. I am rescinding his order with the understanding the young men will leave the country within one week."

I returned to my office with the good news, welcomed with shouts of relief from my staff and the Seabees. I asked my deputy to make sure the President's order was acted on. For myself, however, it was clear that the confrontation with the Foreign Minister contained an implied threat of my recall. I had gone over his head, my principal officer, to the President, to whom I was officially accredited. I had every right to do so, as well as an obligation to protect my staff. But, I knew that by not accepting the dictates of protocol, I had made an enemy of the unrelenting Foreign Minister, by what he would now consider an unforgivable, egregious breach of protocol. This was just another instance in a number of confrontations with Alhaji Koroma and there would be a price to pay in the months ahead.

The next day, the local newspaper regaled the tossing of leones from the Embassy roof and the resulting hysteria around the Cotton Tree. They facetiously captioned their front page story: "The Leone Floats Again!"

With my Sunday School class at age six. Lost Creek Baptist Church, Terre Haute, Indiana, 1934.

At age 14, in the Lost Creek Baptist Church Choir.

At age 17, graduating from Otter Creek High School near Terre Haute, Indiana, where I was one of just two black students in my class. I was voted "Most Likely to Succeed."

My "Prince Consort" James O. Perry, at the age of 21, upon his graduation from Wabash college in Crawfordsville, Indiana. We first met at about this time, and I was impressed by his earnest expression as well as by his big ears.

My Mom and Dad, Flossie and George Norton, Terre Haute, Indiana, 1944. This photo was taken as a gift to my four elder brothers who were in military service during World War II. My parents were married for 55 years, and died just months apart, in 1973.

Aunt Anna Anderson, daughter of my great-great grandmother, Chena. Born in slavery, she became, by her own industry, an educator, linguist, founder and administrator of a Red Cross hospital, and even began formal study of medicine at the age of 60. I found her life story fascinating and inspiring. She died in Louisville, Kentucky, in 1928.

Great Aunt Cynthia Howard, my primary inspiration during my early youth, photographed about 1910. She was the second or third Cynthia in our family line, and I was named for her. She died in 1949.

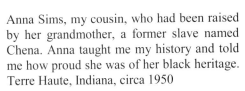

Anna Sims, my cousin, who had been raised by her grandmother, a former slave named Chena. Anna taught me my history and told me how proud she was of her black heritage. Terre Haute, Indiana, circa 1950

The Norton family: my parents and siblings, Burnett, Indiana, 1947.
Back row, left to right: Madonna, Walter, George, Jr., Orville, Otto Shepard (my first husband), James, Iona. *Second row, left to right:* My infant daughter Donna and I, Gertrude (wife of Walter) with baby Patricia, Dad, Mom,   eldest sister Lillian, Doretta (wife of James). *Front row, left to right*: Sharon (daughter of my sister Lillian), Hazel, and Dolores (daughter of my brother Walter).

The Norton sisters. I painted this during my sisters' first visit to Africa.   My father taught me to paint. I developed a passion for painting, and have all my life used it as a personal expression, and to record my impressions of people and events.

Oil on canvas, 1993
36"X54"

My eldest child, Donna.

My eldest son Jim, with his son Bryan, 1985. Jim and his family joined us in Sierra Leone in 1987 while working for Nord Resouces.

Jennifer Shull, daughter of my son James and wife Kathy who lived in Sierra Leone, 1987-1988.

My granddaughter Cynthia Shannon, my son Jim's youngest daughter and the most recent in our line of Cynthias.

My grandson Louis Kent Ross, above, accompanied us to Freetown in 1986.

My grandson Scott was born in Freetown on Nov. 7, 1987. Perhaps he will ask for dual citizenship when he's grown?

My granddaughter LeShan and I, in one of our heart-to-heart chats.

My son, Milo, 1986.

My second family, the Perrys, Houston, Texas, 1971. From left to right: James Perry, Jr., Mark Shepard, and Paula Perry with my husband J. O. Perry and me.

Receiving Indiana State University's distinguished alumni award in 1988, surrounded by my grandchildren, left to right: Clifford Robinson, Raymond Hill, LeShan Shepard, Kent Ross, myself, Celeste Shepard and Pamela Ross Hill. I also received the honorary doctorate of civil laws, in 1987.

Mrs. June Love, my elementary teacher and my first role model. She taught at the segregated one-room, School No. 8, in the village of Burnett where I grew up, outside of Terre Haute, Indiana.

Herbert Lamb, principal of Otter Creek High School during my secondary schooling. My mentor and friend, he devised for me, in the space of 30 minutes, a plan to make me an ambassador, and then helped me to set my goals properly to fulfill it — which took nearly 30 years. Mr. Lamb later became a trustee of my *alma mater*, Indiana State University.

Photo courtesy of his wife, Mrs. Bernice Lamb, Terre Haute, Indiana.

George and Dolores Nichols, Terre Haute, Indiana. George was my first employer, at a time when most white businesses would not hire a black person in any non-menial capacity. They are pictured here at my swearing-in as Ambassador to Sierra Leone, Washington, D.C., July, 1986.

Valerie Dickson-Horton, my best friend, with my husband in her kitchen in Gabarone, Botswana, in 1997. A career Foreign Service Officer, Valerie opened many doors for me.

Dr. Paul Fowler, my professor of political science at Indiana State University in Terre Haute and his wife Alice Fowler, editor of this book, and long time friend and confidante.

My dear friends Marion and Andy Torchia. I was visiting their home when I received the President's first call in Johannesburg, South Africa, 1986.

The house of my dreams in Houston! The room which plagued my dreams for years is on the right side of the house in this picture, on the upper floor. Houston, Texas, 1976.

My children, grandchildren, "adopted" family from Kenya and Ethiopia, and other extended family members, with J.O. and me at a family reunion at our home in Houston, 1978.

J.O. and I led a trade mission to Sierra Leone in 1973. Our children loved to travel , recognized it as a rare privilege, and accompanied us on many trips to Europe and Africa. They had been to Sierra Leone with us before, in 1971, and delighted in being able to expertly tell the members of this trade mission all the "do's" and "don'ts" about the culture of the country.

In my office as Chief, Human Resources Development, United States Agency for International Development (AID), Washington, D.C., 1982-1986.

My first visit to President Reagan's oval office before leaving for post. July 1, 1986.

Taking the oath of office at my swearing-in ceremony as Ambassador to Sierra Leone, in Washington, DC. July 3, 1986.

Presentation of credentials to President Momoh at State House, Freetown, Sierra Leone, July 16, 1986. With this act, I was officially received as the American ambassador by the Sierra Leonean government.

Tête-à-tête with President Momoh after the Presentation of Credentials. I found the president warm and genuinely concerned about his presidency and the future of his people. I left his offices feeling good about working with him and his government.

Partial view of Freetown from the air, 1986.

View of my front verandah overlooking the garden, Lumley Beach, and the
city of Freetown. I spent hours here conceptualizing my garden and contemplating measures to be taken at the Embassy.

A delegation of the US European Command from Stuttgart, Germany being briefed in my office in the Embassy in Freetown before meeting with President Momoh. Left to right: Greg Talcott, myself, Lt. Gen. Crowell, Ambassador Davis, Maj. Gen. Smith, and Brig. Gen. Gleason. November 7, 1986.

Foreign Service secretary Betty VanAusdal from Everett, Washington. My friend and confidante, she served with me in Sierra Leone from 1987 to 1989.

Presenting the first shipment of United States PL480 wheat to President Momoh in Sierra Leone, 1987. Rice was the other major commodity which the United States sold to Sierra Leone.

J.O. and I visiting a Peace Corps project in a school in the regional city of Bo with project manager Peggy Gorth (far right), Peace Corps Volunteer, 1988.

Men panning for diamonds in the alluvial soils of Sierra Leone. These are located outside the diamond fields where the public is free to exploit the diamonds.

Aerial photo of the Sierra Rutile mines in the southern Sierra Leone. This is a multi-million dollar American operation for mining rutile, an ore found in large quantities in only a few countries of the world. Rutile is a source of titanium, used in paints and the manufacture of jet engine parts, 1988.

Visit to a Peace Corps fish pond project. We visited such projects in Bo, Kenema, and Freetown, Sierra Leone. 1988.

J.O. and I with Ambassador Joseph Reed, Chief of Protocol, Washington, D.C. Taken on verandah of official residence in Freetown, 1988.

Meeting with President George Bush after my nomination for a second appointment as ambassador, this time to Burundi, in central Africa. 1990.

Being honored as a Paramount Chief (highly honored traditional regional leader), 1987. I received this honor twice while in Sierra Leone.

Dancers of Sierra Leone performing during my visit to Makeni, 1988.

Photos of the verandah that I had Embassy workers to build to increase our representational space. Pictured is one of the many events which J.O. and I hosted at the Residence, 1987-1988.

Bunce Island fortress, located just outside Freetown. On this island rest the ruins of an 18th century slave castle used to temporarily hold captured slaves until preparations could be made for the infamous Middle Passage across the Atlantic. Historical documentation confirms that this island fortress contributed significantly to the African slave trade, especially in the traffic of slaves for the rice plantations of South Carolina.

This is an upcountry project directed by Joe Opala (second from the right), former Peace Corps Volunteer in Sierra Leone who researched the Sierra Leonean-Gullah relationship and instigated the visit by President Momoh to South Carolina in October, 1988.

A meeting between the Deputy Secretary of State, John Whitehead and President Momoh of Sierra Leone on his first visit to Washington, D.C., October, 1988. Others pictured, left to right: myself, Ambassador Dauda Kamara, Sierra Leone's Ambassador to Washington and Alhaji Koroma, Minister of Foreign Affairs.

The American C-12 coastal security plane based in Monrovia, Liberia which took President Momoh and me on a reconnaissance flight over the Russian fishing trawlers off the coast of Sierra Leone, 1988. Pictured are President Momoh, the American flight commander from Monrovia, and I.

The American International School in Freetown, established in 1986 by the American community. The school accommodated grades K-6 for about 40 children. Dr. J.O. Perry was the first headmaster.

The first teachers of the American International school in Freetown, 1986.

Addressing a woman's international conference in Freetown, Sierra Leone. Photo was taken at the soccer stadium, in 1987. I spoke to many women's groups across the country — and finally learned to replace my uncooperative male translator with a woman!

Tough Choices

Looking back at my first three months in Sierra Leone, I faced some of the most challenging, exasperating, irritating, humorous and informative experiences of my life. During that period, I called upon every skill I had honed throughout the years—diplomatic, interpersonal, administrative, managerial—and many others which I had long possessed but never appreciated. Even those I considered my strong suits—presentation, persuasion and patience—were all sorely tested. I had to apply these skills to their utmost, not only to manage my mission but also to protect it for those Americans who depended on it, and for the image of America as a nation. I had to take care to protect myself as the highest representative of all that was American in this foreign land—even from the unintentional but disruptive and potentially dangerous foibles of my own family.

In spite of incidents I clearly perceived to be challenges to my authority, I was generally pleased with the Foreign Service staff I had inherited. It had not been within my authority to select all employees of the mission, especially agency heads, but I did have power of approval prior to their assignment to Sierra Leone. I could select only the two employees who would work most closely with me and on whom I would have to depend: the deputy chief of mission (DCM) and the Foreign Service secretary.

Before departing Washington for my post in Sierra Leone, I decided not to retain the existing deputy but rather to choose one with more managerial experience and whose skills complemented my own. From a short list provided by the State Department's Committee for DCM selection, I chose another Foreign Service officer, Greg Talcott, who served me well as my deputy for the next two years. The incumbent officer remained at post, however, for the first month of my administration to facilitate a smooth transition, and then departed for another assignment prior to Greg's arrival.

I had attempted to take to post with me my A.I.D. secretary, but her selection was not approved. I, therefore, decided to retain the incumbent secretary for the remaining year of her assignment to maintain continuity in the mission. She had a strange personality, but her professional skills were excellent. She seemed to have the respect of the Foreign Service Nationals (FSN's) for whom she frequently performed nice little favors. She was well organized and punctual. Before I replaced the previous deputy, she had been extraordinarily helpful in getting me settled into my office and the Residence.

With his departure, however, and Greg's arrival, her personality seemed to undergo drastic change, and she began to invade my privacy. I found her in my kitchen late one evening, having entered through the service entrance, in animated discussion with the household staff. I overheard her say to the cook, "Well, each ambassador has his/her own style. I'm sure once we all get used to her ways, everything will be all right." Surprised to see me, she quickly explained that she was there on my behalf, just trying to be helpful.

I was not aware that a problem existed between me and my household staff and would rather she had consulted me about it if she thought one did exist. I considered her presence in my house an impropriety. I took her aside.

"You are always welcome to visit my staff, but I would prefer that you advise me when you wish to visit so I will know you are in the house. No one is to enter this house without my knowledge. It is a matter of security and courtesy. I'm sure you understand."

"Yes, Ambassador, I understand," she said. "But, this is the way I operated with your predecessor and I thought it would be okay." And, then she snorted her way out, this time through the front door.

During the three months of my adjustment period, I was exposed to almost every type of crisis I would face during my ambassadorship to Sierra Leone. Some I had managed to anticipate. My secretary, I felt, would be at the root of more than a few of them in her attempts to help the mission and its staff to adjust to me, and me to them.

My family members, especially the boys, had begun to settle down. Their initial excitement had begun to abate, and they were now looking for friends—and "friends" were looking for them. James and Kent were being openly admired, chased perhaps by women of all ages, which was pretty heady stuff for these young men. James almost immediately became attached to a shy, young woman named Agnes, and the two seemed quite committed to each other. But, Kent, who was just one year younger than James, was busily shopping around.

Anticipating problems down the road, I asked the PSO to brief the boys on local conditions and the importance of being circumspect in Sierra Leone. Afterward, he related to me his discussion with them, which he felt they might not have taken seriously.

He told them that although they were big and handsome, those were not the only reasons for their attractiveness to local women. "You must be aware that because your mother is the ambassador of the United States," he emphasized, "you will receive a great deal of attention. Women of all ages will 'hit' on you, will attempt to get close to you, thinking that they might thereby get closer to her and to privileged information."

He emphasized, "You must be especially careful of the Russian women here in Sierra Leone. Most of them came here from Moscow after having married African men. When these husbands dumped them, they began looking for better mates and tickets to another world. You must be cognizant of Russian women, very attractive and seductive, who are agents of the Soviet Union. They won't appear to be, and that's why you must stay away from them, no matter how attractive, no matter their story. We are in the midst of a cold war with the Soviet Union, as you know, and they are looking for any information that can be used in their name-calling and propaganda campaign against American leadership. They might use you to discredit your mother in this country, for example. It has been known to happen, before."

He said the boys told him about encounters they had already had, and he warned them. "Venereal diseases are also rampant here, not just AIDS but other social diseases for which no cure has been found, a virulent form of syphilis and a rare strain of gonorrhea, for example. Be sure to protect yourselves adequately at all times, and see the health unit immediately if you have a problem. The women are quite promiscuous because of the need for money, and sexual activity is not limited to those known to be prostitutes. Be careful. Consider your mother's image and importance in the country. Do nothing to embarrass her and the American presence here."

He invited them to come to him with any questions they might have and encouraged them to visit the Peace Corp doctor's office periodically if need be. Although I wasn't privy to the total conversation they had, I felt more comfortable after he had lectured them.

I soon found I had not been mistaken about my secretary. I began to have a series of run-ins with her over some things I felt no professional Foreign Service secretary would ever have done, each more egregious than the other. Without consulting me, for example, she accepted social invitations on my behalf that had I been advised, I would not have considered.

On one occasion, for example, she committed me and my husband to high tea with one of Sierra Leone's former U.N. diplomats, Ambassador Terrence Eldridge, who had lost favor with the existing government. A brilliant and well-educated man, he had been driving the diplomatic community mad with his incessant pleas for intervention on his behalf with the Ministry of Foreign Affairs. When I confronted her with this breach and told her to cancel the date for tea, she said she would lose favor with Sierra Leoneans with whom she was building bridges—for me and for our operations in the country.

To save face for her, J.O. and I went to this engagement, and spent one of the most uncomfortable evenings we would experience in all our three years in Sierra Leone. We visited only as long as common sense and courtesy required, but I worried how this one act might be misconstrued by other diplomats and government officials.

Shortly thereafter, I was summoned by the Foreign Minister to his office, just as a courtesy, he said, to discuss relations between his office and the American embassy. He began with the issuance of visas, the fact that long lines formed each day in front of our building, and that lack of waiting space inside forced people to stand out in the rain. He said he had received many complaints and asked if I might do something to relieve this situation. Further, he said, very few visas were being issued by my Consular Officer to solid Sierra Leonean citizens and businessmen who were making proper application for travel to the United States. He had been told, in fact, that the CO looked people in the eye, and flatly told them that that they were lying. She had reportedly instructed her workers to be rude in carrying out their duties. He was certain that his embassy staff in Washington went out of their way to make it easy for Americans to travel to Freetown, and asked for reciprocity in that respect.

I acknowledged that for some reason at this time, there was an inordinate number of requests for visas. Not all requests were being properly completed, requiring second and third visits to the Consular Offices.

"We are discovering an increasing number of forged passports and other documents, which also detracts from staff time and patience. I will, of course, look into the matter of rudeness, which I cannot condone. We have no plans, however, to place an awning over the walk in front of the embassy. Interestingly, Mr. Minister, when I passed through London last week, there were double lines of people, stretching around the block, waiting to enter the American consular office—in the rain, and under umbrellas. They were bundled up against the weather, and waited their turn with little fuss. I would hope you will not interpret the long lines at our embassy as a token of disrespect for the Sierra Leonean people."

He removed his glasses so I wouldn't miss his haughty stare, and then went on to discuss some small matters that might have been more appropriately addressed by our two administrative officers. Finally, he came to the prime issue: my visit to the home of the former ambassador.

"It has come to my attention," he began, "that you recently paid a visit to the home of Ambassador Terrence Eldridge, at his invitation, of course. He is somewhat estranged from the Foreign Office at this time but is yet on our payroll. Because of his peculiar situation and behavior, I thought perhaps we should discuss the matter. As you know, it is the Foreign Minister's prerogative to make appointments of his returned ambassadors to foreign or domestic posts. I would have appreciated your coming directly to me if you wished to support reappointment of this individual. He has become increasingly troublesome and an embarrassment since his recall from New York, and it will take us some time to find a suitable post for him. However, I understand he is now boasting to others in the Ministry that the new American Ambassador had come to his house for dinner. Further, that she has agreed to champion his cause and will take up with the President the matter of his reappointment to the U.N. in New York."

I shifted in my chair, sensing this was not the time for response.

He continued, choosing his words very carefully. "I think we have been experiencing, you and I, some difficulty in the relationship between your Embassy and the Foreign Office. It is not as warm or relaxed as it was with your predecessor. Perhaps I have been negligent in making clear to you the role of my office versus that of the President's Office. You are, of course, accredited to President Momoh's government and you have the privilege or authority to meet with him as you choose.

But, I am your first contact. For most matters of state and small matters which can be settled by this office, I would prefer that you see me first—my door is always open to you, and if necessary I will refer the matter to the President."

He continued, "In this particular situation, the gentleman is my responsibility. Frankly, I found the news of your visit to his home quite disturbing. It lends credibility to his boast of your warm relationship. He is sure that as a powerful ambassador, you can force a positive decision on his behalf. Some might consider this relationship, in fact, an act of meddling in the internal affairs of this government. Of course, I wouldn't go so far as to say that, but of all the diplomats resident in this country, you are the most distant—perhaps bordering on disrespect. I thought it might be helpful for us to have a chat—perhaps a series of chats in the future, to get to know each other a little better and for us both to consider how we might develop a better working relationship."

I was being extremely careful to manage my nonverbal cues, and lowered my eyes until I could mask the anger and indignation I felt. It took a while for me to get my thoughts together. I felt this man did not mean to be helpful, but was himself dangerous to my presence in the country. He was jealous of the close relationship I had developed with the President and was therefore castigating my knowledge of protocol in an attempt to restrict my access to the President. But, to have shown any measure of resentment would not have been productive or sensible.

"I thank you, Mr. Minister, for the opportunity to have this little chat, and for the clarification on the role of your office to the embassy and to myself, as its ambassador. I assure you I have no interest, whatever, in making a case for the gentleman in question. He has become a royal pest to us all in the diplomatic corps. I had never intended to speak to President Momoh on his behalf, and would not misuse my access to the President for such trivialities. It seems to me, however, that by calling me in today, you have given this man cause to assume that I am here on his behalf."

He snapped. "Then, he will soon know that you failed!"

Swallowing hard, I offered gently, looking him in the eye, "I, too, would be pleased for an opportunity to develop a better working relationship with you and the Foreign Office, and I look forward to future chats."

It would not have been prudent for me to explain that the President himself had directed me first to present cases or requests to the Minister's office. If the matter received no response in an appreciable space of time, it should be referred through the President's Protocol to his presidential advisor; further, if the matter called for direct and immediate discussion with the President, I should come directly to him. I recognized this procedure at that time, to be a matter of internal politics.

As graciously as I could muster, I took my leave of Alhaji Koroma, who was rapidly becoming the villain in my affairs.

Rightly or not, I again saw the meddling hand of my secretary in this problem along with others. Her transgressions seemed to multiply. It wasn't working. I had always gotten along well with my secretaries in the past. They tended to follow me, in fact, from one assignment to another and some remained in contact with me through the years. We had provided each other mutual support in reaching our individual career goals. I decided to have a frank discussion with the secretary, to clarify my style, my priorities and the protocol to be followed between us for her remaining year.

I explained to her, for example, that I preferred to personally handle the payroll of my household staff with the assistance of the budget and accounting office, rather than having it pass through her office. I made it clear that she was to make no appointments to my calendar, business or social, without my concurrence, and cited the dinner engagement as an example.

She seemed unnaturally relaxed, and cool, as I went through a number of items, some of which she may have interpreted as diminishing her role in the executive office.

She said, looking me straight in the eye, her blue eyes enlarged and unblinking through her bifocals, "I don't like you,

Ambassador," she said. "I will never like you. There is nothing you can do to ever make me like you. I don't like your kind."

That did It! My kind? What kind is that: black, female, old, fat, Republican, non-career, straight. . .?

She added gratuitously, "No one here likes you."

At that point, I instructed her that unless she were willing to identify the "others" by name, she should speak only for herself. I sat with my mouth wide open while she continued speaking in a monotone with her fixed, wide-eyed stare.

"I don't have to like you to do my job efficiently. I am a professional! And unless I told you, you would never know that I have no respect for you. But, I want you to know that! Now, that I understand better how you wish to operate, there will be no further problems from me. But, please don't ask me to serve you coffee at mornings. I will always serve your guests, of course, as a part of my job."

Reminding her that I had never asked her to serve me anything, I dismissed her from my office and summoned the DCM. "Greg," I was quite upset. "I'm afraid I can no longer trust the secretary to handle the confidential matters of this office, especially those personal matters concerning me or my family. I question her loyalty. Please advise Washington that I would like a replacement for her like today!"

I told him of the conversation we had, and he sat with his mouth wide open. I left it to him to carry out her departure. Later, he told me that when he interviewed her, she seemed astonished that I would have questioned her loyalty. I learned later that the greater problem in our relationship centered around her questionable attachment to the former deputy whom I had decided not to retain. She felt I had wrecked his career and possibly hers as well, and no political appointee should have that right.

As the time went by, her attitude changed and she sought in many ways to ingratiate herself, to overcome a bad beginning. But, Greg and I agreed that she should leave post as soon as it could be arranged.

In the interim, I interviewed other Foreign Service secretaries via letter and telephone, and finally found dignified, talented and discreet Bette VanAusdal serving in Geneva. She came to Freetown as my secretary, confidante, and alter ego for the next two years, with the promise to accompany me to ongoing postings if they occurred. My life in Sierra Leone became better organized and my morale took a definite upswing after Bette's arrival. With her boundless energy, experience and organizational skills, the executive office began to operate more efficiently and cooperatively with other sections and agencies in the mission than it ever had. She made friends with secretaries and administrators in government offices, especially within the Ministry of Foreign Affairs, and things began to go much more smoothly.

I recognized my need for competent staff, and during the first few months took time to know them and their families, and to get a sense of their competency levels. It became clear, however, that my mission—along with other American missions in Africa—was not only understaffed but had an inordinate percentage of first-tour, inexperienced officers. My mission was serving as a training post while being expected to conduct all the normal operations of larger missions elsewhere in the world. The loss of a single officer or a delay in filling a vacancy seriously overworked the few experienced officers I had as well as myself, the Chief of Mission. For this reason, I tried to be watchful and concerned about my officers, especially those on first tour.

Sometime during my first year, I began to receive complaints from American staff and their families about the failure of the general service division to provide normal services to their residences—that is, delivery of water or fuel, maintenance and repairs, etc. Although he was in an entry level Foreign Service position, the General Services Officer (GSO), had been at post longer than I. Nonetheless, his performance as the manager and controller of our warehouses and manager of the general maintenance services had been questioned. I noticed in my initial meeting with the GSO, that he shook almost uncontrollably and perspired profusely for no apparent reason. When I discussed the problem and the status of the GSO's health with his supervising officer, the administrative officer (AdminOff), he told me the GSO was scared to death of me. Not denying that might indeed be true, I investigated further and found he was suffering from alcoholism and deep depression following the departure of his family from post. He was left alone in a house with five bedrooms, large enough to have housed two families, which contributed to his loneliness.

My DCM had oversight responsibility for administrative personnel, and after interviewing the GSO, he recommended that the officer be returned to Washington for medical treatment as quickly as it could be arranged.

I was angry that no one seemed to care enough to provide friendship and support to a fellow officer who was obviously troubled. In the next team meeting, I discussed the responsibility that each has for the other, especially those responsible for supervision of junior or first-tour officers. Washington began a search for a replacement, but advised it would be months before a new GSO would be located and posted to Sierra Leone.

Very shortly thereafter, I became painfully aware through the employee grapevine that essential controls over certain expendable and non-expendable items were lacking in the warehouse. As Chief of Mission, Washington would hold me responsible for establishing and maintaining these controls, so I asked the AdminOff to review his operation with me. Through this process, I came to know that large, costly items such as air-conditioning units, word processing equipment, refrigerators, sheets of plywood, and other non-expendables were simply "being eaten," as the Sierra Leoneans put it, between the port and the warehouse, or after they reached the warehouse. Best yet, I noted that 250 toilet bowls, which the mission couldn't possibly use in a hundred years, had been ordered, received and distributed to parts unknown, and were yet to be located. A large order of plywood, shown on paper as shipped by the vendor and received at the port, never reached the Embassy warehouse.

The mission appeared to have been supporting both local entrepreneurs, and perhaps even international entrepreneurs, as these things—like stolen cars—might be going across the borders to Liberia or to Guinea.

To cap it all off, I received a phone call late one afternoon from someone outside the official community, who urged me to visit the warehouse at the airport. He hinted that some items marked for the American Embassy had been sitting in the warehouse for more than a year, and needed to be checked. Greg, who would normally handle such matters as these, was on leave in Italy. The situation had to be immediately investigated.

I jumped into my limousine, and with the American flag flapping furiously in the wind, entered the port with an urgency that opened gates quickly and without question. The customs officer in charge walked with me through the vast warehouses until he located several shipments duly marked for pickup by the American GSO. They were neither damaged nor opened, but because they were unclaimed would soon disappear into somebody's long pockets or the local retail shops. Here were the WANG word processors, and the split air-conditioners needed for replacements in staff housing. Here were countless numbers of essential items missing for up to one year that the administrative office was preparing to write off as lost.

I returned to the office absolutely furious as I further investigated our management procedures and oversight activities of responsible staff. Clearly, a major administrative snafu had occurred by either the former GSO or the current AdminOff in assigning to a trusted FSN the sole responsibility for both procurement and receiving, which greatly facilitated a number of incredible scams. This was made possible by the negligence of the responsible American officers to apply existing procedures and controls. I found it necessary to report all these matters to Washington and to request a full investigation of our operations in Sierra Leone.

After thoroughly interviewing the AdminOff who had been responsible for oversight of all these operations, I found him culpable of negligence more than anything else. Clearly these scams did not begin with the departure of the GSO; they were long-standing, before his departure and possibly before his arrival. How far back did this begin?

The AdminOff, by his own admission, had left the GSO to his own devices without oversight, because he, himself, was overloaded. Fully perturbed, I sent him home to his residence, to sit there until I could make sense of what was happening. I then located the DCM, vacationing in the mountains of Italy, and after explaining the situation, summoned him to return to Freetown to handle the matter properly through Washington channels.

In the end of the matter, with deep regret, I requested the reassignment of the AdminOff, a black career officer whom I felt responsible to mentor and if possible, to advance. I endorsed his request to be reassigned to a consular position from which he could again move forward on his career ladder. I voiced my conviction that the State Department personnel office was in part responsible for promoting him beyond the limits of his administrative capacity. It was also not possible for him to bear the additional GSO responsibilities, which resulted in giving more authority to the FSN than was warranted or safe.

I was not at all happy about my decision to have this officer recalled to Washington. Following his return, I received extremely negative feedback from black Foreign Service officers in the system who said they expected more from me as a black ambassador. Then, I received a letter from a senior administrative officer in the State Department who commended me for the action taken. The letter read in part: "The way you have handled the mess you inherited is very impressive. You have done the Foreign Service a great duty by 'taking the bull by the horns' before things degenerated even further."

I felt vindicated and encouraged. The State Department also acted immediately to alleviate the staffing problem by temporarily replacing both officers with experienced senior annuitants, to bring matters under control. Then, they assigned permanent officers who in my judgment were competent and took great pride in doing the job right. Larry Palmer joined us as the new AdminOff and Don Ahern was assigned as the new

GSO, both first-tour in those positions. Things began to fall into place.

Two questions continued to nag my sense of order and efficiency. One, the issue of the lack of administrative controls and resulting scams; the other, the question regarding how to attract competent and experienced Foreign Service staff to a small post like Sierra Leone.

Sorry to say, I seemed always to have been alerted to inefficiencies within my mission by some unidentified source outside the mission, rather than through our normal internal reviews. Rumors persisted regarding scams in our Peace Corps operation, for example. This became an issue following the departure of the Director, Dr. Habib Kahn. The rumor involved the operation of the Pharmacy and Mailroom and indicated that pharmaceuticals were being sold from the pharmacy and for profit outside the organization. There was also the rumor that monies arriving for Volunteers at the central office in Freetown never seemed to reach the Volunteers but were indeed cashed, and that mopeds were disappearing from the motor pool.

I advised Peace Corps/Washington of the suspected scams and possible malfeasance and requested that they send a temporary replacement for the departed director with sufficient administrative experience to investigate the rumors and to rebuild the decreasing morale of the Volunteers in the country. They sent Dr. Sarah Moten, at that time completing her five-year tour as Director of Swaziland's Peace Corp. Without favor or apology to any, she immediately upon her arrival began to clean up the operation. She also visited Volunteers in every part of the country, and otherwise improved Peace Corps' outreach to the Volunteers and the communities they were serving. Sarah found additional instances of malfeasance and scams, which she quietly, but efficiently handled within the Peace Corps framework in Washington.

The second question regarding the need to attract competent and experienced Foreign Service staff begged the question of how to make a small post like ours attractive for the next assignment schedule. Personnel studies undertaken by the Department indicated that the lack of an American school at several missions, primarily in Africa, was deeply affecting mission ability to attract qualified staffing. Understandably, no matter how beautiful Sierra Leone was, highly qualified and experienced officers with young children would be forced to decline an otherwise attractive post for lack of a school.

Embassy personnel in Sierra Leone had formed a committee to study solutions to this problem prior to my arrival. They arrived at a consensus that the community would have to establish its own American School with a standard of curriculum and instruction comparable to that of any good private school at home.

Within a week of our arrival in Freetown, they recruited the able assistance of my husband, who had extensive experience in managing and operating private primary schools, and in teacher training. Within six months, the post succeeded in founding a private school, kindergarten through the sixth grade (K-6), supported by a small grant from the Office of Overseas Schools. Founded primarily for Foreign Service dependents, the school experienced phenomenal growth in enrollment and curricular offerings in its first year. It was then opened to all children, including Sierra Leonean children, whose parents could afford the tuition.

J.O., with a doctorate in education and many years of experience managing his own private kindergartens, became the school's first headmaster. He served well in this role for the first two years. But, at that time, serious controversy arose in the official American community regarding the employment of the ambassador's spouse. A restriction did exist prohibiting the in-country employment of spouses of the ambassador and the DCM, but did not apply to private funding. The waiver had been applied for the sake of the school's opening, but the growing level of controversy and antagonism in the school community tended to undermine my own authority. Regrettably, I discussed with J.O. the necessity to submit his voluntary resignation at the close of the second year. With agonizing regret for the deep offense felt by my husband, I recommended to the school board that they find a new headmaster.

J.O. retired again, with little lingering regret, to full days of hiking, swimming and playing tennis at the Marine House, and otherwise living a life of an "international playboy" for the next year.

But, having a school at post began immediately to attract a different variety of professionals, and generally more experienced officers, to Sierra Leone. As the quality of our staffing and the mission's efficiency began to rise, so did the quality of our existence in Freetown.

The environmental problems in Freetown never seemed to cease. Due to the shortage of potable water in the city, especially during the dry season, our water had to be delivered to storage tanks at our residences by the Embassy-owned water truck, which was filled daily at the reservoir. The city's energy sources often failed due to lack of oil in the city, and the periodic shortage of electrical power and power outages became an acute, complicating factor in our operations and lives. The Embassy buildings and all the residences were supported by backup generators, which automatically started up when city power was broken. The heavy smell of diesel and the sound of the motors were nuisances to be endured. The generators required additional cost in maintaining a competent technician to regularly service and maintain them.

The mission also purchased an oil tanker truck, filled from our reserves on the GSO compound, which serviced the generators at the Chancery, other agency buildings, and residences on a regular basis, to ensure a constant supply of electrical power. The embassy support services were adequate and quite efficient, but the mission seemed to use an inordinately large amount of diesel. There was reason to believe that somehow our oil supply was being shared quite generously outside the American community.

So, I decided to ride each of the trucks just once on their rounds to our residences and operation buildings to get a feel for the efficiency of delivery of these essential services. The drivers were greatly surprised—and more than a little suspicious—when without warning, I climbed aboard their rigs in my jeans and tennis shoes.

But, they seemed honored to have me aboard their trucks and appreciative of this unexpected opportunity to engage me in discussion of their personal situations. Following these rides, and as suddenly as it had started, the loss of oil seemed to quickly balance itself, again.

My flagging outlook and energies were tremendously boosted by my new staff and a three-day visit from Dolores and George Nichols, my mentors from Terre Haute, Indiana. It was their first trip to sub-Saharan Africa. Their visit was a heartwarming and encouraging event, enjoyed not only by J.O. and me, but it rejuvenated also my staff, both professional and domestic. Everyone enjoyed exchanges with George, who, as a retired banker and investor, was always professionally engaging. He had many questions about the country, about American foreign policies and mission operations. During their short stay, the President and Lady Momoh hosted a state dinner for the Nichols at the President's official residence, a great honor normally reserved for the very highest level of visiting dignitaries. It surprised us all that the Nichols should have received such honor. Perhaps it was due to a floating rumor that George was my billionaire mentor with loads of money to invest in Sierra Leone. The Nichols departed with a glowing new concept of not only the country, but of the whole African continent. Sierra Leone had indeed won two sincere friends.

It helped, too, that for a few months after their visit, we had a spate of visits from old friends within and outside the Foreign Service: Valerie Dickson-Horton, my good friend over the years, and Sherry Suggs, both stationed with USAID in Mali at different periods of time. Jerry Gaither, a loyal friend from Houston, also came. All three were our former Peace Corps Volunteers in Sierra Leone, trained at Texas Southern University during the 1970's. Rainette Holiman, formerly from Bell Laboratories, also came to visit us after completing her tour as a Peace Corps trainer in Kenya. Shelby Lewis, whom I felt privileged to meet, came through leading a group of black, professional women on a business tour. All encouraged me in the job I now had to do.

Taking time from my official duties to spend time with supportive friends helped me get through this period, as it had throughout my career. I missed, of course, frequent contact with my children. Our youngest son, James, was with us. Mark was in Nepal with the Peace Corps; Donna was married living in Chicago; Paula was teaching school in Houston, and Milo was in California.

I was delighted to learn in my second year, 1987, that my eldest son Jim, and his family would be joining us on a one-year assignment in Freetown. A senior computer systems satellite communications specialist, he had undertaken a consultancy for one year with Nord Resources, based in Dayton, Ohio, which had become the offshore management firm for Sierra Rutile.

During that year, it was such a pleasure to have his family in the country and to get to know my grandchildren, Jenny, Bryan, and Scottie, the latter born during their stay in Sierra Leone. While the bulk of their time was spent at the rutile mine a few hundred miles away, we were frequently able to spend good quality time together during their stay. I was pleased that some of my experience as ambassador could be shared with my eldest son and his wife, Kathy, as it had been with my younger children. A former Marine, Jim was honored that year at the annual Marine Corps Ball as the senior Marine in the country of Sierra Leone. He had the opportunity to use his role as big brother to James and Kent in an important new way, and they had good times together in the way that brothers do.

One day, Jim said to me, "Are you aware that Kent has a girlfriend?"

"You mean Kathryn Smythe? No! He told me something the other day," I said, "about a white woman hitting on him, and then he laughed his strangely humorless laugh. I didn't take him seriously."

"Well," he hesitated. "I don't like to be a tattler about your grandson, but I think you should know that she's a Russian woman who has been in this country for sometime, several years older than he—maybe about 35 years old."

I was flabbergasted and extremely annoyed. I called Kent in and confronted him with the information, which he readily admitted. I asked, "Why are you doing this after having been warned? Why would you wait until somebody else told me?"

He was embarrassed. "It's no big deal, Grandmother, although I did try to tell you. She's nice, doesn't ask me any questions about you or this house, or the Embassy. She's just good company, not somebody I'm serious about. I don't see her now since I started dating Kathryn Smythe. I'd like to marry Kathryn someday."

"But, Kent, after you were told about the harm you could cause me, you still felt free to pick up a Russian woman?"

I understood now his immaturity at only 19 years old, caught up in his maleness, and behaving like the child he was— on one hand enjoying the spotlight and protection afforded by my authority while mischievously seeking ways to get around it. The jeopardy in which he might have placed me and the mission had no meaning for him, and for that reason, infractions were sure to occur again and again. He had been with me at post for the entire first year and, as his "Year Abroad" program, it had been a broadening and deepening experience of value to his future. But, at present, he needed more the benefits of seasoning and motivation.

It occurred to me that it was nearly time for the opening of the fall semester at Texas Southern University, and it was time for him to go back to school. With great regret, I sent him home to his father.

I learned later through my intelligence that the Russian woman was a known Soviet informer.

My Constituency

The combined staffing and family concerns in Freetown kept me plenty busy by themselves. In addition, I also had certain responsibilities and commitments for a much larger and wider-spread community outside the capital city. Wthin the first three months following our arrival in 1986, J.O. and I began to plan our "upcountry" travel in response to various requests from our missionaries and Peace Corps Volunteers scattered all over the country. They wanted to meet their new ambassador. I was also anxious to visit the provincial centers of Bo, Kenema, and Makeni which were well known, historical sites and thought the two purposes could be combined

Several official requests were also being made by the provinces. Whenever possible, we planned these visits to coincide with President Momoh's trips to the interior. Other ambassadors also regularly traveled with his caravan, adding in this way the prestige of foreign interests and potential funding for the constituent cities and regions. These trips gave me tremendous insight into the personality and popularity of his presidency outside the capital. We traveled by automobile wherever the roads would permit, or utilized the four-wheeled van for the rougher terrain. Sometimes we flew to distant sites, utilizing the small Cessna 12-passenger propeller plane, based in Monrovia, available to us if we reserved it well in advance of our travel. We always took with us one or two staff members and sometimes an FSN who spoke the language of the area to be visited.

We made it a point to visit at least once, each of the several American missionary sites in the country, some high in the craggy mountains, others in the heartland of the country, some along the coastlines. Wherever the missionaries had established themselves, the food was always good and plentiful. The buildings were comfortable, some outstanding, especially the churches and clinics. At one time, the missonairies numbered more than 1,000 persons. They were generally well respected by the government because of their work in establishing and staffing schools and hospitals. They would often travel to Freetown to purchase supplies or to pick up shipments, mail or packages; and, whenever they came, they would stop by the Embassy or the Residence to say hello.

On Thanksgiving Day of each year of my tour in Sierra Leone, I would host a huge dinner at the Marine House for the American community and their guests, and many of the missionaries would take that time to visit Freetown in order to join us in giving thanks. A good number of American missionary groups were actively engaged in the country, including the United Methodists, the Catholics, the Salvation Army, the Free Methodists, the African Methodist Episcopalians, the Bahá'í Faith, and other denominations in varying numbers.

We quite often visited the American School in Kabala, located in the northern-most region of the country. This rather prestigious boarding school was established for the education of American missionary children from all over West Africa. It was far from Freetown and as Ambassador, I requested from time to time the use of the small C-12 from Monrovia. The plane and officers were a part of the Defense Department's coastal security program. In this way, we could also comfortably travel to the rural location of Sierra Rutile, a multi-million dollar American mining operation near the southern regional towns of Gbangbama and Gbangbatoke. Rutile is a rare mineral rarely found in deposits sufficiently large to warrant the cost of exploration and mining other than Sierra Leone and parts of Australia. Rutile is an important source of titanium used as a pigment in paint and in the production of light-weight elements of jet engines. We toured the rutile plant on various visits and witnessed the incredible investment of futuristic mining equipment at an operation site far from "civilization." At one point during a period of heightened instability in the country, I was assured by plant management that the operation was well secured by the company's local security force which operated at all times like a small independent army.

We made special plans for more prolonged visits to Peace Corps posts, taking with us loads of peanut butter, crackers, jellies, and M&M's from our storehouse. Volunteers in the most remote areas would come to the towns to join the larger Volunteer groups by bus, poda-podas, or mopeds. These visits gave Volunteers the chance to show us their schools or projects, and to introduce us to their African counterparts. It also offered an opportunity to have a big celebration to which other Volunteers for miles around could be invited. They prepared delicious local dishes with tasty palm oil, rice, various meats, vegetables and fufu.

I never managed to swallow fufu, a staple eaten widely over Sub-Saharan Africa and made from the boiled flour of ground cassava. It was eaten with the fingers, "sopped" in sauces and spicy meats and vegetables, and then "popped" into the mouth. It was tough, glutinous, and rubbery—had no taste, with the consistency of uncooked bread dough. It was, in fact, a preferred substitute for bread, and the Volunteers absolutely loved it. But, the only time I tried to eat it, when I flipped it into my mouth, it never got past my throat—I choked.

We tremendously enjoyed our visits to the Volunteers, and they seemed happy to have us come. They seemed to prefer the economic and social atmospheres in the provinces where the conditions were perceived to be merely simple rather than poor.

There was always plenty to eat that could be taken freely from the land: bananas, pineapples, mangoes, yams, and more. Beef and pork were scarce and therefore more expensive. Chickens were difficult to raise, but could be purchased at a reasonable price. The Peace Corps Office in Freetown provided support services to the Volunteers throughout the country through their regional offices in the regional capitals. This arrangement permitted less centralized administration of their projects and programs and provider quicker access to our many Volunteers.

The Peace Corps medical office, staffed over the years by a number of notable American doctors, took medicines and health information to the regional centers and provided treatment in those areas. One notable doctor, Dr. Mae Jamison, a young black woman who served the Volunteers in 1985, just prior to my arrival in 1986, later became one of America's most celebrated astronauts.

A few newly-arrived Volunteers in Sierra Leone elected to return to the United States immediately, on their first sight of the primitive conditions in Freetown. One black Volunteer reportedly stated her shocked sentiments upon arrival, "Hey, I was not taken in slavery from Africa. I was rescued."

But this attitude was rare; the majority of Volunteers stayed, contributed and extended beyond their two year commitments to finish projects they had begun.

Several Volunteers in the groups J.O. and I had trained during the 1970's at Texas Southern University had married Sierra Leonean citizens and had begun their families in the country. Other Volunteers, rearing families of their own in the country had arrived as early as 1966. They expressed no interest in returning home except for short visits and vacations. Life was good, they said, for them and their children in Sierra Leone.

Some Americans in the country, employed by special projects of American-based institutions, were part of the Embassy's support and security system. The Centers for Disease Control (CDC) in Atlanta, for example, established a River Blindness Research station at Segbwema near the Tongo diamond fields in the northwestern region. Dr. Diana Bennett, the American CDC doctor, managed a small clinic in that area while researching the disease which was quite prevalent along the rivers. Spread by small flies, the disease caused permanent blindness. One of Sierra Leone's most brilliant doctors headed the government hospital at Segbwema. American educated, this promising young man was totally blinded by this disease. Dr. Bennet assisted his hospital as well as others to treat and to study the ravages of AIDS, although the incidence of this disease was relatively low in Sierra Leone. Her small team also conducted studies and treatment of Lassa Fever, another debilitating and killer disease in remote areas of the country. We enjoyed visiting Dr. Bennett, although the stay on the hospital compound was often distracting and not too palatable.

I used these visits to gather rare plants, indigenous to the swamps and lowlands of the region, for transplanting in my garden in Freetown. The provincial visits were rather exciting and festive with lots of drums, dancing, and good food. My visits usually centered around some greater event. But, I also gave speeches about democracy, the rights of women—not always well received by the men—and sometimes on Martin Luther King, Jr., and the power of enlightened leadership.

On two of these trips, I was made honorary paramount chief, once in Port Loko in the Kambia District and again in Magburaka, in the Tonkolili District, receiving all the rights and privileges thereof. One female paramount chief, also a very powerful Parliamentarian, Madame Honoria Bailer-Caulker from Shenge, participated in a number of my visits. She was well-educated and highly respected, having inherited her position from her father in a long line of male chiefdoms. I very much appreciated her advice on the role which women leaders must undertake in a male-dominated profession.

As a part of the naming ceremony, the elders of the community attempted to honor me by carrying me in the "royal" hammock throughout the village. It required six men or more to carry me in this most uncomfortable contraption. I heard one of them gasp, "Um-m, big mama!" My weight was probably greater than any two of them combined, and my rear end kept bumping the hard ground. My dress refused to cooperate. I tried to ride the thing in a more lady-like "side saddle" position, but that didn't work either. I finally asked if I might walk, acknowledging as they helped me out of the hammock, how much I appreciated the honor.

After these visits, I sometimes returned home to Freetown, my face sore from constant smiling and my body slightly bruised in spots from touching. People wanted just to touch me as though it would bring them luck and perhaps healing. My security officer and my secretary who normally traveled with me, tried to keep the crowds at a distance, as did the local gendarmerie, who sometimes unfortunately wielded sticks and whips. I felt guilty of provoking violent assault.

I also often returned home with chickens, eggs, plants, colorful hand-woven baskets and country cloths, and once a valuable, ornately-carved ivory tusk, which by law or precedent regarding its historical value, I was forced to report to the U.S. government archives in Washington. They allowed me, however, to retain the gift of ivory in the Residence to be admired by all the ambassadors who would succeed me in Sierra Leone.

The most extraordinary gift following one of my investitures as Paramount Chief, was a young bull and two cows, with which to begin a great herd and new wealth, befitting of my new station. I tried to refuse this gift, but was advised by the Volunteers that to do so would be a prime insult to the people of the village with whom they lived and worked. This gift symbolized their great respect and honor for their traditional rulers. I compromised by accepting only the bull, and donating the cows to a local home for handicapped children in the area. So to my flock of chickens, including the rooster, Chanticleer, and two goats from previous trips to the interior, I added the bull. My compound was large, but was on a steep, rocky hillside, with insufficient leveled ground to accommodate this menagerie. Besides that, the bull had to be tethered and watered, and cleaned up behind, although his contributions to my flower gardens were valuable and appreciated. My gardening staff thought I was absolutely mad. Embassy officers thought it hilarious and often brought their children to the Compound to see how we were faring.

After a month or so of gathering eggs and suffering the bellowing of the bull and crankiness of my staff, I donated the bull and the chickens to a small orphanage located on the road to the Cape Sierra Hotel. The goats were given to my staff, who immediately barbecued them and took the meat home to their families for a sumptuous meal.

The excursions into the countryside were always exciting, even if a little exhausting. Making the social rounds in Freetown was sometimes no easier. But, for the most part, this was all great fun. We were expected, as the leading American couple in Freetown, to be active in social events and our few absences from such occasions were always questioned. It was incumbent upon all diplomats to attend functions such as weddings, funerals, soccer games, special church services and especially ceremonies at the State House. The Presentation of the Order of Rokel was one of those ceremonies, the most prestigious on the social calendar, at which the President bestowed upon a few deserving citizens the highest award in the nation.

One particular honoree, a Mr. Bangura, whom I remember above all others, nearing 75 years of age, was the eldest living veteran of World War II, having served with the exemplary Sierra Leonean forces in England. A very fine and highly respected gentleman, Mr. Bangura had coveted this high award for years. He reportedly tried every trick in the book to get one, offered to pay handsomely for it or whatever, but never met with success. It was not until 1989, the final year of my ambassadorial tour, that he would finally receive this coveted recognition.

The ceremony was very elegant and very formal, taking place on the grounds of the State House and President's Office. The entire diplomatic community along with two hundred or more of the "who's who" of Sierra Leone were present in their best formal afternoon attire, seated well in advance of the opening ceremonies, facing the stage. There was a roll of drums and we all rose to our feet as Sierra Leone's national anthem was played by the military band. Then President Momoh entered with his entourage. When he was seated, the ceremony began.

He individually bestowed upon several men the Order of Rokel, for various levels of achievement and contribution. With the assistance of Mansour Turey, his protocol officer, the President placed a bright red and white striped ribbon bearing the solid gold medallion around the neck of the honoree and shook his hand. To the beat of drums and applause of all present, each was then escorted triumphantly to his seat in the audience to rejoin his proud family and admirers. It was indeed "old world" pageantry, and tremendously impressive.

The drums began to roll once more. All eyes were on Mr. Bangura, who was next, who listened as though enraptured by the reading of his full name, followed by a listing of his accomplishments and reasons for being awarded the Certificate of Honor. Mr. Bangura, rose, stood tall and straight like the old soldier he was, and marched proudly to the beat of the drums toward the President on the dias. He was escorted by two very tall and polished servicemen, who gently restrained him when he marched ahead too quickly. This was no stony-faced, solemn occasion for Mr. Bangura. No, he was smiling broadly, exuberantly, so proud he was of this honor. The crowd began to titter. Knowing how badly he had wanted this award, we all joined in his exaltation. Finally, amid the blare of ceremonial horns and beating of drums and whir of the national television cameras, President Momoh signaled for Mr. Bangura to come forward. His escorts stepped aside as he mounted the steps.

As the President laid the striped ribbon with the medallion of the Order of Rokel across his shoulders, the unthinkable suddenly happened: Mr. Bangura's trousers fell to his feet.

He could not, of course, stoop to pull them up. The television cameras were upon him recording every move. He was perfectly motionless, paralyzed in disbelief at his humiliation in his own finest hour.

Mansour told me later that the President whispered to him, "Pull up his pants!"

He said he looked into the President's eyes in astonishment, "Pardon me, Sir?"

"Pull up his pants. They've fallen around his feet and he can't move," the President whispered, maintaining all the while the serene smile on his face for the audience and the cameras, as though nothing unusual were happening.

But, the crowd knew something was happening. We all began to applaud Mr. Bangura. Mansour could hardly maintain his composure as he knelt, pulled up Mr. Bangura's trousers and firmly tied the drawstring of the traditional robes he was wearing. The crowd exploded with applause and laughter. Out of respect for the old gentleman, the cameras turned away for a moment to focus on the applauding multitude.

Mr. Bangura never stopped smiling through it all, his eyes riveted on the President. Being an old and disciplined soldier, he stood rigidly at attention, never once attempting to pull up his pants on his own. The ceremony finished, he saluted President Momoh, backed off his three paces, did an about face. Then, snapping his heels together, he marched off the platform, breaking into a wide grin and almost a dance as he returned to his seat, sporting his beautiful, shining award. I shall never forget his joy that day, as well as his chagrin.

* * *

Mr. Bangura waited long and patiently for his moment in the sun, so to speak, and his embarrassment would have little enduring consequence to anyone but himself. But, for those of us in the diplomatic corps, public embarrassment could be a common occurrence if the ambassador were not properly briefed, or as often happened, his words or actions were inadvertently misconstrued.

Nonverbal cues in African societies convey a wider range of meaning than the spoken word, especially where the spoken word or language is foreign, not well spoken, or understood. This happened to me, no matter how careful I was not to give off cues that might have double meaning and contribute to misunderstanding in a cross-cultural setting. And, it happens to most diplomats, even the most seasoned and sophisticated.

In Sierra Leone, as in most African countries, public events were often conducted outside in the open, without cover. Depending on the occasion, the speaker, and the time of day, the length of exposure to the sun could be insufferable. Exposure to the elements, other than rain, seemed to have little impact on our African colleagues and counterparts who were more accustomed to the sun's rays and heat. Western diplomats often found themselves sitting or standing uncomfortably in the hot sun, listening to long, involved speeches being made by high officials. Although audible groans and muttering could be heard in our midst, we all consciously avoided giving nonverbal expression to our discomfort.

As a case in point, I remember one occasion, where I had been standing in the grass for a long time, listening to a long and detailed request for donor monies. I never really heard the speech because my feet had begun to hurt, throbbing painfully with every heartbeat, sweating and swelling in the heels I had stubbornly insisted on wearing. Like Mr. Bangura, I tried to maintain my composure, to look interested and pleasant, shading my eyes from the sun. Finally, I stepped out of my shoes and stood barefoot in the grass, feeling immediate relief, just as the speech came to an end.

The next day, the daily newspaper reported on the Minister's request for donor assistance, noting the responsiveness or lack of interest shown by the assembled dignitaries. The report read, "Judging from the expression on the American ambassador's face, the Minister is not likely to receive assistance from the United States on this measure. She looked extremely pained and uncomfortable, showing great relief when the Minister's speech came to an end."

The press was ever mindful of opportunities to present articles of human interest, although the content of their coverage was sometimes restrained by governmental pressure, especially when the press was viewed as making mischief.

As an example of "freedom of the press," everyone knew, that the Iranian and American Embassies had no dealings our two countries. The takeover of the American Embassy in Tehran nearly a decade earlier continued to emanate bad feelings and hostilities that plagued diplomats in the field.

Once, while the world and the press were watching, I extended my hand in greeting to the newly arrived, very elegant, bearded Iranian ambassador to Sierra Leone. He acknowledged my greeting by bowing from the waist while ignoring my outstretched hand. His interpreter, usually at his side, whispered something in his ear. On-lookers felt strained by this obvious insult to the American ambassador. I started at first to ignore the fact that he shook hands with other diplomats.

Then I said, "So, are you going to shake my hand or not, Mr. Ambassador?"

He turned an ear to his interpreter, and then, with an amiable smile, distinctly enunciated, "No."

Then, I bowed to him from the waist, or as close to it as I could manage, and moved away. The Lebanese ambassador, who also was quite new to the community, took me aside.

"Our colleague's refusal to shake your hand," he explained," was not due to the political impasse between your country and his. It is due to the Islamic religion. The Koran, if narrowly interpreted, as the Iranians tend to do, would forbid contact with a woman other than one's own. In his mind, shaking your hand would constitute making contact with a woman. I am a Christian, myself. But, I was brought up in the world of Islam, and I understand it. Please do not report this incident to Washington as an intentional public insult to the United States."

I felt as though cold water had been dashed in my face. Did he honestly think I would be less insulted by the Iranian ambassador's disdain of me as a woman than as the official representative of my country? Anyway, I thanked him for the pains he had taken to enlighten me. I didn't have the emotional energy to take on two wars in one day.

Although the event was misinterpreted, the Foreign Ministry and the press duly noted potential sensitivities that could easily disrupt the harmony of the diplomatic community in Freetown.

Soon after this event, a particularly distinguished Sierra Leonean citizen died in Freetown and the diplomatic community was called to attend the memorial services being held in St. Michael's Cathedral. The church was absolutely packed. Seats reserved for the diplomatic corps had all been taken when I arrived. I was escorted to a seat behind a center pole, but I was not offended. What was I supposed to see, anyway, I reasoned? Sensing a flutter in the crowd, I turned to see that the Iranian ambassador, also arriving late, was being escorted to a seat right next to me on the same pew. Our eyes met. His face reddened, and I felt mine grow warm. The protocol officer rushed over, profusely apologizing to both of us for the mistake—he had a hard time phrasing it.

"Your Excellency," he said, addressing the Iranian ambassador, "I beg your pardon, sir, there are virtually no seats left, but please come; I will find one for you."

"Your Excellency," I said, addressing the Iranian Ambassador. "Do you mind sharing this pew with me?"

He flashed his amiable smile and in perfect English, responded, "I would be delighted, Your Excellency. Thank you for your consideration."

We thus averted another world war, and relaxed as we sat together in the same pew, all eyes upon us, cameras flashing. We maintained a discreet space between us throughout the service.

Pictures of us as we shared a pew appeared on the televised news that evening and in the newspaper the next day. Fortunately, the accompanying commentary and captions made no reference to the news-making photo, only that members of the diplomatic corps attended the service. After that day, whenever the Ambassador and I met, we bowed to each other and smiled cordially.

The press was normally kind to me, and I received very favorable coverage. To be sure, not all the impressions that my compatriots and the local people formed about me were just products of the very imaginative Sierra Leonean free press. I worked diligently to put a "face" on my ambassadorship, did not stand aloof from the people, and was concerned about those less fortunate in the city and countryside.

Even when not in the public eye, I took seriously my responsibility to support the American missionaries and Peace Corp Volunteers and was truly concerned about their welfare in this foreign land. Thankfully, I saw them most often under the best of circumstances. But, I remember one instance when their suffering pained me greatly and when, even as ambassador, I could do little to help. But, I felt that my presence, simply as a caring person, was needed.

Freetown was not a place where one would choose to be ill or injured. There were few adequately stocked pharmacies; there were few hospitals or clinics and those available often had no power and no water, due to shortages of fossil fuel. Without working telephones, it was often difficult to summon doctors and the quickest way to get help, especially at night, was to drive to the doctor's home or to the hospital. This was not only true for the local population, but even for much of the diplomatic corps and unofficial Americans. It did not so seriously affect official Americans. We had a well-supplied pharmacy, a nurse, and the Peace Corps doctor, who could be easily reached by radio if the telephones did not work.

In this one instance, however, it was the Peace Corps doctor himself, Dr. Alan Zeller, who was hurt, and quite seriously. He was returning from a trip upcountry in a range rover accompanied by his wife, Bette, a Volunteer, and one of their Sierra Leonean neighbors. Attempting to avoid a large convoy of trucks on a narrow turn, the range rover went over the cliff, rolling several times, nearly killing the occupants. I was informed of the accident by a passerby who had been unable to locate the Director of Peace Corps. I instructed the marine guard at post to summon others, and then rushed off to the hospital to see about the injured.

The two persons riding in the back seats without seatbelts, one of which was Bette Zeller, were critically injured. Dr. Zeller, who valiantly tried to remain cheerful in spite of the pain, had a gruesome injury—the skin had been pulled loose from his skull and lay folded over one ear along his neck. His wife had painful internal injuries and a broken pelvis; the Volunteer had a broken arm with internal injuries. The neighbor had a deep burn at the base of her neck where the range rover's hot tail pipe had pinned her to the ground. It was a sad and painful sight, although the four of them remained very brave under the circumstances.

I stayed with them, fanning them, talking to them, clucking in sympathy or whatever else I might do until the hospital doctor was found. With gas lamps, he began to treat the wounded. The Post Security Officer had radioed our Embassy in Monrovia requesting immediate assistance and in a few hours, the C-12 arrived with the American doctor. As soon as the patients' conditions could be stabilized and they could be moved from the hospital, he set up a "M.A.S.H." operation on the Peace Corps compound. He remained in Freetown, treating and keeping a watchful eye on the patients until they could be "medi-vacked" to Germany for more extensive medical attention. This was a harrowing experience which gave me an increasing sense of our frailties and vulnerability, even in a friendly environment, where the capacity to provide necessary human services was less than equal to our own.

Although sometimes there were broken bones from crashed poda-podas, or scraped shins, thankfully nothing so serious as this crash occurred during the rest of my tenure. My husband told me later that people marveled that I would spend so much time at the hospital, trying to soothe the injured and yelling at nurses to find that blasted doctor, find the Peace Corps Director, find some more gas lamps and bandages.

But, in the absence of responsible persons to carry out orders, isn't that what an ambassador ought to do?

* * *

Perhaps the most important means at my disposal as ambassador, for building relationships and the sense of community with my compatriots and Sierra Leoneans, was my role as hostess. Most societies, if not all, hold dear the notion that hospitality opens many closed doors. So, the Official Residence became central to the execution of my representational policy, and a great deal of time and money went into renovation of the space for this purpose. For a variety of reasons, it had suffered some neglect over past years.

The American ambassador's residence was supposed to be the most beautiful of all diplomatic residences, and perhaps it had been in the past. I dare say our gardens initially didn't compete well with Runnymeade, home of the British High Commissioner in Freetown.

It had been years since anything at all had been changed at the Residence, primarily because previous ambassadors had abhorred the disruption that it would entail, the mess of shattered plaster, the nakedness and protracted feeling of incompleteness. All ambassadors before me, nonetheless, had the same responsibility for good stewardship of American properties abroad. It was an aspect of our work for which we were evaluated in Washington. Admittedly, the time and patience required to supervise even the smallest project were in short supply among responsible staff, let alone the ambassador or the ambassador's spouse.

But, both our building and the grounds were impressive. They just needed a little attention to be brought back to life.

I began renovations with construction of a 9-foot perimeter wall, a security project approved by the Foreign Buildings Office (FBO) during my predecessor's tour, although it was never actually begun. But now for security reasons, building the wall became a priority. The kitchen was so small that the staff found it difficult to maneuver, especially when I was also in the room.

Then, as luck would have it, a water pipe broke under the concrete wall between the kitchen and a small bedroom. Since a part of the wall had to be removed to fix the break, it afforded an excellent opportunity to tear out the wall completely and to expand the kitchen space into separate cooking and serving areas. Also, when the new stove arrived, too large to bring into the house through any door or window, I suddenly was given the opportunity to widen the kitchen entrance to bring in the new appliances, including a large fridge, all of which coincidentally had the added benefit of bringing more natural light into the kitchen area.

Unfortunately, for lack of funds, I was unable to do much to change the front entrance that I had deplored since my arrival. But, I did broaden the narrow stoop into a small verandah with a white tiled floor, surrounded on each side with large, potted plants. The existing overhanging roof made it look more gracious and inviting. Guest limousines could still discharge their occupants directly at the front door.

Admittedly, being Texan dictated to a great degree my sense of wide-open personal space. My good friend, the leading builder in Freetown, Mr. Gemayel, who was always generously responsive to my needs and wants, opened a door between the master bedroom and one of the guestrooms. When not occupied by guests, I used the additional space for my studio. It afforded me a full view of the bay where I could paint to my heart's content. And, I did paint, in every spare moment at my command, a large triptych fully covering one wall of that room, and designed it to cover one wall of my living room in Houston.

Prior to departing Washington for Sierra Leone, I had visited the Art in Embassy program with its vast collection of donated and loaned works of art to be exhibited in the representational areas of Official Residences around the world. I chose 29 pieces of fine art: still lifes, landscapes, avant-garde abstractions, etc. The Art in Embassy program shipped them all to me within six months for display in the representational areas of the residence. These paintings covered the bare white walls and were great conversation pieces as well as excellent examples of American art. To these I added my own oil paintings, landscapes and portraits, some of which arrived with my household effects from Houston and others I had painted since my arrival in Freetown. Visitors seemed to love most the triptych of Lumley Bay with its billowing clouds and colorful skies and waters reflecting the setting sun.

During the latter months of my tour in Sierra Leone, I hosted at the Residence and in its gardens, an exhibition by serious African artists. This was a big event in Freetown which received wide publicity and coverage by the local press. Embassy personnel worked together with our talented Sierra Leonean staff in forming committees to judge entries and to serve as curators in selecting and placing the many pieces offered for exhibit. They did an excellent job of culling items that definitely did not qualify as legitimate art. But, presented together with the water and oil canvases were several beautifully woven baskets, country cloth, tie-dyes, silk prints and creations I will not likely display or view in one place again. Fanciful jewelry with artwork in beads and local stones were also for sale.

When the day arrived, more than 500 entries from all over the country had been received and logged. Local artists priced their entries to be sold during the exhibit. Art in Embassy pieces marked for sale by their owners, were also sold to buyers. It was a great day for artists in Sierra Leone and I myself purchased a number of interesting things. Among my purchases was a 6-foot tall wooden carving of a drummer man, his veins bulging from the stress and passion of drumming, and with detailed ropes holding the drum to his shoulders and decorating his drumming costume. It was designed and carved from a single tree trunk by a young man named Marco and his group of young carvers. It was a magnificent museum-quality purchase for my home in Houston. Several large carvings were available for purchase, and smaller carvings of mahogany and ebony woods.

The purpose of the art exhibit was to emphasize the importance of art and artists to any society's growth and development, and to encourage young artists to create. The artists were grateful for the opportunity to exhibit their creations in such a grand setting. Importantly, most were able to sell their artwork at good prices to the many visitors who came to the exhibition from around the country. In this manner, I did my best to improve the suitability of the house as a reasonable representation of America and American lifestyles and values.

The garden was my delight. One focus of my proud stewardship was a system of small holding ponds and waterfalls built in a previously neglected area of the garden. The waters cascaded in stages along the garden as it sharply descended down the hillside of the compound. My gardeners stocked the pools with small catfish and tilapia from steams outside the city. Children from the American school visited on field trips to feed the fish, delighting in watching them rush to get the bits of bread. The fish soon grew large and plump. Then, I discovered that my precious, plump fishes were regularly being eaten for lunch by my greedy gardening staff, who had never considered them a work of art. I had been running a fish farm and soon my fish had virtually disappeared, needing to be replenished.

Visitors to the Residence enjoyed walking down the series of steps to view the exotic plants and water lilies we had imported from throughout Sierra Leone, plucking them from the marshes on our trips to the interior, creating a type of arboretum in my compound. At the bottom of the garden were several huge blue boulders, blue in color, that looked as though they had been blown out of a volcano millennia ago. They formed a natural rock garden, which beautifully accentuated the waterfalls and shrubs.

The landscape design could have been carried out by a contractor, but I enjoyed working from time to time with the gardeners. More to the point, I'm sure I would have had no garden at all, at least not the garden that I wanted, had I not. I was given funding to hire two additional gardeners to help the one regular gardener to keep up the garden. I found it necessary to assign each responsibility for different sections of the garden. Otherwise, one worked while the two others slept.

It was somewhat difficult, however, to maintain my dignity while digging in the dirt in my sweaty, soil-stained shirt and jeans. One unforgettable day, I was preparing the house and gardens for an evening concert by a celebrated lutist, whose stop through Freetown on a six-country tour had been arranged by the U.S. cultural center. I was deep in the garden when the steward informed me that a man had come demanding access to the house. I hurriedly ascended the steep garden steps and must have looked a fright when I emerged at the top.

I recognized the lutist, the guest artist for the evening, who had arrived at the gate, unannounced and unescorted by a mission officer. He was greatly annoyed. His shirt was plastered to his chest with perspiration from the heat. I was about to introduce myself when he demanded, in a loud and strangely commanding voice, to know why he was not being allowed inside the house to deposit his sound equipment and instruments. He faced me, but did not address me.

"This—this person—has been extremely rude to me," he said, pointing his finger at Kamara, who looked as though he might snap at it at any minute.

I said stiffly and not too apologetically, "Of course, you may take them in. Kamara, please take our guest to the performance area downstairs. Use the side door."

The lutist shouted at me with anger, "Why can't I enter through the front door as I should? You look fairly intelligent—perhaps you're in charge here. Why are you people making simple things so difficult? I am the performing artist for tonight. I'm sure the Ambassador would want you to show me every common courtesy."

I felt myself bristling; my hackles were rising. Trying not to snarl, I said in a diplomatic tone of voice. "I'm sure the ambassador would, indeed. Your equipment is large and bulky and difficult to handle through the front entrance and down the narrow stairway inside. The side door is wider and will give you quickest access to the entertainment area where you will place your equipment." I put on my pleasant face. "Everyone is looking forward to your performance tonight. Please take all the time you need to set up your equipment. Kamara will assist you."

Kamara, eyes red with indignation, led the musician's helpers toward the outside staircase, and I returned to my gardening. When I came back up the steps some time later, the lutist had departed.

That night when the lutist arrived for the performance, I met him at the door, now dressed as the American ambassador might be expected to dress as the hostess for the evening. His eyes widened, all the while staring intently at me. Acting as though I had never seen him before, I welcomed him to the Residence, and escorted him downstairs to our waiting guests. I presented him as graciously as I could muster, and he gave an outstanding performance. It was one of the finest cultural affairs I ever hosted at the Residence. I loved his music and my guests were absolutely delighted to have been invited to this *haute couture* event.

During the reception that followed, the musician—whose name I still cannot recall, said to me, "I have a sense, Ambassador, that I've done something to offend you. Would you please tell me what it is? I am deeply sorry, and I apologize for whatever I've done."

I then realized that possibly he did not recognize me as the person he had insulted in the driveway that afternoon. I admit I had made a great transformation from a female African gardener with a few "smarts" to a sophisticated diplomatic hostess. Or, he was just a good actor and had thought his way out of this one! He kept peering at me intently as if trying to remember where he had seen me before. Failing that, how could he identify his own offense? He could only sense that because I was so cold toward him, he had somehow deeply offended me. It would probably dawn on him later, I surmised.

As he departed for his hotel, I thanked him again for a truly great performance. His music had gladdened our hearts and I was pleased he had chosen to come to Freetown. As his car left the gate, I suddenly remembered why I was so insulted by him. I had had a similar experience before.

Once, while living in Nairobi, J.O. and I were invited to a luncheon at the home of a friend, Dr. Preston King, who lived just down the lane from our house. The luncheon was in honor of a British professor who had completed his long-term assignment at the University of Nairobi, and would soon depart for London. Dr. King, a Black American professor exiled in London for refusing to fight in the War in Vietnam, had been this man's colleague at both Suffolk and Nairobi Universities, and had invited us to the farewell luncheon. For this occasion I was dressed in a cool, white outfit I considered appropriate for the occasion.

It was a lovely day—the rain had stopped, but puddles remaining in the unpaved road required some maneuvering around. I decided to walk the short distance down the lane. I saw a car approaching fairly rapidly and I moved quickly to the farthest edge of the lane. The car came as close to me as it possibly could without hitting me, throwing buckets of red mud all over me. It was clearly intentional and I was furious.

When I entered my friend's gate, the same car was parked just inside. I walked into the house seething with indignation, ready for confrontation. It turned out the car belonged to the honored guest, himself. After taking one look at me, he stammered, "Oh, I am so sorry. I was trying to miss the potholes; I could barely see you—I thought you were African."

To a room suddenly grown quiet, he added defensively, "Well—who else would be walking down a muddy lane this time of day? Had I known it was you, I would have stopped. I hope you will forgive me."

"What? Forgive you for thinking I was 'just' an African woman to whom you owed no consideration, no apology? Would splashing her with mud have been of no consequence to you?" I glared at him, mouth open ready to split his ears. My husband, who had arrived before me, placed his finger over his lips, bidding me not to spoil the party. I was not an ambassador at that time, and could not invoke executive privilege as excuse for the behavior I was contemplating. But, I wore my muddy dress all that evening just to remind that unspeakable Brit of his folly. I had found it impossible over the years to completely erase that incident from my memory.

The American lutist, no matter how pure and sweet his music, fell into the same insensitive category as the British professor. I sighed wearily, shut the door and went to bed. I made a note, however facetiously, to take my makeup kit, my wide-brimmed floppy hat, and especially my white gloves the next time I went to the garden on a Sunday.

Unfortunately, I caught malaria three times during my tour in Sierra Leone. The doctor asked that I refrain from working in the garden during early hours of the day when malarial mosquitoes lurking in the damp undergrowth were most likely to be active. Luckily for me, my body responded to the suppressants and treatments prescribed by the doctor and I suffered no long-term consequences. I refused to be exiled from my garden, although I did become more circumspect, and thereafter, for the most part, supervised the gardeners from the balconies.

I reinforced the order, however, that the guards were to admit no one through the gates when I was in the garden, even if they arrived in a U.S. or Sierra Leonean government van.

PART THREE

IN THE AFFAIRS OF MEN

Rice Politics

Sierra Leone was known as the "rice belt" for centuries, and rice to this day is its staple food. Its farmers throughout its history were well trained to grow rice and the environment is conducive to production of both marsh and tasty dry-land rice. The prowess of the Sierra Leoneans in the production of rice in the soft, watery deltas along the Atlantic coastline had made them particularly attractive to slave traders from the Americas. Historically, Sierra Leone had always boasted of being food self-sufficient. Its rice staple production was more than sufficient to meet consumption demands and allowed a surplus for sizable commerce with other West African countries, primarily its neighbors, Liberia and Guinea.

Early in my tenure, however, rice suddenly became scarce. It could hardly be found on the market, especially in the regions where the need and use were greatest. It was rumored that a lively black market was flourishing, supported by a few wealthy Afro-Lebanese families. They, along with native merchants, were accused of selling the rice across the border at more than triple the local price. According to the rumor mill, the same merchants had bought up remaining stocks and stored them in hidden warehouses. They artificially created a shortage to boost the price of rice within the country, while at the same time increasing available stock for export to Liberia and Guinea.

Some people claimed to have undeniable proof of the existence of these syndicates and of the burgeoning market in rice. The Lebanese with whom I talked said local merchants, especially the market women, were selling the rice across the border in larger quantities than ever before, where it was in great demand and could be marketed in hard foreign currency, such as U.S. dollars or French francs. According to Lebanese merchants, responsible government officials actually knew about these transactions and were partner to the scams, hoping that potential social instability caused by the rice shortage would encourage the United States to unload their surplus at cheaper prices on the Sierra Leone market. It was clear that merchants of all nationalities and ethnic groups across the country were all wildly speculating in rice. The poor rural people, primarily women, children and the elderly, were suffering for lack of it.

Eventually, the Government of Sierra Leone formally requested that the U.S. provide shipments of rice to be sold at a reduced price through our U.S. Public Law 480 (PL480) program. This program allowed American farmers to export their surplus grains to developing countries of the world for sale at a reduced price. Wheat was already being shipped to Sierra Leone to supply the wheat mill operated by American entrepreneurs. The GOSL requested also an annual consignment of rice through the "Food for Peace" program, not to be sold for profit. This rice was distributed directly through the Catholic Relief Service, although other nonprofit agencies were allowed to compete for the distributorship. Both programs were administered through the U.S. Department of Agriculture and the U.S. Agency for International Development.

By 1988, the rice shortage had become critical. Heavy rains in the rice producing areas of the country had virtually destroyed the crop. People were hungry, not starving, but hungry enough to threaten the security of the country. Tighter controls on rice prices and distribution were established and administered by the military, who as a special category, were receiving larger consignments of rice as a part of their payroll. They were happy. Professors at Fourah Bay College, who might also have intervened on behalf of the poor, also received a 100-kilo bag of rice each month as a part of their monthly stipend. They also were quite happy. No one in positions of power and authority seemed overly concerned about the less fortunate peasant class that formed the bulk of the population.

Rice politics emerged as a game between the government and the entrepreneurs. The government began to purchase more rice for consumption from the U.S. and other rice-producers like Mainland China, Taiwan, and Thailand. There were numerous stories that rice shipments were being hijacked at high sea, in reality just a few miles off shore, preventing anticipated shipments from reaching port.

Whenever U.S. ships arrived with a load of rice, I would go down to the port and greet the ship, watch its unloading process, get my pictures taken with the stevedores, even once with President Momoh, for good public relations on both sides. The United States Government and I, as ambassador, were praised highly for our generosity and for the quality of our long-grain rice. The truth of the matter, as explained to me by our Foreign Service Nationals, was that Africans preferred the local rice, whose grains are softer and stickier and more edible with the types of traditional sauces prepared. Therefore, people would trade two bags of PL480 rice for one bag of Sierra Leonean rice when it could be found.

PL480 rice was not absolutely free to consumers. It was sold throughout the country at a reasonable price agreed upon by the Government of Sierra Leone and the U.S. Government through the American Embassy. It allowed the local distributor a small margin of profit in distribution costs through creative management, and gave the participating company an ounce of prestige in having a contract with the American mission.

Several local contractors were competing for the right to distribute American rice throughout the provinces promising to ensure even and fair delivery to selected sites. USAID and the Embassy were reviewing a number of applicants, with an eye to bringing in not only the best distributor, but also to giving small advantages to new entrepreneurs who showed some stability and eagerness.

One day, I received a call from a Ben Kamara, a local rice dealer whose conveniently packaged plastic bags of rice were sold locally as "Uncle Ben's Rice." He said he had been a very close friend of the previous ambassador and wished to get to know me. My staff had earlier advised me that Ben Kamara was our current PL480 rice distributor, a nephew of President Momoh, a strong member of the ruling All Peoples Congress (APC) party, and just recently named Member of Parliament-at-Large. All of this at least spelled caution in dealing with Ben. With some misgivings, I gave him an appointment.

When Ben arrived at the Embassy, he was dressed to the "T," down to the diamond stickpin in his tie. I was impressed. He was of average height and weight, quite good-looking, relatively young and worldly-wise, "smooth" in other words. I somehow felt that my desk with its duress button made me less vulnerable to his charms as he sat before me.

"Your Excellency, thank you for this opportunity to speak to you directly like this. I have visited this office many times in the past, but somehow it looks very different. You've added a lot of little touches; perhaps some of the furniture is new? Anyway, I'm sure that your sense of interior decorating is far superior to your predecessor's. We used to play tennis together, you know—he's quite good. Do you play?"

"Yes, not well, but I enjoy the game." I was practicing being inscrutable.

"You are known everywhere as a woman of impeccably good taste, Your Excellency, and a woman of distinction in every sense. I wanted to bring you a special gift of welcome, one most fitting to your station. I am told that you and your husband have vast holdings in the United States. It is always difficult to find a gift for someone who already has everything. But, here is something that has been in my family for a very long time, Your Excellency. It has great value, and I would not offer it to just anyone, I assure you. Let me show you."

He brought out a small packet of indigo cloth, which he carefully and slowly untied and spread out on my desktop. He had my full attention. In the cloth was one of the largest, most perfect diamonds I had ever seen. It was uncut, about the size of an English walnut, completely outside the range of my imagination. I sat stupefied for several seconds staring at the brilliant flashes of light and color emanating from the stone.

"It is indeed beautiful. Was it found in this country?"

"Of course," he said smiling proudly. "Here! Please hold it and examine it more closely. Look at it—it's flawless! The Lebanese manage somehow to get these for themselves—illegally, of course, but my company is licensed to mine and to market such gemstones, and I do pay the assessed taxes. I would not operate illegally, I assure you. I would be honored if you would accept my gift. It is an uncut diamond, which I will have cut and set for you as a ring or a pendant, however you wish."

"I know it's rude of me to ask this question, Mr. Kamara, but can you give me an idea of its worth?" I asked. Some years prior, when I was serving in Ethiopia, I had purchased a smoky topaz from Madagascar, a semi-precious stone just about the same size. It had cost me a small fortune and didn't come close to the beauty of this flawless diamond.

"Oh, that doesn't matter, Your Excellency. This is a gift from me to you. If you'd rather, no one need know about it. It's probably better that no one knows. I just appreciate being able to give it to you. Please accept it."

I sat looking at him for a moment; he was smiling affably with a 'trust me' look in his big brown eyes. Finally, I said. "It's a truly magnificent stone. I have never hoped to see or to own anything so perfect and so valuable. But, you should know, Mr. Kamara, that I cannot accept it."

He sat upright in disbelief.

"My government forbids me to accept gifts of value greater than $250," I explained. "If I should accept it, it would be in the name of the U.S. Government and would be turned over to our archives in Washington. I'm sure you understand the reasons behind these restrictions, Mr. Kamara."

"No, I don't, Your Excellency, and I am truly hurt that you would refuse it." He looked incredulous.

"Not as hurt as I am, Mr. Kamara," I assured him. "I would love to accept it from you as graciously as you have offered it. But, I cannot."

"You must be the first one, maybe the only one to play by those rules, I can assure you, Madame Ambassador," he responded.

I sensed that I had just demoted myself in his eyes. He managed to look hurt, with the slightest hint of moisture in his eyes as he carefully returned the gemstone to its blue wrapper. Was he suggesting that my predecessors in Sierra Leone had accepted such gifts from him? I could not ask, of course.

We engaged in light discussion a bit longer, about rice politics in Sierra Leone, about the upcoming lottery on contracts for distributing PL480 rice. He expressed his interest in maintaining the contract he currently held but would be willing to subcontract to women and other groups as might be required. Finally, he thanked me profusely for allowing him the honor of visiting me and expressed hope to see me again soon.

Backing out the door, he implored, "Your Excellency, I beg you to reconsider my offer."

Bette's eyebrows went up. When she returned from escorting him downstairs to the door, she said, "What was that all about? Was he asking you to marry him?"

"Almost," I responded. I returned to my desk in deep reflection.

When Diamonds were King

Diamonds were king in Sierra Leone. They were used to buy many things and people. When the country gained its independence in 1961, it became the world's second largest exporter of diamonds—gem stones, number one in quality. The country's wealth of natural resources, particularly gold, diamonds, bauxite and rutile, brought new prosperity in mining and increased employment for local people. Sierra Leone was known as a leader of African nations and Freetown a great commercial capital in West Africa. By the 1980's, however, due to mismanagement of its natural resources and widespread corruption at the top, the government was nearly bankrupt.

The first diamonds were discovered in 1930, alluvial diamonds buried in the wastes and soils flowing from the mountains with the heavy, seasonal rains. In heavy storms, the diamonds are said to have rolled into the streets for anyone to claim as his own. Alluvial digs are yet conducted freely along the roadsides, but as the government grew in strength, the diamond fields were restricted to licensed miners. One great stone found in the Kono region in 1972, the "Star of Sierra Leone," weighing close to 1,000 carats (one-half pound), is yet the largest uncut gem diamond found in the world. It was sold to a British museum, where it is displayed in splendor.

Before my arrival, a former governor of the Central Bank of Sierra Leone had made it difficult to illegally remove diamonds from the country, and set up controls to prevent merchants from bypassing the stringent taxation process. Interestingly, in 1985, this same governor of the Central Bank, who had not at all been a careless or bumbling sort, mysteriously fell to his death from a second story window of his home, still sitting in his chair.

In 1986, during my first year as ambassador, a powerful and well-trained West Indian banker, Sir Victor Edward Bruce, was appointed successor to the deceased governor of the Central Bank. In little time, things began to fall into place and the Central Bank became more efficient and regained people's trust. Just as a precaution, when Sir Victor Bruce arrived in Freetown, he chose not to live in the designated house owned by the Bank. He moved with his family into another well appointed home. Like his predecessor, he began to establish and enforce new regulations on the commerce in gold and diamonds, and began to bring in new monies to fill the coffers of the government. He won the respect and trust of donors and of European banks. The economy began again to flourish.

But, within the year, he too, mysteriously died in his home from carbon monoxide poisoning. While his wife was away on holiday, he had reportedly lit a charcoal burner to dry out dampness in the house. The deaths of both bankers were officially classified as accidents. Understandably, no one of repute or integrity wanted to fill that vacancy.

Diamonds were powerful. They replaced the floating currency, the leone, and were being used to barter goods and favor inside and outside the country. It was no small wonder to me that the rice distribution contract, which could bring millions of leones or better, millions of U.S. dollars from across the border in Liberia or French francs from Guinea, could warrant an offer the size of the diamond offered to me by Ben Kamara. The level of intrigue and the breadth and depth of collusion in this country was unfathomable to expert observers.

I sat long at my desk, musing over this state of affairs. If this corruption continued or worsened, the public was sure to rise up against the merchants and eventually the government itself. There were rumors of coup-plotting upcountry among the Mende, who were striving for power and control over the diamond fields. And, among the Temne, the other powerful group who wanted control over the distribution and pricing of rice. The situation became quite tense. The issue of control of the diamonds seemed beside the point, except where they were used to control the distribution of rice. It was food and access to food, which ultimately would control the balance of power in Sierra Leone, and in the world.

President Momoh once said to me quite poignantly, "There will never be peace in this country until all the diamonds are gone."

He could not predict when that was likely to happen, when deep shaft mining of diamonds had not even begun. Deep mining could not be done so secretly nor "tiefing" (stealing) not so easily hidden.

American businessmen were also involved in the illegal diamond-trafficking and when they ran into trouble in the country as visiting businessmen, they became the responsibility of the Embassy through its Consular Office. The responsible government agency would advise Barbara Johnson, our Consular Officer, when an American citizen was jailed or imprisoned. She would arrange a visit to the prison to assist the prisoner, although she could not negotiate his release without pursuing resolution to all charges.

A businessman from Texas, introduced to me as Mr. George Peterson, arrived in country accompanied by a student he had met in Texas, who said he had an uncle, a "chief," who had access to diamonds in the Kono Region. Mr. Peterson did not consult me or the consular officer about the veracity of the student's story or the advisability of going to the Kono area. He had visited Freetown in the past and had established his own connections. He arrived with a briefcase bulging with large denomination American dollar bills, made his contacts, and set himself up comfortably in a hotel to do business.

The student introduced the American merchant to his "uncle, the chief," who displayed some sample diamonds and invited him to travel upcountry where he could choose the diamonds he wished to purchase, as a matter of good business.

One week later, the Foreign Ministry advised Barbara that an American businessman had been jailed for illegally negotiating for diamonds in the restricted diamond fields. Learning it was indeed Mr. Peterson, Barbara visited him in jail—bearing toilet paper, soap and other toiletries—to ensure he was being treated properly while his case was pending. The briefcase full of money had disappeared. As a normal consular procedure, Barbara offered to notify his wife and family back in Texas. If they would guarantee reimbursement of his ticket, the Embassy would negotiate his voluntary departure and return home from Sierra Leone.

He said, "Oh, no. There's no need for that. I'm quite comfortable here. My friends come to see about me from time to time and have presented my case to authorities. It's a big mistake. I was operating on American business principles. The student abandoned me; the uncle took advantage and turned me in to the police as a shyster. Me, a shyster? I am not interested in leaving this country until they return my money or give me the diamonds I purchased. But, thanks anyway. I'm not unhappy, otherwise. I'll just stay right here."

Less than a month later, Mr. Peterson telephoned Barbara. "Please contact my wife in Texas to send some money through the Embassy. I'm ready to leave here. Life is not so good in jail unless you have money to pay for services."

Barbara immediately contacted the wife, who thought it hilarious. "In jail?" she said. "Well, of course, I'll send him the money and guarantee his ticket if he will tell me where he has hidden the diamonds from his last trip to Sierra Leone."

When this message was relayed to Mr. Peterson, he was quite angry and refused to comply. Instead, he asked Barbara to contact his son in another state, who eventually guaranteed payment for the fine and the return ticket. Mr. Peterson was released from jail and left the country, with barely a word of thanks to the Consular Officer.

This is just one of many stories related to diamonds and various American business attempts to deal outside the established legal channels. For some, it apparently has worked. Black market diamonds were attainable, but the game had to be played according to set rules, which guaranteed marketeers their share. The Government officially marketed its diamonds through DeBeers, with Maurice Templesman in New York and the Oppenheimers in South Africa.

Although rarely discussed in the context of Sierra Leone's vast wealth, the incredible deposits of gold in the country drew unscrupulous speculators as well. Once when J.O. and I visited the spectacular Bumbuna Falls in the northern Koinaduga District, we were invited to stay in the guesthouse of an Italian mining company near Lake Sonfon. These private Italian engineers had been contracted by the GOSL to build a huge water delivery system in that area. We were impressed with the huge reservoir built by the Italian engineers, much like Boulder Dam in Colorado. They found it necessary to bore through the mountain to establish the huge turbines, which would control the flow of water from the reservoir. The European-type village they had built to house their expatriate employees was cool, comfortable and efficient and we enjoyed their hospitality.

Freetown operated an indigenous rumor mill—and a rumor spread that the Italians had stumbled upon the mother lode of gold in the mountains they had accessed—whether accidentally or with some prior knowledge of its existence—while boring and tunneling through the hard rock. They reportedly separated out the gold over a period of time and removed it from the country. J.O. and I considered the possible credibility of the rumor when we learned that this vast water delivery project had folded due to lack of continued government funding. The lovely little village was abandoned, and the engineers returned to Italy.

Sierra Leone undeniably had a wealth of natural resources and minerals. The unethical collusion of government officials and private entrepreneurs with speculative counterparts inside and outside the country, continued to defeat the nation's ability to provide the most fundamental elements required for economic growth, such as a renewable source of fresh water. The people as a whole continued to suffer from lack of knowledge of the machinations going on around them. In the meantime, seeds of unrest were planted and flourishing around the countryside. The question among my compatriots was when it would indeed explode, and the consequences that war would have upon the simpler populations of Sierra Leone.

Groping:
An Indiscriminate Sport

Both men and women in Sierra Leone were quite curious about the persona of a female ambassador. I was not their first one, but I was black which seemed to place me in a more accessible category. Sierra Leone, like Africa in general, can be said to be a "man's world," a country where even the most educated and sophisticated men revere themselves almost as gods, caretakers of the earth—and certainly of women. Men thought themselves to be answers to everything a woman could ever want and, therefore, nothing they might do could be considered offensive. They respected only the protection created through ownership by another man. I remember that one man once told me smugly that a woman could never hope to enter heaven except on a man's coattail. He said the Bible said so, and I searched in vain for a biblical reference, which might seek to attribute such fundamentalist drivel to God, Himself.

Being U.S. ambassador did not completely protect me from indignities suffered by other women. My husband traveled with me on most occasions throughout the country and was normally at my side or close by. But, once I was escorted to my car by a local official who did his share of out-of-view groping, as he handed me graciously into my seat. He did not apologize, in fact, smirked as though he had done me a great favor. I smoldered in deep contempt, not only for him but for myself that I did not immediately, for fear of creating an international incident, kick him in the balls. The withering look I gave him only made him feel victorious.

After a few such groping sessions on the dance floor, I wanted almost immediately to excuse myself from public dancing. Once at a large public celebration, I had to refuse an otherwise genteel offender, a high ranking government official, who took great umbrage at my refusing to dance with him. I did steadfastly refuse, explaining that I had been experiencing some vertigo.

"Just what kind of ambassador are you," he yelled to my embarrassment, "that you can refuse to dance with your host?"

My husband lightly touched my elbow guiding me away from the irate official. From that point early in my tour, however, I could not accept an invitation to dance with any other man, other than my husband, for fear of creating greater insult to the official. It soon became common knowledge that the American ambassador did not dance—like some people don't drink?

I never kidded myself that I was so physically attractive that men couldn't resist groping me. It was not due to physical attraction at all. It was a question of power, of touching a power source and wielding a modicum of control over it. These incidents gave me greater insights into the role of women in Sierra Leone and the things they were forced to endure, without the protection of prohibitive laws.

During my three years at post, I received many invitations to speak to national and local women's groups. Men also attended these meetings, quite often serving as interpreters. Once I visited a small village in the north of Sierra Leone to dialogue with an active woman's group on maternal/child health issues. The dialogue changed rather dramatically to a discussion of male/female issues and especially the issue of polygamy. Very few of the women spoke English, so I requested assistance from the official male interpreter of the local language provided by the government protocol office. He followed my speech in English with his translation, mimicking my own vigorous body language on points I wished to emphasize. The women laughed at his humorous antics, and for the most part were respectful as they listened, but they were less than responsive. I wondered about that.

Lt. Kula Samba, an army officer, the First Lady's representative and unofficial interpreter, was permitted to accompany me to one such occasion in her hometown. Once again, I spoke through the official male interpreter to a rather unresponsive group of women on the individual rights and responsibilities of women in the modern society. Lt. Samba suddenly spoke out, "That's not what she said."

And, she stood and proceeded to give a different twist to my words in Mende. The startled interpreter first tried to hush Lt. Samba and then to plead with her to inform me that he dared not tell the women what I was saying. The men in the village would beat him to death, thinking the words he spoke regarding the rights of women were his own.

From that time, Kula Samba traveled with me and gave my words the intended interpretation, which was likewise supported by the First Lady. Even with Kula, whom I trusted, I could only surmise what the women were actually being told. I learned how deeply unhappy women were in the rural areas, the physical injuries they suffered at the hands of their husbands, the indignities of polygamy, and the treatment they received as chattel resulting from the "bride price" exacted by their families.

Many died in childbirth, a large percentage of deaths caused by the unyielding scar tissue formed from the practice of female circumcision, which made the birthing process difficult or impossible. Even women from the most sophisticated families of Sierra Leone endured this circumcision and only recently had female doctors begun to challenge the tradition.

Rural men had witnessed the horrible crippling and disfigurement of newly born children, affected by the heavy, backbreaking toil of pregnant women in the fields, carrying firewood and water. Many seemed unable to associate cause and effect, or just didn't care.

Once I encountered a young woman walking down a dirt road near Freetown, obviously in a late-term pregnancy, leading a small child by the hand, a baby on her back and a huge basket of produce on her head. Her husband walked along ahead of her, with very little in his hands.

I said to him, "Your wife is struggling with her heavy load. Unless you help her, the new baby could be born with defects, or your wife could die in childbirth."

He turned to look back at her, and said to me with a blank expression, "Well, in that case, I'll just get another."

I gave many speeches in Sierra Leone on the plight of women around the world and the pain they endured. Women's organizations soon learned of the horror I felt, and of my desire to do something to bring about change. The Women's Bar Association of Sierra Leone invited me to give the keynote address at their international conference in 1988. I considered it a great honor to speak to this large gathering of female barristers, all English-speaking, from Europe, Asia and several African countries, including a large audience of women from Sierra Leone.

The Hall was packed when President Momoh arrived to open the conference. He praised the planners and conveners, stating the importance of women to work diligently to improve women's conditions in the world. His remarks were well received and he was given a standing ovation.

The President's protocol officer and speechwriter, Mansour Turey, smiled smugly to himself. He smiled encouragingly at me as I was introduced to the crowd as the conference keynote speaker.

As I rose to go to the podium, the President also rose, choosing that moment to signal his officers that he was ready to depart the hall. As an act of respect, everyone throughout the audience also began to rise.

I leaned over to him, "Mr. President, please don't leave," I whispered. "Mine is not a long speech—at the most 20 minutes, but parts of it I have written thinking it would be of interest to you. I beg of you to stay, if you will."

He looked surprised. "I have another pressing engagement, Madame Ambassador," he said, "but if it will be no longer than 20 minutes, of course I will stay."

He sat back down and a murmur went through the audience as they all sank into their seats again.

The title of my speech was "The Role of Women in a Democratic Society." I began with the premises that the President established and praised in his opening remarks; i.e., the value of women in the society and his gratitude for their contributions to the growth of the economy. Then I chose examples of female leaders in democracies around the world noting the leaderships of Indira Gandhi, Golda Meir, Margaret Thatcher, and Benazir Bhutto. I noted acts of inhumanity, highlighting the horrible mutilations of women through circumcision, imposed upon young women by older women; of the horror of sati, wife-burning in India; of the defeating practices of polygamy around the world, not excluding the traditionalism of African societies, both Islamic and Christian.

Then, I expounded on wife beating which I considered the most egregious of all insults to women, a practice assumed by men to be their right in societies around the world. I had my eye on Mansour, the president's protocol officer, since I could not be so brazen as to eyeball the President on this taboo subject. Mansour was incredulous, with a look of shock on his face. As I continued to speak, he began to slide down in his seat, his face barely showing above the edge of the table.

The women in the hall were applauding vigorously, rising from their seats and remaining on their feet until my speech was finished. I charged the women to take the lead in their own affairs—in health, education, in the preparation of young women for nontraditional careers. Using the same phrases I might have used in speaking to women at Chatham College and Spelman, I challenged them to use the foundation of law, through their Bar Association to reach women and others sympathetic to their causes. I urged them to establish legal clinics for women throughout the country to treat injustices of the past. They stood continuing to applaud long after I had returned to my seat.

The President rose again—and so did everyone. He shook my hand and said. "Thank you, Madame Ambassador, for approaching a difficult and emotional subject that I have not found easy to broach. I have learned a lot today from you on this form of abuse as practiced around the world. It needs to be changed here in Sierra Leone and I am grateful to you for bringing it out in the open." Then, followed by his entourage, he left the hall.

Mansour stopped at my chair on his way out. He said, "I couldn't believe you were saying those things. Nobody talks about wife beating, Ambassador. Agreed, it's uncivilized and we all know that it is widely practiced. Several women die each year with no recourse, but it isn't talked about. I thought I would go through my chair, but His Excellency didn't seem offended. You pulled it off, by making it appear a worldwide crime against women, not endemic to Sierra Leone alone."

It had been important to me that the President remain throughout my speech to tacitly endorse its principles before the entire female audience. Mansour's reaction, however, left me wondering whether I might not have hit some personal as well as political nerves.

I think I made a difference in Sierra Leone in the way women are treated, but how can it be measured? I did notice before departing Sierra Leone, growing numbers of young women leaving the country for legal training in Western countries and returning as barristers. But, I was unable to affect age-old traditions and practices among the poor, rural, and uneducated women whom my voice rarely reached in the countryside. Certainly, with respect to many towns in Sierra Leone and in Africa in general, Freetown was quite liberal, having had a woman mayor in the early 1980's. Curiously, some months following my speech, one woman was named to Parliament, and two were named ambassadors to European posts. I guess the President was indeed listening.

Fish Poaching and
the Russians

President Momoh's protocol officer telephoned my secretary early one morning, saying the President wished to speak with me at 11:00 am. He asked whether the time were convenient for me. All ambassadors recognized the call from the State House to be a command performance and therefore, we always responded very quickly to the President's request.

In most cases, I could predict the problem he wished to discuss. I knew this day, for instance, that the country needed more rice and he would surely ask me to request some $6 million in assistance from the U.S. Government. I normally went alone to the President's office when responding to his summons, but otherwise would take along one or another of my senior officers, depending on the nature of my visit.

I entered the gates of the fortress-like State House, my driver John pulling up the Oldsmobile limousine smartly to the front door. The armed presidential guard opened my car door, helped me from the car and waved my driver on to the parking area. As always, someone from protocol was standing in the doorway to greet me and to escort me to the President's third floor office. Some days, the elevator worked. This was not one of those days.

Depending upon which diplomats you met arriving, waiting or leaving the State House, one could determine what was bothering the President that day. The Soviet Ambassador was just leaving as I puffed my way up the stairs, and we exchanged greetings, while trying to double guess why the other was there.

The Korean Ambassador was sitting in one of the waiting rooms as I passed by. I was placed in a different room, but by now, I had gotten the picture. The subject today was going to be fish, most likely the poaching of fish in Sierra Leone's territorial waters. Everybody was doing it, but the two most egregious exploiters were allegedly the Koreans and Russians. Both loved the shrimp and unlike the local fishing trawlers, their heavier foreign trawlers would drag their metal nets along the bottom of the lagoon, their steel nets dredging up not only the mature shrimp and fish but also the young crop, destroying the breeding grounds. The local independent fishermen and the factory, managed by a local Afro-Lebanese millionaire, had recently reported drastically reduced catches of large shrimp and game fish for local consumption and export.

I anticipated the question and began to form an answer to the President's request before I entered his office. He sat behind the high desk much like the judge's bench in an American courtroom. Seated around him were the official note taker, the Minister of Agriculture, National Resources and Forestry, Souffian Kargbo, and the Minister of State for Presidential Affairs, Dr. A. K. Turay, the President's closest advisor. All stood and nodded their greetings as I took a seat.

The President spent a few moments discussing generalities. Then, smiling, he said, "Thank you, Ambassador, for coming to see me today. I hope I haven't disrupted your busy day. We have a problem we wanted to discuss with you. I guess you met your colleagues going out, so you have some idea of the reason I have summoned you."

I smiled, "It is always my pleasure, Mr. President."

"As you know, fishing in this country is a major industry. We have always had a great surplus, allowing us to develop a thriving factory and capacity to export a sizable surplus of large game fish to Europe. Suddenly, we find that our supply is diminishing; the breeding grounds are delivering no where near their normal yield. We suspect the Koreans are over-fishing and we have just charged them to curtail their large catches or to forfeit their license to fish in this country. The Russians, we suspect, are also over-fishing; but, our searches have found nothing out of the ordinary. In fact, their trawlers never seem quite full."

I waited for his request. When none came, I asked, "What can we do to help you, Mr. President?"

"Americans are very resourceful people," he chuckled. "We have greatly appreciated the attention you have given to our many requests. Today, I am asking your assistance in studying this matter. Help us to discover what is happening to our fish." He leaned toward me, emphasizing the seriousness of his problem.

"How often do you survey your waters, Mr. President?" I asked cautiously.

"We have no means of surveillance, Madame Ambassador. As you know, we have no airforce. I have asked your government for a small fixed-wing plane and also a patrol boat, with no real response." (I walked right into that one!) "The Chinese have now agreed to give us two patrol boats, but we have no idea of their condition. Our one boat has been in dry dock for over a year, and repairs are impossible for lack of parts. We had two boats at one time, but we cannibalized one to save the other, to try to have one working boat, without success." He was watching me carefully with a slight smile.

Although I didn't disclose anything at that moment, Washington had indeed responded negatively to the request for a fixed wing plane, but was seriously considering the patrol boat. Perhaps for this occasion there was another option.

"Mr. President," I asked, "would you consider taking a flight in our plane, the C-12, just for an hour or so over your fishing waters to see what's out there? I can arrange for the plane to come from Monrovia in two to three days. I will go out with you. Let's start with that, if you wish to do so."

He was quite happy with that suggestion and Dr.Turay, sitting quietly in the corner, signaled with his eyes to the President that he should go. I suddenly felt that these two old foxes had just "snookered" me.

"Yes, I would," said President Momoh. "I appreciate your gracious generosity, Madame Ambassador. Just let Dr. Turay know when the flight will be feasible."

I took leave of President Momoh with the certainty he had already considered the use of our plane from the onset and had even set me up to make the offer. He already knew, of course, when the plane arrived and departed Sierra Leone since permission to land a foreign aircraft had to be granted by his government. He may have also traveled similarly with my predecessor on the plane.

I was aware from our own intelligence that the Russians had anchored a fish-processing factory ship just beyond the government's surveillance capability and were doing a lively business of packing and freezing fish for the Russian market. From our purview, taking the president on a tour of his territorial waters, where he could judge for himself whether agreements were being abrogated, was a helpful ploy. It was certainly much more politic than presenting the President with information leading to his direct confrontation with the Russians. For his part, having the Americans as witnesses to the presence of the factory ship was useful to substantiate, if need be, the illegal presence of Russian fishermen in Sierra Leonean waters. We were credible witnesses.

Within the next few days, the C-12 arrived with its two commanders. The President joined me and the crew at a small airfield just outside the city. He seemed a little jittery, I thought, perhaps not totally trusting the Americans, or perhaps fearful of small planes. But he was a Major General, after all. I expected him to show no fear, no real emotion at all. He was quite engrossed in viewing the terrain below him and pointing out familiar sights to Dr. Turay, who accompanied us.

When he spied from the air the large Russian factory ship, however, he became quite emotional. The ship was surrounded not only by the licensed Russian trawlers, but also by Sierra Leone's largest fleet, unloading their day's catch onto the Russian factory ship. To the President, the cause of the shortage of fish in Freetown was finally clear.

We circled the ship several times. Our pilot informed President Momoh he was taking pictures of the giant factory ship and the attending trawlers, which the President could have for his own records. When we landed, the President was furious. He understood now to what extent the Russians had deceived him, and he knew also how his own countrymen were contributing to the poaching. We left him and his advisors to their machinations, but as we parted, they were already deep in Krio, no doubt talking through next steps.

In the next few days, I received an official visit from the President's protocol officer who stated stiffly and unequivocally, "The President requests that, as part of our military assistance program, you recommend to your government that they provide a fixed wing aircraft or a fully-equipped patrol boat to help guard against the poaching of our fish. His recent trip aboard your C-12 provided compelling evidence and reason that we must as a government have the capacity to survey our own waters to determine our vulnerability or to prevent greater losses. You witnessed yourself the egregious acts of some nations, with the help of our own citizens, to take undue advantage of our inability to catch them in the act."

I immediately forwarded the President's request through State Department channels, and provided information to support the request. In the following weeks, the question was fully vetted in Washington and Stuttgart, but they considered the aircraft still out of the question. Later, we learned that the ICAO (International Civil Aviation Organization), a U.N. body based in Montreal, did provide a large, refurbished helicopter to permit the President quicker access to remote areas of the country, an act of largesse they had provided only two or three countries in the world. An American pilot with experience in Vietnam was hired to ferry the President around the country and over coastal waters.

The two boats provided by the Chinese, required refurbishing, but all instructions for their handling and repair were written in Chinese. This delayed for several months the independent operation of the boats by the Sierra Leonean navy. The U.S. Government in time provided a patrol boat and the technology, and brought in instructors to train the navy to operate it and keep it in good repair. This, finally, was an elegant compromise.

The Government of Sierra Leone lodged a very stiff protest to the Russians and developed other ways and means to deal with their own poachers. Poaching came to a standstill until the poaching groups could figure out how to manage it without being caught.

Without the complicity of the factory ships, the fishing industry again began to look to its own population for its livelihood. Fish and shrimp were again to be found on the streets and in the fish markets at reasonable prices. Seafood in Sierra Leone was most valuable as a commodity for export, however, not as a foodstuff. Fish was eaten primarily by people living in Freetown and along the coast, delivered by local fishermen in their dugouts. The population in the interior fished the fresh water rivers and lakes, not relying upon the markets of Sierra Leone for this produce. But, for a brief period, at least, the fishing industry normalized.

The Gullah Connection

Soon after my arrival in Sierra Leone in 1986, Joe Opala, an energetic and imaginative Peace Corps Volunteer, came to see me in my office, loaded with documents. As a trained anthropologist, Joe had researched independent slave movements in the United States from the Carolinas and Georgia down to Florida, where the slaves intermarried with Seminole Indians. From Florida, the black Seminoles became divided, some going to Oklahoma, the state where Joe was born, others to Texas. The Texas group became special soldiers, called the Seminole Negro Indian Scouts. I suspected Joe might possibly be searching for his own roots, as he retraced their movements backward from Oklahoma to Charleston, South Carolina.

He discovered in Charleston's archives a wealth of information on the slave trade in that area, particularly about the Gullahs or "geechies," people who spoke a distinctly different language, who were inhabiting the Sea Islands off the coast of South Carolina. He concluded, along with other researchers, that, unlike the majority of blacks in America who could not identify their African roots, there was a direct verifiable connection between Sierra Leone and the Sea Islanders. He joined the Peace Corps, requesting assignment to Sierra Leone, where he continued his research. He learned about an old slave fort, Bunce Island, which had historically figured in the European slave trade. After many visits to the ruins of the fort on Bunce, he was convinced that there was indeed a direct linkage in slave traffic between this small country in Africa and the State of South Carolina.

During his Peace Corps assignment, he learned to speak with some fluency the Mende and Krio languages, and gathered further information from oral historians and storytellers throughout the country. When Joe finished Peace Corps, he returned home to Oklahoma for a period of time establishing his research strategy, linking with researchers at the University of South Carolina and gathering funds to promote further research. He returned to Sierra Leone to continue his research in concert with researchers at Fourah Bay College who were also pursuing this phenomenon in their history.

He presented to me a summary of not only his work but also a composite of all research done by both Americans and Sierra Leoneans on this possible connection dating from the late 1700's. He told me the story of the Amistad Revolt and the history of Sengbe, a Sierra Leonean, including Sengbe's contributions to the establishment of churches in Sierra Leone through the American Missionary Society. He presented me with a booklet called the *Amistad Revolt,* authored by Arthur Abraham, a Sierra Leonean, with Joe's collaboration. J.O. and I were amazed at what we did not know.

I took this entire information home with me from the office for bedtime reading. J.O. and I read through the documentation, and found Joe's facts amazingly convincing and compelling. The information was all there, in writing, fully documented by American history, the marketing and trading of this special group of rice-growing slaves. Flyers in the Charleston archives announced the arrival of ships in the Charleston harbor bearing human cargo from Bunce Island. Slave bills advertised the range of costs for male and female slaves and for children arriving directly from Sierra Leone. The old papers described the slaves as rice growers, who could and did develop South Carolina's rice economy. This information verified a direct and unmistakable link between Bunce Island and Charleston. How could it have gone undiscovered or forgotten for so many years? The question, now, was how to make this discovery known to the Gullah descendents and their ancestors on both sides of the ocean. How could the American public be made aware of this startling revelation in a positive manner?

Strategizing, Joe asked for my help in getting the White House to offer an official invitation to President Momoh to visit the United States for the first time, and then to convince President Momoh that he should go to Hilton Head in South Carolina.

I was unsuccessful in securing the official White House invitation. I had already been advised before coming to Sierra Leone that such a visit would be next to impossible to negotiate. Only under very rare circumstances are more than two state visits traditionally arranged each year, which involve great cost to the United States government. Foreign presidents who wish to visit are, therefore, encouraged to arrive in the United States by other channels and means, and may request an appointment through their ambassadors to meet with the American president at some time after their arrival in the country. In this case, President Momoh already had plans to address the General Assembly of the United Nations in New York, and could extend his travel to Washington where he could be received by President Reagan.

It was not a difficult task to convince President Momoh to go further to Hilton Head. He had also reviewed the indisputable research that I had sent to him. His special advisor, Dr. A. K. Turay, an American graduate and former professor of linguistics at Fourah Bay College, had conducted a part of the initial research effort. He supported my efforts in urging the President to take the trip sooner than later.

On the other hand, President Momoh was being strongly advised by Foreign Minister Koroma not to combine his visit to the United States with a visit to the Sea Islands. He argued that it was not a good political move. Considering the history and racial biases of the United States against its former slave population, visiting the Gullahs might place President Momoh in an unfavorable light for meddling with U.S. domestic policies. His sterling argument was that the President's visit might encourage hundreds of Gullah descendents to "return home" to Sierra Leone. Who was prepared to handle the cost of repatriation and resettlement? But, Dr. Turay prevailed and preparations began for President Momoh's first trip to the United States.

On October 16, 1988, President Momoh addressed the Thirty-fifth Annual Session of the General Assembly in New York City. I was there. His speech was well delivered and well-received by members, and he felt honored and empowered by this opportunity. The next morning, I joined his flight to Washington, D.C., where meetings had been set up with President Reagan and other government officials. We lunched with Under Secretary John Whitehead and other State Department officials and met with Sierra Leonean students in the D.C. area.

While in Washington, Foreign Minister Alhaji Koroma requested a meeting with the Acting Assistant Secretary of State for African Affairs, Ambassador Ken Brown. As a normal courtesy, Ken asked that I attend the meeting. When Minister Koroma arrived with three other Ministers from GOSL in his wake, and found me also sitting there, his face fell and he looked both bewildered and angry.

They chitchatted briefly about the President's first visit to Washington and conditions in general in Sierra Leone. Minister Koroma said, "Things are going as well as expected, although I am concerned about current relations with your embassy. I regret I must report to you the unparalleled audacity of your ambassador whose relationship with my office, I believe, cannot be mended. Therefore, I..." His voice trailed off into space.

Noting the look of shock on my face, Ken responded, "I'm frankly surprised to hear this. We think back here in Washington that she is doing a fine job in carrying out the conditions of our foreign policy, and has become a strong advocate for Sierra Leone in the Department. She is well qualified, you know, for the position of Ambassador, has close access to your president, and we are quite pleased with her performance. Ambassador Perry has arranged an unprecedented visit for President Momoh to the Sea Islands which required a great deal of negotiation on both your side and ours. President Momoh's ambassador to Washington has praised highly the work of Ambassador Perry on behalf of Sierra Leone."

Breathing deeply, I interrupted. "I'm surprised to hear this, Mr. Minister. I am not aware of a problem that exists between us. What is the problem as you see it, Mr. Minister?"

Minister Koroma glanced at the faces of the Ministers he had brought with him for support, who all looked down at the toes of their shoes, avoiding his gaze. He glared at me and stammered, "You dislike me intensely and you do not show respect for me or for my religion."

I was flabbergasted with this charge which had no precedent, no frame of reference in our relationship. I had no basis for response or for further questioning.

The Minister then requested a private meeting with Ken Brown, and I never learned what was discussed or how the matter was resolved. I was not recalled nor chastised in any manner and received no feedback from the private meeting.

That evening, I related the incident to Dr. Turay for the advice of the President. The whole matter set a damper for me on this glorious visit to the Sea Islands, and not wishing to make it worse, I did not pursue the issue during the President's visit.

Libations to the Ancestors

The next morning, I joined President Momoh's entourage to Beaufort, South Carolina. When our plane arrived in Beaufort, we traveled by cars in convoy to Hilton Head in the Sea Islands off the coast of South Carolina. President Momoh's large entourage of supporters and journalists was met with great excitement, and some anxiety. The news had been spread among the Gullah people that "the President of Africa" was coming to reclaim his own. That raised some fears as well as joy. Some thought he had come to take them back to Africa, and few expressed a desire to go.

But, undeniably, this was one of the greatest days in American history, and I was there. Blacks during slavery in America had a wistful vision for generations, that some day, a great king of Africa would come to tell them their names, to reveal their origins and to restore them to their people. For the few remaining black families of the Sea Islands and their many descendents, that day occurred on the 20th day of October, 1988. Here on their own soil stood Major General Joseph Momoh, President of Sierra Leone, a powerful warrior, an honest and caring African leader who had come to fulfill a mission for his people: to find their children who had been lost and assumed dead for many generations. No one knew what had happened to them. Now, the oral historians and story tellers would have a new story to tell their children. He had come to meet the children of those lost, to restore to them their names.

President Momoh appeared larger than life in the common room of Penn Center on St. Helena's Island, filled with both young and elderly descendants of the original Gullah inhabitants of the Sea Islands. Several in the room, a number over 100 years old, still spoke remnants of a strange dialect inherited from their slave parents and grandparents. Rice growers they were, whose knowledge and backbreaking toil in slavery had made South Carolina "rice king."

With the advancement of rice technology and the end to slavery, these ex-slaves were resettled on tracts of land on the Sea Islands off South Carolina, Georgia and Florida. Isolated from the mainland by choppy coastal waters and lack of transport, they existed for many years in a time warp, retaining much of their original language and traditions. Most of the old settlers, who really could have told the true story, had long since passed away. Their children had departed the islands for better education and employment elsewhere, but many returned this day for this historical celebration.

President Momoh gravitated toward those still speaking bits of their native language which they called Gullah, and which he called Krio, which seemed to be related. Those who had remained on the islands still practiced unique traditions and customs whose origins were unknown. Their African heritage was evident even in their patterns of basket weaving and rice winnowing, strangely spiced dishes, and other traditions brought by their foreparents on the slave ships directly from Sierra Leone.

The archives at the Port of Charleston had yielded for researchers a treasure of authenticated shipping notices and slave papers noting the direct transport of slaves from Bunce Island in Sierra Leone. The process for unloading and auctioning their human cargo, left no doubt in the minds of researchers as to the origins of the Gullahs, or "Geechies" as they were sometimes derisively called. Research had indicated, additionally, that their ancestors from the eastern Mende areas and the southern regions of Sierra Leone were called by similar-sounding names: Galla and Kissi.

The room became silent, waiting, watchful, as this giant, black man approached the lectern in the far corner of the room. He said nothing for a moment or two looking out over the hundreds congregated before him. Eyes brimming with tears, his voice resonant with emotion, he began to speak to them in Krio, the *lingua franca* of Sierra Leone: "Kushé-O."

They answered in chorus in Gullah, "O-Kushé," which was also the correct response in Krio. Then they all cried; he shed tears, too. So did I. The air in that room was charged with emotion. What a glorious moment in history! And I was there.

Taking a glass of water, President Momoh approached the entrance to the building. As we all watched, he performed an ancient, African ritual of pouring libations to the ancestors, both those in Africa and those who died in America. He asked them to calm the troubled and restless spirits of those who had passed long ago, that their souls be reclaimed and reunited with those who remained yet alive, both in America and Africa.

As the drops of water spilled upon the earth, he chanted words of an ancient tribal prayer or song. He rejoiced with those African mothers of old that their lost children had been found. He soothed the spirits of those proud old African mothers in America who had suffered centuries of slavery and degradation. Then he asked the spirits of both the living and dead to come together, promising to reunite their children once again in their native land.

The audience was mesmerized by the pouring of libations to the ancestors—a foreign tradition yet so familiar and fitting for this occasion.

Then, returning to the lectern, this stately African president stepped out of his kingly character into his role as redeemer. He sang, in a quavering voice, an old spiritual, the way he had been taught as a child by the missionaries, "Swing Low, Sweet Chariot, Coming for to Carry me Home." The Gullah community then sang to President Momoh a number of hymns and spirituals, those heavy with deep yearning and abiding faith, expressing generations of longing and pain and hope: "Sometimes I feel like a motherless child, a long, long way from home," and "Steal Away." He listened with deep humility as the eldest citizens gave oral histories of their sojourn in America.

Dr. Emory Campbell, Director of Penn Center on Hilton Head, spoke in the language taught him by his departed mother who had learned it from her mother. "We always knew we talked different from others and we were belittled for it by our teachers and people from the mainland," he said. "But none of us knew our language came from Africa, none of us knew we came from Sierra Leone. How I wish my old mother could have been here today."

The television cameras, from local stations and from the United States Information Agency in Washington, were there recording it all. I was there as President Reagan's personal representative to Sierra Leone. Although I could take no credit for the years of scholarly research that culminated in this moment, I could be credited for having brought it all together, for completion of its final stages. I had used the considerable coordinating and negotiating powers of my office as U.S. ambassador, to make it all happen. Bringing them all together again was the essence of my mission and a highpoint in my life as a diplomat.

As we prepared for the return flight to Washington, President Momoh said to me, "It is time to close the circle. When we return to Freetown, we will begin to plan the return home for the Gullahs. We will welcome them with open arms, and everyone in the country will celebrate their return. We will need your help to establish a new relationship with our people in America, to enhance our renewed family ties."

It would be more of a "ceremonial" return than an act of repatriation. I regretted that my tour as ambassador would have ended by the time the Gullahs would visit the country. I hoped, without giving voice to it, that my successor would know the significance of that planned return and would willingly provide the support and assistance required.

After a great meal of traditional Gullah dishes, including many rice dishes and sauces similar to those in Sierra Leone, we left the Gullah population jubilant and at peace with themselves. A plan was formulating among them to send a delegation within a year "home" to Sierra Leone, not to stay, but to set foot on the soil of their ancestors. This had never happened before in the history of slavery in the United States that an identifiable group of descendents of slaves had been united as a group with their legitimate African families. Under the leadership of Marcus Garvey, many had returned to the shores of Africa, settling on the coastlines of Liberia and Sierra Leone, for example. Most had not returned to the land of their ancestors, but rather to the Continent. More recent arrivals of Africans to the United States were well aware of their roots, but none had histories dating back to three to four centuries.

It became clear to me that not all slave records had been destroyed, as I had been taught, and evidence of slave origins could be found, if researchers were willing to commit themselves to the task. I found myself searching for Gullah meaning in the unfathomable name of my great-great-grandmother, Chena. I listened, in memory, for Gullah intonations in the distant sound of my great-aunt Evie's voice; I wondered whether my great-great-great-grandmother, Catherine Hill, a slave in North Carolina in the late 1700's and grandmother of Grandpa Josh, might not have had some connection to the Gullah people of the Sea Islands.

Although the likelihood of my ever confirming that my ancestors came from Sierra Leone was perhaps small, I departed the Sea Islands off the coast of South Carolina with a deep sense of completed mission, pride, and belonging.

* * *

Shortly after our return to Freetown, I was summoned to the President's office, although no reason was given. Only A.K. Turay was there with the President. With an absence of formality, and with a sense of sadness, President Momoh introduced the topic.

"Madame Ambassador, A.K. has told me a devastating story about our visit to Washington and your encounter with Minister Koroma in the State Department. I was not aware of this incident until just a few days ago."

I glanced at A.K. He said apologetically, "I couldn't tell the President about this while he was on tour. It would have interfered with that powerful moment in history. I thought it best to wait until our return, when we had time to think about the consequences of the Minister's action."

Then, while the President listened, A.K. repeated what I had told him of Minister Koroma's discussion with Acting Assistant Secretary Brown in the State Department. I confirmed the gist of the story.

President Momoh expressed his great embarrassment. "It was probably best that I didn't learn of this matter until I returned to Freetown, or I would have handled the matter then and there. The Minister did not discuss with me his intentions and I would not have endorsed under any circumstances what he did, or his castigation of you and of your work here in Sierra Leone as U.S. Ambassador."

Speaking very softly and directly to me, he continued. "I wish to apologize for this offense created by Alhaji Koroma. There is no apparent reason for his undiplomatic behavior toward you. I have summoned him to my office and will address him directly on this matter later this morning. It cannot go without notice from this office."

With great humility, he continued, "I called you in firstly to apologize for all of us. You are accredited to me and my government, not to Mr. Koroma, and he had no authority to speak for me. You are a good ambassador, from my perspective, the best we have ever had. Secondly, among my people there is a tradition that when someone has deeply offended another, the victim of the offense may decide the punishment. Please tell me what you believe to be an appropriate punishment for Minister Koroma's offense to you."

I looked again to A.K. for guidance. I wished I had known about this right of mine to hang the Minister by his "unmentionables." I would have already dreamt up a fitting insult. But, instead, I said. "I thank you for your apology, Mr. President, but the offense is not of your making. I admit that I was extremely embarrassed, Mr. President, but primarily because I thought his threat of recall was endorsed by you. Now that I know it is not true, I must demand an apology from Mr. Koroma, although I would much prefer his removal as Foreign Minister."

We all laughed nervously.

"In good conscience, I cannot ask that," I continued, to dispel any misinterpretation of my position on the issue. "I must leave it to you, Sir, to decide what punishment would be appropriate to the crime, so to speak."

We shook hands as we parted. I felt better. This meeting was proof positive of the President's trust and respect for me and the American government, and the strength of our relationship. I never knew whether he confronted the errant Minister and whether the Minister's hands were slapped. There was no forthcoming apology to me from the Minister.

However, the definite rift between the President and Minister Koroma significantly widened. The President's attempts in later months to remove this apparently powerful Minister were not immediately successful. He was a Mende, and as such commanded powerful tribal and party support. However, with the death of Siaka Stevens, in 1989, just prior to my departure, President Momoh assumed the full leadership of the ruling political party. Alhaji Koroma was subsequently removed from the Office of the Foreign Ministry.

A Fond Farewell

It was August, 1988, and we were entering the final months of our tour in Sierra Leone. The three years of my assignment had gone by quickly. I began to take stock of my accomplishments. The conditions of the Chancery and the Residence were testimony of my stewardship. I had left little for the incoming ambassador to correct or to rebuild, but a lot to maintain.

We began to plan our farewells to all our friends in Freetown and throughout the country. We traveled to the provincial capitals of Makeni, Bo and Kenema, and to smaller towns where our Volunteers were assigned: Tikonko, Kpetema, Banya Junction, Mattru Town, Yamandu and Segwema. We visited again Mattru Hospital, and flew to Kabala to say farewell to the American School and the missionaries located in that area. Later that year, we made our final trips outside the country to Rwanda, Guinea and Liberia.

In November, 1988, George Bush won the election for President of the United States. We watched the elections on television and the jubilant celebrations by Bush supporters throughout the country. In preparation for his takeover of the government on January 20, 1989, Mr. Bush and his transition team had begun to make tentative appointments to his Cabinet and other critical posts. It was not a reasonable assumption that, because the Republicans had retained control over the White House, persons appointed by President Reagan should necessarily expect a chance of reappointment. We were prepared to return to our children and grandchildren and to take up our lives again in Houston.

We took a vacation break in late November, 1988, and flew to Kathmandu, Nepal, for a ten-day visit to Mark who was serving with Peace Corps, high in the foothills of the Himalayas, overlooking India. Before returning to Sierra Leone, we would also visit India, Hong Kong and China, walking along the Great Wall and feeling ourselves to be a great part of history.

This was the trip of our lives. I felt deeply the mysticism inspired by that area of the world, and spent some time in reflection. While in Nepal, I discussed with Milton Frank, the American Ambassador, the possibility of reappointment as ambassador to another country. I had already submitted my resignation to the Bush transitional team, postdated January 20, as required, but having never been one to depart one phase of my life without some plan to take me into the next, I felt daring. From Nepal, I sent a message to Washington stating my interest and willingness to serve the Bush administration.

Upon return to Freetown, I received a call from a close political ally in D.C., advising me to get to Washington quickly if I intended to be considered. It was Christmas time and a difficult time to leave post. But, I left Freetown immediately on a ten-day visit to Washington, where I consulted with a number of old friends who were said to be close to the "throne." Mr. Bush was indeed selecting persons of highest intellect, experience and competence to flesh out his new administration. Heading this "sifting" effort was Chase Untermeyer, also from Texas, who was temporarily operating from space in the offices of the Republican National Committee.

I called for an appointment, and in the next day or two, was graciously received by Chase in his office. In the course of the dialogue, I told him of my desire to continue serving in the capacity of ambassador somewhere in Africa.

He stated quite emphatically, "President Bush will not reappoint ambassadors who were appointed by President Reagan. That isn't the way the game is played. Changes in the administration can be as drastic under a new president from the same party as one under a different political party. For most appointees, their resignations as of January 20, 1989, will be accepted."

"I understand," I said. "But I came to Washington in 1982 as a result of a letter of encouragement written by Mr. Bush. I was hired by Frank Ruddy, Assistant Administrator of Africa Bureau, and my appointment was supported by the White House. In fact, Frank gave me a note written by you recommending that he take a look at my résumé for a position he had in education."

"Me? I certainly did not!"

I persisted. "The handwritten note attached to my résumé said, 'Frank, this looks like a live one'."

Chase laughed, looking more closely at me. "You're from Houston, you say? Have we met before?"

I shook my head. "I'm sure I would have remembered."

"Well, again, in spite of all you might have been told, Mr. Bush has made it quite clear he will reappoint only a few key and outstanding people from the past administration. Therefore, I cannot encourage you to hope for anything when you finish your tour in Sierra Leone. President Bush will be looking for the best people he can find for all positions he must fill. But, for the sake of argument, tell me what makes you special—what makes you stand out from the crowd, that might convince Mr. Bush that he should consider you among those few?"

"Well, aside from the good and outstanding job I'm doing in Sierra Leone, I am the only black woman appointed as ambassador to a foreign country during Mr. Reagan's administration—not another, even from the career Foreign Service." Is this called *playing the race card*, I asked myself?

"Secondly," I continued. "I campaigned in Houston for Mr. Bush's nomination for the presidency, and continued to work for his election as Mr. Reagan's vice president. When I was a young woman, I set a goal to become ambassador in 25 years. I spent those years preparing myself, to prove myself worthy of appointment. I wrote Mr. Bush, when he was Vice President, advising him I wished to be considered for appointment, and it surprised me that he answered. I have a copy of his letter, making it clear that he as Vice President was not in a position to appoint ambassadors—only the President had that prerogative. But, he would give me an opportunity to serve the administration in other categories of appointments. That's where you came in as Director of Presidential Appointments, and so the note sent to Frank Ruddy resulted in my being hired as Chief of Education and Human Resources Development in the Africa Bureau of A.I.D. It was a mere note attached to my résumé, but a very powerful one, that brought me to Washington and I worked for four years, before the White House noticed me. President Reagan then appointed me ambassador to Sierra Leone."

He was still shaking his head, "Well, you'll have to produce that note to convince me. At any rate, I can appreciate your argument and I will pass it on to Mr. Bush, but at this point it changes nothing. Thank you for coming by, Cynthia, and if anything at all changes, I know where you can be reached."

I left his office, mentally preparing myself to leave Sierra Leone at the end of my tour in July 1989. Perhaps I should return to Texas Southern University where I might continue to work making a difference in this crazy world. I had had a good life. I had reached my life's goal, and had proved I could make a difference at a very high level, that I could assist an African government to move toward democracy while I served faithfully the policies and values of my own country. I had reason to be proud of my accomplishments as an ambassador and as a human being.

Amazingly, Chase had already called by the time I returned to Freetown. When we were finally able to make contact with each other, he advised me—to my obvious delight, that Mr. Bush would like to consider me for another posting.

"Where?" I had completely lost my cool, so excited I was to have another opportunity.

"I will give you five choices and you decide, okay? First, Burundi, a small country in Central Africa."

"Oh, I have always wanted to go there—it would be a new country for me."

"Well, would you be willing to go there, should the President decide to appoint you?"

"Of course, I would be honored," I said. What are the other countries?"

"Oh," he said firmly, "I can't tell you that. You've already agreed to go to Burundi."

It was clear no amount of argument or pleading was going to move Chase from the position he had taken. Anyway, I was pleased to go to Burundi, no matter the opportunities that I might have had in another country. I was elated. I thanked him profusely, although I don't know to this day what happened to change his mind about my reappointment.

"You do realize, I'm sure, that you can't broadcast the fact that you are being considered for this post. Until the President himself calls you, your lips must be sealed. I wish you all the best, Cynthia."

Bette, my secretary, was sitting on pins and needles, so to speak, and when I buzzed her, I blurted out, "We're going to Burundi, Bette! Will you go with me?"

Without hesitation, she replied. "Yes, of course."

Then, I informed J.O., who simply said, "Oh, my!"

Our lips were sealed. Bette and I returned to the extensive planning required for my final Independence Day celebration in Freetown.

President Bush telephoned me in February, 1989, just two weeks after Chase's call, and formally requested that I serve as his ambassador to Burundi. Having gone through this process once before did not diminish my joy, my excitement over receiving his call. I lived at the highest peak of emotion for the next several weeks, trying to complete my programs in Sierra Leone while preparing to go on to French language training at FSI (Foreign Service Institute) in Washington, or elsewhere.

The 1989 Fourth of July celebration in Sierra Leone was one of the largest celebrations ever given at the Residence in

Freetown. My reappointment had now been officially announced, and we were scheduled to depart post in August. The Independence Day celebration was also a combined farewell to our many friends in Freetown whose individual farewell invitations for dinners and receptions we could not accept, given our very tight departure schedule. But, we felt an obligation to attend those offered by the Diplomatic Corps and by government officials. A number of ambassadors were departing post at this time, some for further postings and others taking retirement, and we were compelled to attend their farewell dinners and receptions as well as our own.

We were absolutely fatigued, but loved the showering of warmth and goodwill by the people with whom we had shared our lives over the past three years. Nonetheless, saying goodbye, not knowing if we would ever return, was very difficult.

* * *

The day arrived to make my farewell call on the President. I did not find it a pleasant task. I knew he still needed my presence and influence to support the democratic process which would yet sustain severe opposition from the several political factions in the country. I learned that President Momoh had requested the State Department to extend my tour by one year. But, the process had already begun for replacing me in Sierra Leone, and considerations for my next post were also moving along. So, the Department was reluctant to consider the request.

In my shining limousine, I entered the gates of the old fortress for the last time as ambassador, taking note of everything, etching it into my memory. Everyone at the State House knew I was departing and saluted me as I went up the stairs to the President's office.

Strangely, I do not recall what I wore, something I normally note on special occasions. I took with me my deputy, Gary Maybarduke, who would be Chargé d'Affaires upon my departure. It was his first visit to the inner chambers of the President's office. I presented him to the President, and then to

Foreign Minister Alhaji Koroma, and to A.K. Turay, my friend. When we sat, I began my farewell speech. It wasn't really a speech, not a prepared one at least. There seemed to be no need for formality in this, our last meeting.

"Mr. President," I began. "This is a day in our relationship that I suppose no ambassador finds pleasurable, least of all, me. I have thoroughly enjoyed my three years in Sierra Leone, and I believe my presence has made a difference. My government has been pleased with the progress you have made in your push toward democratization. I believe the relationship between our two countries has greatly improved during my tenure, and will continue to improve as time goes by."

I paused, trying to find the right words. "As you know, I have been appointed by President George Bush as Ambassador to Burundi and I am pleased that I merit in his eyes a second posting. My successor in Sierra Leone has been named, Johnny Young, a highly respected career diplomat with years of experience. This will be his first posting as ambassador. He is also an African American, your third in succession." Everyone smiled.

"I present to you, Mr. President, Gary Maybarduke, who will serve as Chargé d'Affaires until Ambassador Young's arrival." I gulped a bit with no small emotion. "I will always consider one of my greatest achievements as Ambassador to Sierra Leone, the reuniting of your people with the descendents of the Gullahs in South Carolina, symbolically bringing together the spirits of the ancestors and soothing the wounds that occurred over the centuries. You will always loom large in my memory as the "Great President of Africa" who came to America to claim his own. I wish you greatest success in your continued administration, and if democracy prevails, Sierra Leone will have regained its position of power and leadership on the Continent. I am pleased to have been accredited to your government. May God bless."

He responded, also without a prepared text, and I believe from the heart. "Your Excellency," he said. "All of Sierra Leone has greatly benefitted from your presence from the first day of your arrival, not just my administration but also the people. They love and respect you as a person, as well as American Ambassador. You have traveled widely, participated with the people in the villages in various ceremonies; you have been honored twice as Paramount Chief, an honor not to be taken lightly. You have understood our needs and have responded with the largesse allowed by your government. I know that the position you have taken sometimes with your government on our behalf has not always been well respected, but you have been an excellent envoy for President Reagan and the American people.

"Our relationship is different from that which will exist with those who will come after you. Our careers started together, yours and mine. I had been President only months when you arrived, and I believe we have matured together; we have worked as a team for the betterment of all.

"I, too, will always remember with deep humility our visit to Hilton Head and the reclaiming of our family in that place. I regret you will not be here to welcome the return visit of the Gullahs to the home of their ancestors, but we will remember what you did to bring it about. May God bless you and your wonderful husband in your new assignment in Burundi. Come back to see us sometime in the future. Please accept this gift as a token of our high esteem for you, your Excellency."

I bowed to him and shook his hand as I accepted his gift, thinking that our relationship throughout the three years was somewhat like Anna and the King of Siam, both tough and endearing in good and bad times. After shaking hands one last time with his Ministers and cabinet members, I departed the President's office. All the military guards stationed around his office came forward one by one to shake my hand and to bid me farewell. I passed through the gates to their salutes for the last time, and as the limousine passed the great Cotton Tree in the Square, I recalled my arrival three years previously. It was a sad moment. But, it was time to move on.

I returned to the Residence to find a huge container that had been delivered just inside my gates for shipment of my personal and household effects. Although two weeks remained before our departure, the move to Burundi had already begun.

I was advised within that week, that the State Department had approved intensive language training for me and I was authorized to take four weeks of French language training in the City of Ville Franche on the Côte d'Azur. J.O. and I decided to go to France prior to returning to Washington, and to have a week-long reunion with our six children in Paris and Nice, prior to beginning the French training. Mark, who was fluent in French, had completed his Peace Corps tour in Nepal and would join us for the month of our training at the Institute of Languages in Ville Franche.

We waited until the last three days to say farewell to my staff at the Embassy, USAID, USIS, Peace Corp, and their various associated agencies. It was a difficult and emotional task for us all. There were many testimonials and tears, and I received so many gifts of baskets, cloth, carvings and other works of art that another carton had to be created for a later air shipment. But, saying farewell to our faithful household and gardening staff was far more difficult and poignant for us. Boima, the most serious member of my staff, gathered all the others in the foyer to say farewell to us. They told us how much they had learned from us because we cared and took time to teach them. They felt they had been treated as friends, not servants, that we had allowed them to offer us advice and to hold conversations with us. We had cared for their families, supplying bags of rice from our own pockets, and making sure they themselves and their families received regular medical attention at the embassy clinic. They were sorry that we must go, and asked that we remember them always.

Then Boima, the cook, asked if they might have a word of prayer with me as we departed. I was totally humbled by this gesture of their caring, and as Boima prayed, we all shed tears that we must part, perhaps never to meet again.

* * *

Our plane to Paris was scheduled to depart early in the evening on August 18, but my chauffeur suggested that we leave for the airport early that morning, to reduce the stress of hurrying and to avoid the normal crush of people boarding the ferry to Lungi Island. He remained with us for the remainder of the day. Although the helicopter service was available, we chose to take one last ride on the ferry, to bid farewell to the looming "lion mountains" and to savor the memorable vision of Sierra Leone's beautiful coastline.

We took a dayroom at the Lungi Hotel, to complete our meetings with Bette, my secretary who would rejoin us later in Burundi and Gary Maybarduke, in whose hands I was leaving the mission. A number of local Lebanese businessmen and women also met us there to add their farewells.

Suddenly, there was a rush of people at the hotel, some bearing champagne and waving flags. Tony Yazbeck, a Lebanese businessman and financier who among other things, managed the helicopter service, had generously offered free trips to Lungi Airport for any of the Embassy staff who wished to say goodbye to me there. We were nearly overwhelmed with their expressions of love, respect and regret.

We finally boarded the plane at 6:00p.m., August 19, totally spent, our minds already beginning to focus on the move to Burundi, to a new experience, a new President, a new language and new goals as United States Ambassador. But, our spirits remained with the President and people of Sierra Leone, wishing for them continued harmony and growth. Sierra Leone would always remain for me the culmination of a lifelong goal, and the substance of dreams for a lifetime: Sierra Leone, a beautiful country and beautiful people, a wonderful, mystical interlude in our lives.

The Epilogue

I regretted I would not be in Sierra Leone to welcome the first contingent of Gullahs in 1990. But, I had helped to lay the groundwork for their visit and to secure funding on their behalf.

As I prepared to leave Sierra Leone, I completed a self-evaluation, an accepted custom in the State Department, detailing as one of my greatest achievements the role I played in re-uniting the Sierra Leonean people with the Gullahs of South Carolina. My self-evaluation would serve as a basis for my formal evaluation being done by the Department. However, I was told flatly by the desk officer in Washington—herself a descendent of the Gullahs—that even though my actions were indeed laudable, I would receive no praise from the State Department for having done so.

"First of all," she said, "You were not sent to Africa as the President's emissary to reunite former slaves with their roots. It was never stated as a part of your evaluation criteria. You are being favorably evaluated for having unprecedented access to top decision-makers, including the President, which facilitated American policies with the government. You are commended for encouraging and facilitating the move of the government from autocracy to democracy, for championing the rights and welfare of Americans abroad such as Peace Corps, for your outstanding stewardship and the care you have given to the enhancement and beautification of government properties abroad, and for otherwise representing the best that America offers, culturally and diplomatically. There is a place on the form, however, where you are encouraged to write anything you feel was significant but omitted from your evaluation."

As it turned out, my final evaluation did make mention of my role in the Gullah reunion with their homeland, although no appreciative detail was given. Nonetheless, I consider among my greatest accomplishments in Sierra Leone the reuniting of the Gullahs with their ancestors.   Since I have not yet determined where in Africa my roots lie, I am at liberty to share the jubilation of the Gullahs, and to choose any country on the Continent I wish to call the home of my ancestors. Or, best of all, I can choose them all.

I salute the United States of America as the home of my birth and the land of opportunity which I shall always be honored to serve, and to which I pledge my allegiance.

But, easily the crowning achievement of my diplomatic service as Ambassador to Sierra Leone during those three years centered around the goals I had expressed to the journalist in Terre Haute prior to my departure for Sierra Leone. What did I hope to achieve, she asked, as Ambassador of the United States to Sierra Leone?

As though she were again facing me, I answered:

"I set a 25-year goal to become ambassador and I persevered to reach it, not just once but twice. I fulfilled my purpose to make a difference in my lifetime, by setting in motion those policies and practices that expressed most eloquently my concern for fairness in the world. I exercised every power at my disposal to improve the quality of life for all people. I utilized every available forum to serve as a fitting spokeswoman and representative for my country and I satisfied my aim and hope to be a symbol of what America offers—freedom to become. That's what America is all about."

The successes I could point to at this phase of my life were due in great part to the philosophy given to me by my friend and mentor, a true philosopher, Herbert Lamb. "You must," he said, "perceive all things as being equal, and then act on faith. Although there will be political considerations, concentrate on doing the right thing. If you meet up with a brick wall, believe it doesn't exist and walk through it. 'All things being equal' has to do with the rightness of human existence, of seeing one's self equal to all others with a God-given right to pursue one's own destiny and place in this world."

I relived the morning of August 18, 1989, when J.O. and I departed the Residence for the ferry dock in Freetown. Hundreds of schoolchildren lined the streets, waving, shouting, and singing as our limousine whizzed by:

"Goodbye, Cynthia. Farewell Cynthia. We love you."

"I love you, too, children of Sierra Leone," I whispered as I returned their wave through the bulletproof glass. I could not ignore the threat I knew existed to the country's stability, which could forever impair the welfare and the lives of those happy, innocent children. But, it was time for me to leave.

I blew them a farewell kiss with a prayer: God grant that, All Things Being Equal, you will live in Peace.

The Afterword
The President's Call

Freetown, Sierra Leone, February 1989

The call came on a Sunday morning. I was deep in the bowels of my garden working with the gardeners to reset some flowering shrubs, when Kamara rushed down—he would never yell to me, no matter how urgent—to say that the marine at post needed to speak to me immediately on the radio. He brought the hand-held radio down to me.

"I hate to bother you on the radio, Madame Ambassador," the marine was speaking rapidly, "but your lines are down and I couldn't get through to you."

"That's fine—what's up?"

"President George Bush is on the line here in the Embassy and wants to speak to you. What shall I tell him?"

"Are you kidding?" I screamed. "Tell him I'm coming to the phone. It will take me at least 15 minutes to get there from here. Ask if he can hold until I get there."

There was a moment of silence while the marine inquired.

"Madame Ambassador, President Bush says he will hold."

My hands were full of plants and dirty gloves. My hair was wild and matted with perspiration. I hadn't yet had my bath. Thank God he wouldn't be able to see me on the telephone! I ran up the steps, yelling at J.O. to come quickly; there's an emergency—it was Sunday and although the limousine was parked in the garage, there was no driver. He didn't work on Sundays unless I needed him.

"Let's take the van," I said to a bewildered J.O. "You drive and I'll explain everything along the way. Go! Go! Go!"

Everybody in Freetown knew George Bush was on the line, even those who weren't supposed to be on our frequency— even those who didn't have a radio. The van careened down the mountainside, J.O. blasting the horn, people in their Sunday suits jumping off the tarmac, chickens squawking, feathers flying trying to get out of the way. When I told J.O. what the urgency was all about, he drove even faster and more erratically. We made it in fifteen minutes flat.

I rushed to the privacy of my office, leaving J.O. with the Marine. "Hello."

President Bush was still on the line. Breathless, I apologized for keeping him on hold so long.

"That's alright, Cynthia." He said, "Your marine has explained the circumstances. As you might know, we're very busy here trying to put our new administration in place. There's a lot to be done. I understand you know Chase Untermeyer. I've known Chase for a very long time and I trust his judgment. He's told me about the good work you've done in Sierra Leone, and he seems to think you would do a good job out there for us. We need a good, solid and concerned ambassador out there to help Burundi to put together a democratic government and to avoid a disastrous ethnic war that has been brewing for some time. We think you can do that. So, I'm calling to ask you to go to Burundi as my ambassador. Would you be interested in doing that?"

"Yes," I hastened to respond. I was quaking in my tennis shoes, and happy he couldn't see me in my shorts, which were too tight and covered with smudges. "I would be honored to serve your administration anywhere, Mr. President, but I would be especially pleased to go to Burundi. Thank you for considering me, Mr. President."

Now didn't seem the time to call him George, but looking back, I think he might have expected me to call him by his name.

He continued, "You've spent a lot of time in your career in various parts of Africa. Do you know Burundi? How about your French?"

"I have never been there, but always wanted to go to Central Africa. Thanks for giving me the opportunity. I studied French in my school days, but will certainly need additional training before going to Burundi. When am I expected to arrive there?"

"Well, as you know, the process here will take some time, and you will want to give your language training sufficient time. Someone from Chase's office or the State Department will be in touch with you further. It's been good talking with you, Cynthia. I look forward to seeing you soon in Washington. Farewell, and God bless."

"Thank you again, Mr. President. Goodbye, and God bless you too."

I remembered to say that, this time.

Author's Note

Peace, in Sierra Leone, was not to be. The following notes were excerpted from an article by Professor Joe Opala, and appeared in the *Washington Post*, Outlook, May 14, 2000:

In 1989, President Momoh's government continued to disintegrate, rapidly becoming dysfunctional, having no money to pay civil servants, police, and school, and no money to import oil for electricity and gasoline. The people became increasingly disgruntled. In 1990, President Momoh made the fatal mistake of mixing in the civil war in neighboring Liberia, whose leader, Charles Taylor (later becoming president), punished Momoh by sponsoring the invasion of a ragtag group of disgruntled Sierra Leonean exiles called the Revolutionary United Front (RUF). Led by Foday Sankoh, a cashiered army captain and psychopathic killer, the RUF rampaged through the rural villages of Sierra Leone, murdering, raping and mutilating innocent people.

In 1992, a group of young officers staged a coup, forcing President Momoh to flee the country, and to take up exile in neighboring Guinea. Within two years, the new junta had lost control of the government troops, who pillaged whole cities, factories, mining operations, while maintaining control of the capital city and the major diamond mining areas. In 1996, with U.N. peace-keeping forces in control, a free democratic election occurred placing Kabbah at the head of the government.

In May 1997, Kabbah's government was toppled by the stronger RUF, who opened the prisons and armed the most hardened criminals. Since that day, Sierra Leone has become a collapsed state and anarchy reigns. Sankoh's army has brutalized the people, chopping off the arms and legs of thousands upon thousands of innocent children, brutalizing the people and committing other unspeakable atrocities within the land.

In the year 2000, in spite of U.N. attempts to maintain a negotiated peace agreement and to restore Kabbah as elected head of the government, the pillage and murdering has continued, primarily over the control of the diamond mines and the natural wealth of Sierra Leone. Kabbah's new government has proven to be weak and ineffective against renewed efforts of the RUF, to destabilize the country. At this writing, there is no peace.

The Author's Notes

My six children are all productive members of society and find satisfaction in their respective careers. From them, J.O. and I have derived, as of the year 2000, eighteen grandchildren and ten great-grandchildren.

After leaving Sierra Leone in 1988, my eldest son, Jim, and his wife, Cathy, resettled in Terre Haute, Indiana. He is now a senior computer productions specialist and they have five children.

My daughter, Donna, a human resources management executive, settled in Michigan. She has three grown children and a new toddler, Kamryon, the light of her life.

My son, Milo, a computer management executive, resides in Houston with his wife, Toya, and three of four daughters.

My daughter, Paula, is a kindergarten teacher in Houston, and has two boisterous young children.

My son, Mark, is an epidemiologist, and resides in Houston with his Ethiopian-born wife, Mirchaye.

My son, James, a senior computer analyst, returned from Sierra Leone to Houston, married his sweetheart, Nina, and is now the proud father of three.

My grandson, Kent, the carefree teen who took his "Year Abroad" in Sierra Leone with us, is now a successful software manager in Indianapolis. He and his wife, Celeste, have a son.

My granddaughter, LeShan, the subject of "Passing for Black," matured into a balanced, thoughtful and wise young mother, and resides in Terre Haute, Indiana. She takes pride in her multi-ethnic history, her individuality, and her young son.

THE APPENDICES

Black career women

Cynthia Perry: 'I was born for a purpose'

BY GAY E. McFARLAND
Chronicle Staff

CYNTHIA SHEPARD PERRY has an almost evangelical fervor when she speaks of her mission in life: unifying the world.

The holder of a Ph.D. in international education from the University of Massachusetts is currently director of the Center for International Student Affairs at Texas Southern University. And she has just returned from a four-year stint with the United Nations where she acted as an administrative officer for staff training; and career development in Africa.

> Fourth of five

"I was born for a purpose," she says in her beautifully articulated voice.

"I was not a biological accident. I was planned and I was made to feel very special — and I have a mission in my life. When you have something very deeply spiritual inside you, you cannot afford not to use it."

Mrs. Perry (whose professional name is Dr. Shepard Perry) said that when she was 25, she came to a crisis. "I knew I had to do that meaningful thing in my life. I had an obligation and I had to fill it. When I was 27, I made a conscious decision to move on. I went to a professional counselor and he asked me what I wanted to do with my life. I told him I wanted to be the American ambassador to Kenya."

He advised her to get her doctorate degree in international politics and to space herself so that her education would be over with by the time her child-bearing years were over. Then, he said, she would be in a position to know people in the international field who could help her.

"It took a lot of sacrifices and some loss to get my Ph.D.," she said. "I was married to a man at the time who did not want to be married to me if I pursued my degree. I sacrificed a lifestyle to get the degree.

"The man I am married to now (Dr. James O. Perry, certification officer for TSU and education professor) is a man who would facilitate my freedom." James Perry, who was Mrs. Perry's childhood sweetheart, also served with the United Nations.

Cynthia Shepard Perry says that her sphere of influence has changed since she's no longer with the U.N. "In Africa, I had the whole continent as my sphere of influence." But now, she has a population of over 2,000 international students and their problems to deal with at TSU. And she feels her strong training will help her.

The Perrys have three international students living with them in addition to their own children. And she says that universities and public schools need to be more sensitive to the needs of international students.

"We rather choose to make foreign students Americans. Then the students don't want to return to their own countries. There are many (students) who could be equipped for re-entry (to their own countries). When they go back, they have culture shock — they've gotten used to comfort and security and plenty."

Mrs. Perry had a little difficulty with that feeling when she returned to the United States less than two months ago after having lived out of the country for four years. "When I came back here I was so overcome by the plenty. I would buy six and 10 of certain items in the supermarket. In Africa, small things like a bottle of

catsup would cost $3 and $4 and you grabbed as many as you could because they wouldn't be there when you went back."

She says, "I need to have the kind of interaction I have with the three (African) children who are living with us. We can become very insular, you know. The United States is the land of the gods, but until you see the sufferings of others, you don't really know that."

"I have a major philosophy: I believe in one God and the oneness of mankind. There are major cultural differences between people but the role my life must follow is to do as much as I can to unify people. I'm very deeply interested in my career in the sense of contribution."

Mrs. Perry pauses. "I resigned my position at TSU to go with my husband to Africa. Then, when I became involved with my U.N. position, I intended to remain with the U.N. for the rest of my life. My husband and the children returned (to the U.S.). And while being with the U.N. was my life choice, I had a sense of guilt because I think that nobody but a mother can fulfill the role of a mother. My husband put no pressure upon me to return. But with the world unifying role I play, if I neglect the family, then I lose my credibility."

Dressed in an soft flowing African dress called a bouba and surrounded by African tie dye art and copper plates and handwoven baskets, Mrs. Perry said, "At this point, I don't really see much difference between being a U.N. member and an American. I'm proud to be an American now and I would represent the United States now if I were asked."

Cynthia and James Perry have an "extended" family. Makonnen Assefa, back row, left, 17, his sister Nardos, 15, center, are both from Ethiopia. Right, back row, is Mary Opembe, 18, from Kenya. Seated left, Paul Perry, 17, Dr. James O. Perry, Dr. Cynthia Shepard Perry, and right, Mark Perry, 15. Seated on the floor is James Perry, Jr., 11.

Houston Chronicle, February 8, 1978

Appendix A

Career women

(From Page 1)

At the time she asked the counselor for guidance, Mrs. Perry set a 25-year life goal for herself. "I was to reach that goal by age 52. I'm 49 now. And at this point I'm going to set another 10-year goal."

She says she's working toward people looking at each other as people — not as races. "The kind of one worldism I'm speaking of is based upon a spiritual basis, not a political one. I do not believe that I will see (this unity) in my lifetime.

She walks gracefully through her expansive home near TSU. "I was one of nine children. By the time my mother was 33, she had had the nine children. I lived on a farm when I was a child. And I always knew I was special. My father told me that someday I would be great."

She credits her parents not only with giving her inspiration and helping her live up to the courage of her convictions, but also to her interest in art and music. She is a painter — "by avocation, not vocation" — and plays, the piano, clarinet and organ.

The household she and her husband maintain is run something like a mini-U.N. "I speak bits and pieces of several languages — Swahili, Krio, Anharic and I studied Spanish. I speak a little French and of course, English. A total of eight languages are spoken between all of us."

The kids have their household duties to perform and even dating has been worked out on a contractual basis. "But some of those stipulations can be amended by the necessary number of signatures," she says smiling.

Writing a book is on her mind — a fictional account based on fact and experiences she had in Africa. She tells a horrifying story of an African woman who, because of tribal customs, was forced to take a back-seat to a second wife and ended up burning the husband up in the house. "I want to do a book on the radical behavior of African women. In this country we have never known oppression as women as the African women do. The women are beginning to break loose a little there though and I'm glad."

The director of international student affairs says that she's seen her own share of racial discrimination in her life time. And she is working to eradicate that. "But I have to say that if I could live my life over again, the only thing I would change is that I'd start earlier."

THURSDAY: Women in the financial world.

Houston Chronicle, February 8, 1978

THE VICE PRESIDENT

WASHINGTON

March 4, 1981

Dr. Cynthia Shepard Perry
Dean, International
  Student Affairs
Texas Southern University
Houston, Texas 77004

Dear Dr. Perry:

        Thank you (and our good mutual friend, Jim
Bowie) for your interest in a position in the new
Administration.

        I have asked another good friend, Mrs. Loret
Ruppe, the Director of the Peace Corps, to consider
you for either the Africa regional directorship or the
directorship of Peace Corps programs in an African
country. With your great experience in Africa, you
know how vital the Peace Corps is and how important it
is to American relations with the nations of that
continent.

        The other positions you mentioned in your
letter -- Ambassador to Nigeria or Kenya, or an AID
directorship in Africa -- are not as easily attainable
as might be something at Peace Corps.

        Thanks again for your letter.

                                Sincerely,

                                George Bush

cc: Mrs. Loret Ruppe

President taps ex-resident for African post

Former Terre Haute resident Cynthia S. Perry has been nominated by President Reagan to be the next U.S. ambassador to Sierra Leone.

The Indiana State University graduate would serve a three-year appointment beginning in July in the west African country if the nomination is confirmed. She would replace Arthur Lewis, whose term expires next month.

Perry, contacted at her Washington, D.C., home, said her confirmation hearing is scheduled before the Senate Foreign Relations Committee during the second or third week of June. Republican Sen. Richard Lugar of Indiana chairs that committee.

If her appointment is confirmed, she will be sworn in July 3 and be in Sierra Leone by July 15.

"I've been excited so many weeks, I can't bear it much longer," she said.

Perry, 57, has been serving since 1982 as chief of the Agency for International Development's bureau on education and human resources for Africa. As part of the State Department, she works with 43 African nations to develop education and training programs.

Sierra Leone will be familiar territory for Perry. She worked there and trained Peace Corps volunteers for the country.

"Then, to my great surprise and joy, I learned I was to be nominated ambassador," Perry said. "It's really an honor."

The president called and asked her if she would like to serve, she said. That call followed a series of White House interviews and a question by an aide at the end of one asking if she'd be interested in becoming the next ambassador.

In the years since her graduation from ISU, Perry has been a professor and dean of student affairs at Texas Southern University in Houston, worked for the United Nations Economic Commission in Ethiopia, and done consulting work for firms involving 23 African countries.

Her permanent home is in Houston with her husband James O. Perry, formerly of Evansville. She has six children and six grandchildren. A son, James O Shepard Jr., still lives in the Terre Haute area. So do two brothers, George Norton and Orville Norton, and a sister, Iona Wilcox.

She receive her bachelor's degree from ISU in 1968, majoring in English and minoring in social studies, after having started degree work in 1946. Master's degree work was incorporated into the doctorate of international education she received at the University of Massachusetts.

Appendix D

UNITED STATES SENATE
WASHINGTON, D. C.

RICHARD G. LUGAR
INDIANA

May 16, 1986

Dr. Cynthia Shepard Perry
Department of State
Agency for International Development
Washington, D.C.   20535

Dear Dr. Perry:

In reading over the resume that we received with
your nomination, I noticed that you are from Terre Haute
and lived there until 1968.

It is always a great pleasure to me personally to
see fellow Hoosiers given positions of importance and
authority in the field of foreign affairs. I look
forward to your confirmation and appointment, and wish
you the very best for your term as Ambassador to
Sierra Leone.

Warm regards,

Sincerely,

Richard G. Lugar
Chairman
Foreign Relations Committee

RGL:pclp

Appendix E

June 16, 1986

Dear Madam Ambassador:

I want to extend to you my personal best wishes for the success of your mission in the Republic of Sierra Leone. As my personal representative there, you, along with the Secretary of State, share with me the responsibility for the conduct of our relations with the Republic of Sierra Leone. I know we share a mutual conviction that carrying the American message of hope and freedom and advancing United States' interests abroad reinforces the foundations of peace. Together we are pledged to work for national strength and economic growth and to promote the values undergirding our Nation's unity and security.

I give you my full personal support as Chief of the United States Mission in the Republic of Sierra Leone in the exercise of your strong statutory mandate under section 207 of the Foreign Service Act of 1980 (22 U.S.C. 3927). I charge you to exercise full responsibility for the direction, coordination, and supervision of all United States Government officers and employees in the country or organization to which you are accredited, except for personnel under the command of a United States area military commander, personnel under the authority of the Chief of another United States Mission (for example, one accredited to an international organization), or personnel detailed to duty on the staff of an international organization. I expect you to oversee the operation of all United States Government programs and activities within that responsibility. I have notified all heads of departments and agencies accordingly and have instructed them to inform their personnel in the United States and abroad.

So that you can ensure effective coordination of all United States Government activities within your responsibility, I ask you to provide strong program direction and leadership of operations Mission-wide. Please instruct all personnel under your charge: it is their duty to keep you fully informed at all times about their activities so you can effectively direct, coordinate, and supervise United States programs and operations under your jurisdiction and recommend policies to Washington.

You will receive policy guidance and instructions from the Secretary of State, who is my principal foreign policy spokesman and advisor, or from me directly. I expect you to report with directness and candor. I want to emphasize that the Secretary of State has the responsibility not only for the activities of the Department of State and the Foreign Service but also, to the fullest extent provided by law, for the overall policy direction, coordination, and supervision of the United States Government activities overseas. There may be developments or decisions on which personnel under your authority disagree. The Secretary of State and I will always welcome the opportunity to consider your recommendations for alternative courses of action and policy proposals.

As you assume your duties, I know that you will do so with a strong commitment to impartial and equitable treatment of all U.S. Government personnel under your jurisdiction. Should any perceived inequities be amenable to elimination or mitigation by appeal to or negotiation with the host government, I urge you to pursue this course in a manner consistent with your authority and with international law and established customary practice. Recognizing that various agencies operate under different legislation and regulations, should you consider legislative or executive policy changes to be desirable in this connection, you should recommend such changes through the Secretary of State. Additionally, fair treatment of all U.S. Government personnel regardless of race, color, creed, sex or national origin epitomizes our belief in and adherence to the principles of equality of opportunity, a value and concept that form an important element of the American democratic tradition.

As Commander-in-Chief, I have authority over United States military forces. On my behalf you have responsibility for the direction, coordination, supervision, and safety, including security from terrorism, of all Defense Department personnel in the United States Mission to the Republic of Sierra Leone, except those forces under the operational command and control of a United States area military commander and personnel detailed to international organizations. Defense Attache offices, units engaged in security assistance, and other DOD components attached to your Mission, as well as other Defense Department activities which may have an impact upon the conduct of our diplomatic relations with the Republic of Sierra Leone fall within your responsibility.

It is imperative that you maintain close relations with concerned United States area military commanders and Chiefs of Mission accredited to international organizations. A copy of this letter is being disseminated to them. You must keep each other currently informed and cooperate on all matters of mutual interest. Any differences which cannot be resolved in the field should be reported by you to the Secretary of State; unified commanders should report to the Secretary of Defense.

I expect the highest standards of professional and personal conduct from all United States Government personnel abroad. You have the authority and my full support to take any action required to ensure the maintenance of such standards.

Your mission is to protect and advance the United States' interests abroad, and you will receive the resources necessary to accomplish that mission. At the same time, I expect that these resources will be used in an effective and efficient manner, and that they will be directly and carefully related to priority policy and program activities. You should inform the Secretary of State when you believe that staffing of any agency is either inadequate or excessive to the performance of essential functions.

I am confident that you will represent the United States with imagination, energy, and skill. You have my full personal confidence and best wishes.

Sincerely,

Ronald Reagan

The Honorable
Cynthia Shepard Perry,
American Ambassador,
Freetown, Republic of Sierra Leone.

Appendix F

ABBOTT WASHBURN

JUL 31 1986
4822 BROAD BRANCH ROAD, N.W.
WASHINGTON, D.C. 20008
(202) 944-7593

RECEIVED JUL 2 0 1986

July 26, 1986

Dear George:

By great good fortune I lunched with your Texas friend, Dr. Cynthia Perry, before she went to West Africa as Chief of Mission in Sierra Leone.

What a dynamic and impressive lady!

So heartening that there are Republicans of her caliber and achievement who are willing to accept appointments to struggling Third World countries in wretched climates.

By coincidence our daughter Julie, who graduated magna cum from Mount Holyoke on May 25, has just been posted to Sierra Leone as a Peace Corps Volunteer. She's scheduled to teach biology at the secondary level, upcountry somewhere. She said she wanted "a taste of the real world" before tackling graduate studies two years from now.

Letter from Ambassador Abbot Washburn to President Bush. We met again in Sierra Leone when he came to visit his daughter, who was a Peace Corps volunteer

We know quite a number of her generation who seem to have found a nice balance between practicality and idealism. Like Julie, they are not ashamed to enjoy the good things of American life and to work for them, but they also want to _serve_ in ways that will help the less fortunate.

A comforting thought for the future.

Good luck on your Middle East foray.

Yours,

Abbott

Ambassador

very nice !

The Vice President

of the United States of America

8-6-86   GB

Ambassador returns to Texas Southern

By JIM NEWKIRK
Post Reporter

Dr. Cynthia Perry set her sights on the lofty goal of becoming a U.S. ambassador 30 years ago when she was a young woman with three small children.

On Monday, she returned to the campus of Texas Southern University as the current U.S. ambassador to the African country of Sierre Leone.

"When the day came that the president did call me, I was still saying I can't believe it, I can't believe it . . . He did call didn't he?" Perry told a gathering of TSU students and former colleagues.

Perry, who formerly was director of the Center for International Student Affairs at TSU, has served 11 months of a three-year assignment and is the only black female serving as a U.S. ambassador.

"The image that people have of an American ambassador is that they ride around in long limousines and fly the American flag," Perry said.

While Perry admitted there is "a little of that," she has found her duties ranging from negotiating economicand political matters for the interests of the United States to hosting elaborate receptions for foreign government and diplomatic officials.

It's a lifestyle Perry said she planned on years ago.

"One day, I woke up and said to myself there must be more in life for me. Even though I was happy as a wife and a mother, there was still something unfulfilled," said Perry.

After returning to school, she found there were only two ways to become an ambassador. She could work her way up the ranks in the State Department or try for a presidential appointment, she explained.

Perry said she cultivated political

CYNTHIA PERRY:
Goal achieved

connections and served the Republican Party for 30 years. She also worked at a number of jobs in the State Department, at TSU and at International Business Machines, all of which she found comfortable.

"Just at the moment when I had said to myself I've tried hard enough and haven't made it, and I'm going back to Houston because I was tired of living in Washington . . . almost the next day I got a telephone call asking me if I wanted to be an ambassador," she said.

Her husband, Dr. James Perry, a retired TSU professor who taught at the university for nearly 39 years, joined her in Sierre Leone.

As in much of Africa, Perry said apartheid in South Africa and the deadly disease AIDS are very much on the minds of the people of Sierre Leone.

She said much concern has been expressed about AIDS in Sierre Leone, but authorities there have yet to document their first reported case.

THE SECRETARY OF STATE

WASHINGTON

December 22, 1988

Dear Madame Ambassador:

These have been good years. Strong American
leadership has had much to do with the progress we
have achieved. Your own contribution to our foreign
policy through your work in Sierra Leone has been an
important part of that leadership, and I want you to
know that I am aware of and appreciate your efforts.
Please extend my special thanks to James for all of
his work to promote healthy US-Sierra Leone relations
and improve the lives of our people in Freetown.
O'Bie and I salute you and wish you all the best in
the years to come.

Sincerely yours,

George P. Shultz

The Honorable
    Cynthia S. Perry,
        American Ambassador,
            Freetown.

Map of Sierra Leone